Dylan Thomas

Titles in the series Critical Lives present the work of leading cultural figures of the modern period. Each book explores the life of the artist, writer, philosopher or architect in question and relates it to their major works.

In the same series

Dylan Thomas

John Goodby and Chris Wigginton

REAKTION BOOKS

For Jenny Wigginton

Published by Reaktion Books Ltd
Unit 32, Waterside
44–48, Wharf Road
London N1 7UX, UK

www.reaktionbooks.co.uk

First published 2024
Copyright © John Goodby and Chris Wigginton 2024

Printed and bound in Great Britain by Bell & Bain, Glasgow

A catalogue record for this book is available from the British Library

ISBN 978 1 78914 932 6

Contents

Abbreviations

N1–N5   The 'N' + number designation is the standard critical
        shorthand for Dylan Thomas's poetry notebooks, into
        which he entered fair copies of his completed poems,
        with a date (and sometimes where he was staying when
        he made the entry), between April 1930 and August 1935.
        Six are known to have existed during this period, of which
        five survive.

N1   This runs from 27 April to 9 December 1930, N2 December
        1930–1 July 1932. Between this date and 1 February 1933 a
        notebook is missing. N3 runs 1 February 1933–16 August
        1933; N4 23 August 1933 (though its first three entries are
        dated 17, 20 and 22 August) to 30 April 1934; N5 summer
        1934–August 1935.

N1–N4   These were sold by Thomas himself to the Lockwood
        Memorial Library at SUNY Buffalo in 1941, and published
        by Ralph Maud as *The Notebooks of Dylan Thomas*
        (New York, 1967) and *Poet in the Making* (London, 1968).

N5   This was not known about until November 2014, in
        Thomas's centenary year, and was bought by Swansea
        University at auction; it was edited and published by
        John Goodby and Adrian Osbourne as *The Fifth Notebook
        of Dylan Thomas* (London, 2020).

Dylan Thomas among bomb-damaged buildings in Soho, London, 1945.

Introduction: An Intricate Image

Dylan Thomas is one of the best-known poets of the twentieth century – perhaps, to the general public, *the* best known. His work is something of an exception to the rule that modern poetry is an elite art that is inaccessible to most people. On the contrary, Thomas's work – his later work, in particular – appeals very directly via its obvious empathy, humour and verbal brio, while also fulfilling the traditional expectation that poets should speak movingly and memorably on the traditional lyric themes: birth, death, love, joy, faith and loss. More than this, beyond his fame as a writer, Thomas has become a cultural icon, an embodiment of what it means to be creative, his life an allegory of its glories and its perils, simultaneously inspiring and cautionary.

In this biography, the chief focus is on Thomas as a writer, although we trace the developments in his later years that would make him a cultural phenomenon after his death, and we return to these in our conclusion. The Thomas legend – the seedy glamour of a rambunctious lifestyle and spectacular, premature demise – is the lens through which many view his writing, however, and has shaped what is read, namely a small number of texts written largely during his last decade (the radio features *Return Journey*, *A Child's Christmas in Wales* and *Under Milk Wood*, and poems such as as 'Do not go gentle into that good night', 'Poem in October' and 'Fern Hill'). Moreover, the authority of these later pieces to stand in for all of his work seems to be underscored by the much-loved LP recordings he made of them in his rich, resonant voice.

Without dismissing the legend or neglecting the later works, this biography breaks with the soft-focus figure beloved of the cottage industry that has grown up around Thomas and the equally caricatural dismissal of him as a drunken windbag that is still rehearsed occasionally by critics and reviewers. Over the last twenty years, as new and more up-to-date critical studies and editions of his work have appeared, these flip-sides of the same dud coin have slowly been replaced by the discovery of Thomas as the serious and brilliantly playful creator of a unique kind of apocalyptic, surreal regionalist (surregionalist) Modernism, a follower of the Joycean 'revolution of the word'. When we ourselves helped to initiate the process of retrieval at the turn of the century with a collection of essays, we were careful to keep our distance from the toxic seepage of the legend.[1] Now, twenty years later, we feel the time is ripe to present a fresh account of the life in the light of a new understanding and many fresh discoveries.

Yet in doing so we realize that many of the questions about Thomas will remain unanswered. A cursory glance at his *Collected Poems* and *Collected Stories* suggests why this is so. In the first of these, anthology favourites like 'Fern Hill' sit alongside some of the most opaque poems ever written in English. While a common poetic of process and signature style links almost all the poems, they display a range in level of difficulty unmatched in the work of just about any other poet. The difference in demands made on a reader by 'The hunchback in the park' on the one hand, and 'Altarwise by owl-light' on the other, is not so much a gap as a yawning chasm. The same applies, only more so, to the short stories. Those written between 1934 and 1938 are among the most experimental fictions of the decade. Suddenly, however, in 1938, there was an abrupt switch to the genial, accessible style of the stories of *A Portrait of the Artist as a Young Dog*. Indeed, we know that while Thomas was finishing the most difficult of the early stories, 'A Journey in the Direction of the Beginning', he began writing the first *Portrait* story, 'The Fight'. To make matters still more difficult, these developments are not straightforwardly chronological. Even as he was writing the condensed lyrics of his first collection, *18 Poems*, in the winter of

1933–4, Thomas was also producing equally accomplished but less ambitious and more straightforward pieces, such as 'The hand that signed the paper'. And before he began writing his experimental stories, in 1933, he had written highly polished stories in a mainstream style, such as 'After the Fair'.

What this tells us about Thomas is disconcerting to literary critics and historians, who like to see in writers evidence of an organic, coherent stylistic development, and to biographers, who prefer to describe lives that, however conflicted, ultimately centre on a stable identity. Thomas offers no such certainties. He had few qualms about using relatively simple poems from an earlier period to bulk out his second and third poetry collections; although compulsion was involved – he had to build, quickly, on his earlier success – he was not concerned (as most poets are) by stylistic inconsistency. Indeed, he seems to have embraced it. In the case of his stories, the sudden switch is even more disturbing for those who believe that soul-searching invariably accompanies a radical change of style. From whichever direction they approach Thomas, readers can be left wondering whether what they are witnessing is versatility or opportunism, or even if such loaded terms apply in his case.

The same kind of uncertainty, or ambivalence, can be found in the writing itself. Even the most forbiddingly dense of Thomas's poems intrigue and attract readers, lavishly offering the traditional rewards of poetry – compelling articulations of verbal music, colour, image, metaphor, rhythm and so on.[2] There is a tactical reason for the apparent conflict between resistance and allurement; difficulty halts the reader, enforcing a pause in which she has to relish the language for its own sake ('love the words', as Thomas advised the actors at a rehearsal of *Under Milk Wood*) before rushing to impose discursive sense. This, in turn, derives from Thomas's insistence on the materiality of language, his belief that it is not a cerebral, neutral conduit of meanings but an object in the world of objects it reports on, consisting of the 'shapes of sound'.[3] But the taste for paradox, which helps to determine the switchback, sweet-astringent qualities of the writing, its stylistic polarities, paradoxes and taste for forked statements and ambiguous themes, goes deeper than mere tactics;

it seems strategic, the work of a self that is multiple, chameleonic, game-playing.

This is how we understand Dylan Thomas. Although he seems at first sight to be a distinctive individual with a set of clearly defined traits, on closer examination his 'character' shimmers and dissolves into multiple personae, rather like a Cubist painting. His correspondence illustrates this quality, virtuosically reattuning itself to the wavelength of each recipient, just as his empathic social skills meant that even one or two brief encounters with him left many believing he was a bosom friend. Thomas's friend and first biographer, Constantine Fitzgibbon, notes revealingly that the multiplicity of the memories of Thomas he came across when writing his biography 'belong not to one man but to six or eight'.[4] It is perhaps no coincidence that Thomas's features, which also seem fixed and clear in photographs, have proved so hard for artists to pin down. The seated sculpture of Thomas in Swansea Marina has been described with some justice as a portrait of the artist as someone else (or, as James A. Davies diplomatically put it, 'the chair is excellent'), and the bronze face of Thomas that forms the annual Dylan Thomas Prize trophy has more in common with Morph, the animated plasticine figure created by Tony Hart for the BBC children's television programme *Take Hart*, than with the poet.[5] Joking aside, we might conclude that while there was a basic Dylan Thomas identity – we have no deconstructionist, Death-of-the-Author axes to grind here, and there is, in any case, a consistency in the style of Thomas's utterances and actions, if not their substance – it was a tricksterish one: fluid, compulsively playful, mercurial.

The problems involved in trying even to provisionally describe and analyse Thomas have not deterred biographers, who have been attracted by the colour and sensation of his life like moths to a flame. There are numerous short or partial accounts and memoirs, and three full-length biographies – by Constantine Fitzgibbon (1965), Paul Ferris (1978) and Andrew Lycett (2003). Each has its merits and demerits, but none pays critically informed attention to Thomas's writing. This is where our biography attempts to fill a gap and satisfy a need. It cannot offer a day-by-day, week-on-week account of Thomas's doings. The existing biographies do this perfectly well (although we have nevertheless drawn on material that has emerged since the last biography).[6] Instead we have for the first time integrated a critical knowledge of Thomas's ambiguous, complex writings and their contexts within the narrative of his life. The life is read in the light of his work, rather than the other way around, following the imperatives of Thomas's dedicated artistry, and bearing in mind W. B. Yeats's argument that while a poet 'writes always of his personal life, in his finest work out of its tragedy', he is 'never the bundle of accident and incoherence that sits down to breakfast; he has been reborn [in his work] as an idea, something intended, complete'.[7] In doing so we hope we have shed new light on what motivated and informed the work and suggested why Dylan Thomas made the sacrifices he did for his 'craft or sullen art'.

1

Young and Easy: Childhood, 1914–25

Dylan Marlais Thomas was born on 27 October 1914, a few weeks
after the start of the First World War, at 5 Cwmdonkin Drive, a large
semi-detached house with sea views on a steep hill beside the local
park in the 'middling prosperous' Uplands suburb of Swansea.
He was the second and last child to be born to Florence ('Florrie')
Thomas, née Williams, and David John Thomas ('D.J.' or 'Jack').
Nancy, their first, had been born in 1906.

At the time of Dylan's birth, Florrie was a 32-year-old housewife.
D.J., at 37, was an English master at Swansea Grammar School.
They were both from working-class backgrounds, their fathers both
railway workers, and were Welsh- as well as English-speakers. D.J.
had grown up in Johnstown, a village near Carmarthen, nearly
50 kilometres (30 mi.) west of Swansea. Florrie was from the St
Thomas's area of inner-city Swansea, near the docks, although
her family originated in rural Carmarthenshire and many of her
relations still lived there. D.J. had been a scholarship boy; he had
won a place at Aberystwyth University, and in 1899 was awarded
the only first-class degree in English given by the University of
Wales that year. He was also something of a dandy, a member
of a choir and a good pianist. He met Florrie in 1901 at the Easter
Fair in Carmarthen, according to one family account; she was
then working as a seamstress for a draper in Swansea.

D.J. and Florrie married in 1903, in all likelihood because the
mores of their time and place dictated that they had to; records
of a miscarriage in 1904 show that Florrie had become pregnant
out of wedlock the year before. It is likely that D.J., who would

have been seen as a catch for Florrie, felt some resentment at having to marry. He resigned himself to his lot, as he saw it, but seems to have nursed ambitions to be an academic, and looked down on the profession of teaching, as well as on most of his colleagues at the grammar school. Over time, the tension arising from the disparities between the couple grew, reaching a peak when Dylan was a teenager. However, the brick-built 'villa' in Cwmdonkin Drive, bought in the spring of 1914 after a decade of renting, was a commitment by D.J. to the future and to the status quo. He made the middle downstairs room his book-lined study, and increasingly retreated there from the rest of the family. Arrival in the Uplands had established the family in 'the upper of the lower half' of society, albeit in rather straitened circumstances.[1] They employed a once-a-week washerwoman, a wet nurse when Dylan was born and a live-in maid, whose duties could include minding him when he was small.

The name Dylan, common enough now, was very rare in 1914. It was D.J.'s choice, and was derived from a collection of Welsh medieval tales, *The Mabinogion*. In one of the tales, the magical infant Dylan ap Ton (Son of the Sea Wave) is given birth to by the maiden Arianrhod as she steps over a sword, and makes for the sea immediately after being baptised; once there, 'he took on its nature and swam as well as the best fish'.[2] It was one of a number of gestures D.J. made to assert his roots in the face of the anglicization and petit-bourgeois conformity he part-embraced, part-resented. His son would occasionally allude to the name in his poems.[3] Dylan's middle name, Marlais, was another such gesture, but a more personal one.[4] It was derived from D.J.'s great-uncle William Thomas, the sole distinguished figure in the Thomas family tree. He had been a Unitarian minister in Cardiganshire in the mid-nineteenth century, a champion of the rights of his congregation against their Tory landlords; he wrote poetry and prose in Welsh under the bardic name Gwilym Marles, taking 'Marles' (its Welsh form) from the Marlais stream near his birthplace in Brechfa.

Despite making a point of naming their children in this way (Nancy was also given Marles, the Welsh spelling of Marlais, as a middle name), D.J. and Florrie did not pass on a knowledge of Welsh to their children, since it was then widely believed that the language, associated as it was with poverty and backwardness, would be an obstacle to a child's life chances. Dylan is highly likely to have gleaned a limited listening knowledge of Welsh during the summer holidays he spent with relatives in rural Carmarthenshire (he puns and plays occasionally on Welsh words in his poems, and uses scraps of Welsh in some prose pieces). But it would be wrong to exaggerate the significance of this. 'Dylan' was pronounced 'Dillon' in the family, not in the Welsh way as 'Dullan', and Dylan and Nancy were sent to elocution lessons – even the Swansea accent was to be purged.[5] D.J.'s ambitions for his son included sending him to the University of Oxford, a stage of anglicization beyond his own, obeying the requirements of gentility even if he himself did not fully comply with them. Yet it was precisely this suburban Anglo-Welsh identity, so self-cancelling and so much a part of D.J.'s frustration, that his son would startlingly repurpose in the hybrid, mongrel energies of his writing.

Early childhood

These matters were, in any case, minor ones during Dylan's early years. The golden haze he cast over his childhood in his poetry, fiction and radio broadcasts was largely justified. The family had problems paying the mortgage and living on D.J.'s salary; he may have had to give Welsh lessons, the family took in a lodger at least once and they were sometimes given money by relatives. But they suffered no major tragedies. D.J. was not conscripted in the First World War and remained in work throughout the economic turmoil of the 1920s and early 1930s. Photographs of Dylan as a child show a small, appealing, wide-eyed boy with golden ringlets and Florrie's snub nose; the contrast between his angelic appearance and his behaviour was also noted. Thomas's story 'Patricia, Edith and Arnold' (featuring a fictionalized four- or five-year-old Dylan) suggests a propensity for asking awkward questions of adults, and a taste for mischief.

This was in stark contrast with D.J., who was a stickler for rules and conventions however much he disliked them, and a noted disciplinarian at work. He stood out as the school's martinet and he kept strict order in the classroom. His temper and sharp, sarcastic tongue made him feared not only by pupils but by his colleagues. One story goes that the headmaster once caught Dylan hiding behind a bush near the school entrance. When Dylan admitted that he was about to play truant, the headmaster simply replied, 'Don't let your father catch you,' before walking off.[6] But to Dylan D.J. was a supportive and a loved, if gruff and distant, father. The bond between them was their devotion to literature; D.J. had made a point of inculcating a love of it in his son from his earliest years, reading the Bible, Shakespeare and other poets to him even before he could understand them, and he also passed on to Dylan his love of language and wordplay.[7] One of his pupils recalled D.J. telling his class to read the dictionary as they would

Dylan Thomas: a portrait of the artist as a young boy.

David John ('D.J.' or 'Jack') Thomas, *c*. 1950.

any other book, for interest and enjoyment, and this became a habit (and a piece of advice to impart to others) with Dylan too. Once Dylan could read, at the age of three or four, D.J. gave him the unchecked freedom of his library. Sternness and indulgence overlapped. When Dylan started writing poetry, as he did from around the age of eight, D.J. – and Florrie and Nancy too – encouraged his efforts.

Florrie, in her turn, supplied the vivacity, spontaneity and warmth her husband lacked, mollycoddling Dylan and fostering his expressive gifts and social skills. Her urge to spoil him was intensified by a belief that he was 'delicate' and suffered from the respiratory illnesses that ran in her family. Dylan would later deploy this to impress friends by predicting his own early, tubercular-romantic death, but there was truth in it, as his bouts of bronchitis and his early death would show. Nancy was distanced from her brother by the difference in sex and age, and has been largely ignored by biographers. But she, too, excelled at English at school, and joined local dramatic societies, acting as a trailblazer for Dylan. When he first visited London, he stayed with Nancy and her husband, Haydn Taylor, and despite the fact that their paths crossed infrequently thereafter, he maintained cordial relations with her throughout his life.

There is no doubt that Dylan was precocious. As a child he would ask for a subject in order to show off his skill by making up a jingle on it. Often he would use the pieces of card around which his father's laundered shirts were wrapped to write on (he was still using these as late as 1935, when he met Vernon Watkins). Juvenilia written at ten or eleven years old, such as 'La Danseuse' and 'Decision', has

Florence ('Florrie') Thomas, c. 1900.

survived, fair-copied on lined notepaper. Some pieces have minor corrections, most likely by D.J. They are highly skilled pastiches of existing verse styles – largely comic, elegiac and nature poems – and will be discussed in the next chapter. For now, however, it is important to note that Dylan was not simply a bookish child, as his early commitment to poetry might suggest. Rather, as he grew up he engaged in all the physical, outdoor pursuits available to him, and in coastal, countryside-surrounded Swansea, these were many and varied.

The 'reservoir park' of Cwmdonkin opposite Dylan's home became his first playground, his 'world within the world of the sea-town', containing 'refuges and ambushes in its miniature woods and jungles', a 'small, iron-railed universe of rockery, gravel-path, playbank, bowling green, bandstand', nursemaids, swans and an 'ancient keeper known as Smokey', memorialized in 'The hunchback in the park'.[8] Further inland, over the top and

Drinking fountain, Cwmdonkin Park, Swansea, 1950s.

behind the 'uglier side of [the] hill' down which Cwmdonkin Drive ran, the countryside was still undeveloped, while at the foot of the road lay the shopping centre of Uplands Crescent.[9] Here the local cinema was to be found, a 'flea-pit picture house', where the young Dylan watched silent-era comedies and horror films, or, with his friends, 'whooped with the scalping Indians' of the westerns.[10] Across the main road that ran from Swansea to Gower were other parks: Brynmill, with its aviaries and a lake; and, further down the seaward-facing slope, the sweeping grassy expanse of Singleton Park, with its botanical gardens and trees. Below that was the 'long and splendid-curving shore' of Swansea Bay, 8 kilometres (5 mi.) of beach stretching from the docks near the town centre in the east to the seaside village of Mumbles and its pier in the west.[11]

The sensory vividness with which Dylan Thomas recalled his childhood – its smells, tastes and textures as well as its sights and sounds – is matched by the physicality of his poetry, not only through its often powerful rhythms and musicality, but in its insistent rooting of thought in sensuous experience, as well as its concrete imagery. Thomas has a writer's self-consciousness, but it is an unusually embodied one, with a creaturely sense of the world and the body within it. This immersion in bodily processes and the physical world is described in 'The Peaches':

I felt all my young body like an excited animal surrounding me, the torn knees bent, the bumping heart, the long heat and depth between the legs, the sweat prickling in the hands, the tunnels down to the ear-drums, the little balls of dirt between the toes, the eyes in the sockets, the tucked-up voice, the blood racing, the memory around and within flying, jumping, swimming and waiting to pounce. There, playing Indians in the evening, I was aware of me myself in the exact middle of a living story, and my body was my adventure and my name.[12]

'The Peaches' is set in the rural hinterland of his extended family west of Swansea, in the Llansteffan peninsula near Carmarthen, an area dotted with aunts, uncles, cousins and more distant relatives.

It was visited by the young Dylan both with his parents and without them during the summer holidays, and was a vast adventure playground, less restrictive even than Swansea. The relatives he stayed with included his aunt on his mother's side, Ann Jones, who lived at Fernhill farm; she and the place would be memorialized not only in 'The Peaches' but in the poems 'After the funeral' and 'Fern Hill'. The area as a whole is the setting for many stories: both in Thomas's early Gothic-Modernist tales, such as 'The Orchards', 'A Prospect of the Sea', 'The Burning Baby' and 'The Map of Love', located in the imaginary Jarvis Valley, and in later, more straight-forward ones, such as 'A Visit to Grandpa's', which mention real places. Florrie and her sister part-owned a cottage in this area, in the hamlet of Llangain, and Thomas sometimes stayed there. As this suggests, his early surroundings were stimulating and shaped his work in many ways. More than a backdrop, what was crucial about them was the juxtaposition of many different topographies – suburban, rural, industrial, coastal. They reveal themselves above all, perhaps, by the presence of the sea in his work, so richly symbolic of origins, adventure, sex, the unconscious and death, and also of the liminal zone of the shore, neither land nor sea, but both.

At the age of seven, Dylan was sent to the local dame school run by Mrs Hole in Mirador Crescent, near the foot of Cwmdonkin Drive. It was a conventional establishment – days began with a Bible reading and prayer – and it gave its charges a grounding in basic subjects as preparation for Swansea Boys' Grammar School and Girls' High School. Dylan recalled it as

> firm and kind and smelling of galoshes, with the sweet and
> fumbled music of the piano lessons drifting down from upstairs
> to the lonely schoolroom where only the sometimes tearful
> wicked sat over undone sums, or to repent a little crime – the
> pulling of a girl's hair during geography, the sly shin-kick under
> the table during English literature.[13]

Here he made several friendships, including those with Ivan and George Grant-Murray, whose father ran the town art gallery, and

Jack Bassett (the Jack Williams of 'The Peaches'), whose father was Swansea's Lord Mayor. The most important friendship was with Mervyn Levy, later a painter and one of the 'Kardomah Boys', who moved to London and shared digs with Dylan and Fred Janes in 1934. The school allowed Dylan to develop his literary and theatrical abilities and exercise his powers of invention. But he had already begun educating himself at home, and with only a little exaggeration he would tell an audience at a reading how 'my proper education consisted of the liberty to read whatever I cared to. I read indiscriminately and all the time, with my eyes hanging out on stalks.'[14]

Dylan developed a talent for entertaining, enhanced by a well-developed sense of humour and gifts for mimicry and story-telling. His angelic appearance belied a strong mischievous streak; he relished fibbing to the extent that he took pleasure in having to devise elaborate ways of justifying the initial lie. He also had a taste for adventure that made him prone to minor disasters; when he was eleven he suffered the first of a number of bicycle accidents necessitating hospital treatment for broken bones. It was also around this time that he began to develop his bad-boy persona, fictional-izing a role that he would later, to some extent, be imprisoned by:

I let Edgar Reynolds be whipped because I had taken his home-work; I stole from my mother's bag; I stole from Gwyneth's bag; I stole three books in three visits from the library, and threw them away in the park; I drank a cup of my own water to see what it tasted like; I beat a dog with a stick so that it would roll over and lick my hand afterwards; I looked with Dan Jones through the keyhole while his maid had a bath; I cut my knee with my penknife, and put the blood on my handkerchief and said it had come out of my ears so that I could pretend that I was ill and frighten my mother; I pulled my trousers down and showed Jack Williams; I saw Billy Williams beat a pigeon to death with a fire-shovel, and laughed and got sick; Cedric Williams and I broke into Mrs Samuels' house and poured ink over the bedclothes.[15]

'D. M. Thomas', the improbable under-fifteen school mile winner in 1928.

Although small and apparently puny, Dylan was fiercely deter-
mined. Unlikely though it seems when faced by the portly figure
of the adult poet in photographs taken after his mid-twenties,
in June 1926, aged eleven, he was the victor in the under-fifteen
mile race at school sports day, a feat he repeated in 1928 and 1930.
He cherished the achievement, perhaps relishing its apparent
incongruity; his first win was reported, with a photograph of
him crossing the finishing line, in the *Cambrian Daily Leader*,
and he carried a yellowed clipping of the article in his wallet
all his life. In retrospect, it can be seen to embody the single-
mindedness he would bring to bear on his self-making as a
poet in his teenage years.

Contraries

Although Dylan's childhood was sheltered and nurturing, it was not completely idyllic. The mismatch of his parents made itself more apparent as he grew older, and this was reflected both in how the family behaved and in Dylan himself. Florrie did not, and could not, share D.J.'s intellectual interests. She had no interest in reading and was married to an academic manqué. They managed to get along, and were complementary in many ways, but there was little meeting of minds. Her gift for telling stories and her exuberance could annoy him. While she gamely put up with his disapproval and withdrawal, keeping the household running and engaging with neighbours, friends and relatives, D.J. grew to be defined by his frustration. Yet biographers have exaggerated the gulf between Florrie and D.J. in search of a clash of temperaments, according to conventional models by which the artist is formed. D.J.'s tendency to shut himself away in his study was not unconnected with the fact that, as a teacher, he had a heavy marking load, and while his social life favoured just a few drinking cronies, he had other pleasures. Even so, his world-view was a grim, deterministic one, drawn from Schopenhauer, Carlyle, T. E. Huxley and Hardy (Haydn Taylor noted that D.J. read and reread *Jude the Obscure* with 'morbid satisfaction', and claimed to detect 'no sense of any shared "homely" atmosphere . . . this was not a family that went off to the seaside in the summer or played foolish games around the fire at Christmas').[16] Nancy and Dylan preferred to go to friends' houses rather than bring them home. Personal and historical developments only intensified D.J.'s view of existence as a cosmic black joke. Dylan would tell how, when the weather was bad, his father would stand at the window, shaking his fist at the sky, exclaiming angrily: 'It's raining, blast Him!'[17] On the other hand, D.J.'s anger was the source of his energy and drive, and a version of his determinism permeates his son's early poems. And while Dylan evolved a more benign vision of the universe in his later poems, he would regret the fact that the dying D.J. had relinquished his anger in 'Do not go gentle into that good night'.

If D.J. was an agnostic, even an atheist, Florence was a solid chapelgoer, keen to expose her son to religion. As soon as he was old enough, she began taking Dylan to services at the Paraclete Chapel in Newton, where her brother-in-law David Rees was minister. In August 1933, when he was eighteen, Dylan would refer to his uncle, in a satirical poem, as 'Reverend Crap', but in 1950 he was clear about his debt to the rhetoric of religion and the Bible, describing how, when he was a child, 'the great rhythms had rolled over me from the Welsh pulpits, and I read, for myself, from Job and Ecclesiastes; and the story of the New Testament is part of my life'.[18] In this sense, Florrie's influence on Dylan's poetry, while indirect, was almost as strong as D.J.'s. He would recall it, years later, in 'Poem in October':

> And I saw in the turning so clearly a child's
> Forgotten mornings when he walked with his mother
> > Through the parables
> > > Of sun light
> > And the legends of the green chapels
>
> And the twice told fields of infancy . . .[19]

As his friend Bert Trick was to put it later, 'On the one hand he was in revolt against his father's agnosticism. On the other hand he was in revolt against the narrow Puritan conventions of his mother's Congregational background, and it was from these tensions that the personality of Dylan Thomas developed.'[20]

Recollections and recreations of childhood

What is striking about Dylan Thomas's writing on his early years is not so much that there was a good deal of it, as that he did so in two very different ways. The first way – the one referred to so far – was broadly realist. It is the style found in *A Portrait of the Artist as a Young Dog* (1940) and such radio broadcasts as *Reminiscences of Childhood* and *Return Journey*. Before this point, with the exception of his juvenilia, his work was in the dense, Modernist-Symbolist experimental 'process' style he had forged in 1933 – the style of his first collection, *18 Poems*, with which he established his reputation. In this early style, too, he wrote about the earliest period of his life, but in a much more radical way than in the stories and broadcasts after 1938, or in well-known poems of the 1940s, such as 'The hunchback in the park' or 'Fern Hill'.

This is because the process poetry, in particular, focuses on the very earliest stages of our lives, starting with conception and progressing through gestation, birth and breastfeeding to the acquisition of language. It is about the origin of our being – that is, it is *ontogenetic* – and draws on then-recent discoveries about the sexual organs, nerves, glands and hormones involved in reproduction, on embryology and on theories of neonatal mental life associated with Freud. Thomas effectively puts popular science at the service of lyric poetry. Of course, we know about this period of our lives only because of what science can tell us about it; we have no personal memories of it because it occurs before we have a sense of self or memory. Philosophers, theologians and psychologists had speculated about this period of our lives in the past, but before Dylan Thomas poetry had not.

Thomas's aims can be summed up in the title of one of these poems, 'I dreamed my genesis', which suggests the primary role of 'dream', or the imagination, in filling in the blanks.[21] The result is a poetry that ostensibly takes its cue from biology and psychology, but richly exceeds and complicates the facts they supply, and gives our early existence a mythic, doomy grandeur. The first poem in this vein, 'Before I knocked' of September 1933, does avail itself of a specific identity – that of Jesus Christ. Thomas uses the device of dramatic monologue because Jesus, as the Son of God, existed before his incarnation and is therefore capable of speaking of his conception and his life in the womb. He foretells his suffering and passion, but gestation, nevertheless, is exciting, a 'salt adventure/ Of tides that never touch the shores . . . made the richer/ By sipping at the vine of days'.[22] And although it is a 'Jesus poem', as Thomas described it to Pamela Hansford Johnson, it conflates Dylan Thomas himself, and (by extension) ourselves, with Jesus.[23] In one typical pun, for example, Christ speaks of 'the Jordan near my home', where 'Jordan' is slang for a chamber pot as well as the sacred biblical river.

The ontogenetic poems that follow dispense with Jesus as a device, but further explore the mixed attitudes towards entering into existence, and being embodied, which it opened up. The foetuses of 'I see the boys of summer' seem to usurp their mothers' bodies, to 'split up the brawned womb's weathers', reducing them to their animal function as 'dams'.[24] Birth is the loss of uterine bliss and oneness with the mother in 'Where once the waters of your face', in which the 'green unraveller', inexorable process, cuts the umbilical cord, severing 'the channels at their source/ To lay the wet fruits low'.[25] In 'A process in the weather of the heart', 'each mothered child/ Sits in their double shade', within the womb-tomb.[26] Going a stage further, in 'My world is pyramid', the speaker envisions Freud's traumatic Primal Scene – a child's imagining of his own begetting, his parents 'rotating . . . horning as they drill/ The arterial angel', 'fellow[ing]' him, a 'cripple' because made up of their 'broken halves'.[27]

The First World War and origins

A historical primal scene, as well as a psychological one, lies behind many of these poems. As the phrase 'snipped to cross the lines' in 'Before I knocked' hints, the painful, even nightmarish life of the embryo is often likened to the trench warfare of theFirst World War. Gas, barbed wire, guns, periscopes, shells, wounds, bodies abandoned in no-man's-land – all the horrors of trench warfare recur in these poems. Our origin and the violence of birth are presented as inextricable with the conflict. The speaker of 'I dreamed my genesis' tells us:

> I dreamed my genesis and died again, shrapnel
> Rammed in the marching heart, hole
> In the stitched wound and clotted wind, muzzled
> Death on the mouth that ate the gas.[28]

The link is made more tangentially, and for a later stage of child-hood development, in Thomas's first radio feature, *Reminiscences of Childhood*:

> I was born in a large Welsh industrial town at the beginning of
> the Great War . . . This sea-town was my world: outside a *strange*
> Wales . . . beyond that unknown Wales lay England . . . and a
> country called 'The Front', from which many of our neighbours
> never came back. At the beginning the only 'front' I knew was
> the little lobby before our front door. I could not understand
> how so many people never returned from there; but later I grew
> to know more, though still without understanding, and carried
> a wooden rifle in Cwmdonkin Park and shot down the invisible
> unknown enemy like a flock of wild birds.[29]

As so often, what is serious and grandly impersonal in the poetry
has become personal and self-mockingly humorous in the post-1938
prose. But there is no doubt that from childhood onwards Thomas
feared the war, and in adolescence he came to share his generation's
conviction that a second world war, in which they would be herded
to slaughter as their older brothers, fathers and uncles had, was
imminent. These poems – written at the moment when that threat
suddenly loomed larger, with the rise of fascism in the early 1930s
– understand war as a sickness that has infected even the unborn.

Yet the lives that awaken in these poems, rather than being
crushed by historic fate or wholly constrained by biological or
psychological determinism, are charged with verbal invention and
are full of dreams and projections that explore the unknowability,
the 'salt adventure', of our lives. This appears as a source of hope,
a space in which creativity may flourish. There is, too, a distrust
of hyper-rationalism, of the belief that science can explain all the
mysteries of existence. Thomas, we might say, uses science to oppose
a reductively scientistic outlook (and it is revealing that in 'I dreamed
my genesis' and other ontogenetic poems, such as 'In the beginning
was the three-pointed star', the biblical language associated with his
mother and churchgoing mingles with the science-based rationalistic

view of the universe that Thomas would have associated with his father).

Hence the imaginings of what happens in the womb. Are 'the mushroom features' of those we will love after we are born shown to us there, like photographs, as the fourth sonnet of 'Altarwise by owl-light' claims?[30] Or, as 'When all my five and country senses see' argues, do our senses intermingle synaesthetically, allowing us to experience more richly than after we are born, when four of them succumb to the dominance of sight alone and, as a result, 'love [is] drummed away/ Down breeze and shell to a discordant beach'?[31] Or do we even get to foresee a film of our future lives projected by God on the womb wall, as 'Then was my neophyte' has it – a film that we then forget, although we carry forebodings from it out into the world?[32]

What these poems offer – as we shall see in later chapters – is an exploration of the meaning of existence at a time of uncertainty and threat, of new knowledge and persisting ancient mystery. A specific historic context is suggested, but what is being discussed has universal resonance, and it is Thomas's achievement to articulate fears and hopes we still share. In general, for all the charnel imagery and fatalism, they tend to face towards the future, albeit with ambivalence and no little trepidation. In 'When once the twilight locks no longer', after passing through nightmares, the speaker exhorts himself to 'wake to the sun'.[33] Rather less abruptly, in 'From love's first fever', the positive aspects of gestation and growth are rendered with a curiosity and tenderness that are both physically particular and reverential: blood 'bless[es]' the heart, hair 'hatches', gums grow, sex-glands are 'hallowed', and the embryo is symbolized benignly as a ripening fruit, a 'plum', which drops 'like fire from the flesh', moving from 'darkness . . ./ Into the sided lap of light'.[34] Thomas believes that the neonate understands the universe as a unity: 'earth and sky' are seen 'as one airy hill' (as the steep, one-in-six gradient hill up which Cwmdonkin Drive climbs may have appeared to the infant Dylan), on which 'sun and moon shed one white light'. After birth, the 'hill' and 'light' divide, yet without trauma:

The sun was red, the moon was grey,
The earth and sky were as two mountains meeting
. . . And the four winds, that had long blown as one,
Shone in my ears the light of sound,
Called in my eyes the sound of light.
And yellow was the multiplying sand,
Each golden grain spat life into its fellow,
Green was the singing house.

'Sound' is crucial here; aural awareness leads to language acquisi-
tion, as the child 'learn[s] man's tongue', and the 'singing house'
of the world, but also of poetry as a birthright. Language has its
contradictory and negative sides, being a 'stony idiom' as well
as 'many sounding minded'. Yet 'the tears of spring' eventually
dissolve to become 'one sun, one manna, warmed and fed'.[35]

Into language

The meaning of Latin *infans*, the source of 'infant' in English, is, as
Thomas knew, 'without speech'. The key moment in being able to
imagine the mystery of experience before language is, paradoxically,
when we acquire it. In a remarkable passage in his 'Poetic Manifesto'
of 1951, Thomas describes his love of language in terms that suggest
that words offer a recovery of, or a substitute for, the unity of self
and universe the newborn child loses when it leaves the womb. He
describes his fascination with words as material, palpable 'shape[s]
of sound' and 'sound[s] of shape' (echoing 'light of sound' and
'sound of light' in 'From love's first fever'):

I wanted to write poetry in the beginning because I had fallen in
love with words. The first poems I knew were nursery rhymes,
and before I could read them for myself I had come to love just
the words of them, the words alone. What the words stood for,
symbolized, or meant, was of very secondary importance. What
mattered was the *sound* of them as I heard them for the first time
on the lips of the remote and incomprehensible grown-ups who

seemed, for some reason, to be living in my world. And these words were, to me, as the notes of bells, the sounds of musical instruments, the noises of wind, sea, and rain, the rattle of milkcarts, the clopping of hooves on cobbles, the fingering of branches on a window pane, might be to someone, deaf from birth, who has miraculously found his hearing. I did not care what the words said, overmuch, nor what happened to Jack & Jill . . . I cared for the shapes of sound that their names, and the words describing their actions, made in my ears; I cared for the colours the words cast on my eyes . . . I fell in love – that is the only expression I can think of – at once . . . And, when I began to read . . . I knew that I had discovered the most important things, to me, that could be ever . . . My love for the real life of words increased until I knew that I must live *with* them and *in* them, always. I knew, in fact, that I must be a writer of words, and nothing else. The first thing was to feel and know their sound and substance; what I was going to do with those words, what use I was going to make of them, what I was going to *say* through them, would come later.[36]

Thomas's explanation of his pre-linguistic love of language is in some ways paradoxical. Is it possible to recall loving the sound of words just before we understand them? Perhaps. Whatever, the belief is central to his feeling that the words *as sounds*, as pleasure, preceded the meanings attached to them. They were 'many sounding minded', as 'bells . . . musical instruments, the noises of wind, sea, and rain, the rattle of milkcarts, the clopping of hooves' and so on, bringing all these disparate effects into one system of suggestive bliss. Theorists of poetry have argued that the bliss of infancy before the acquisition of language 'exists only as a memory trace marking its loss', and that to gain language is to fall from this enviable state because we are taught to use language in an instrumental way: this word means that thing, and not any other thing, for example.[37] They have argued that the appeal of lyric poetry is that it tempts us to get caught up again in those aspects of language that we learned to forget, returning us to 'the very threshold of that forgetting'.[38] There is truth in this; lyric poetry certainly encourages us to consider language in a non-instrumental way. But Thomas, in his account, never 'learned to forget' his awareness of language as play and sheer wonder, and this was continuous with his desire to write poetry. Language was not a fall, but a restoration of a sense of oneness with the world and the 'bliss of infancy'. There is, of course, always the suspicion that the 37-year-old poet may have been presenting his infant self in a way that would justify the kind of poetry he came to write; as we shall see in the next chapter, his first efforts at poetry show a pleasure in words, but hardly let them off the leash. However, as an account of the kind of ontogenetic poetry Thomas came to write in the autumn of 1933 with 'Before I knocked' – his poetic birth, or origin, as an original poet – they make perfect sense.

The Great Hall of Swansea Grammar School, 1950s. The school motto was 'Virtue and Good Literature'.

2

Eggs Laid by Tigers:
The Apprentice Poet, 1925–32

In September 1925, a few weeks before his eleventh birthday, Dylan
Thomas entered Swansea Grammar School, a boys-only school
within walking distance of his home. Its ethos and curriculum were
conservative and traditional, but its disciplinary regime was liberal,
even lax. The school's function was to turn out solid middle-class
citizens – solicitors, bank managers and accountants – and prepare
its most academically able charges for Oxbridge. Thomas settled in
swiftly. As D.J.'s son, he would have had to deal with suspicions of
favouritism, but these were defused to some extent by his charm and
intelligence and the fact that it was soon clear to his schoolfellows as
well as the masters that, while he benefited from the connection,
he was a genuine nonconformist. Increasingly, as the curriculum
failed to interest him, he ceased to apply himself to academic work.
Nevertheless, his later boast that he was always top in English but
bottom in every other subject ('thirty-third in trigonometry') is to
be taken with a pinch of salt.[1] In reality, Dylan was intellectually
curious, but in an eclectic way, and in subjects (such as Egyptology,
insects, films) that might be of use to his poetry, if unlikely to crop
up in the classroom.

Thomas's energies were already primarily focused on poetry,
and he was able to get away with his poor performance (and the
truanting it developed into in the higher forms) partly because no
one, staff included, wanted to incur D.J.'s wrath. There are signs
that D.J. might have welcomed disciplinary intervention by others,
but it is unlikely that it would have had much effect. Dylan was
determined on his course, and D.J. was unable to enforce his will at

home either, although he seems to have attempted to occasionally, in a dutiful way. The result was a kind of unspoken connivance between them, a trade-off, whereby D.J.'s desire that Dylan should excel academically was never enforced as long as he was outstanding at English. The upshot of this was that in the summer of 1929 Dylan failed the Central Welsh Examining Board exam for the school leaving certificate, a prerequisite for moving up to the sixth form to prepare for university. D.J. wanted his son to go to Oxford, and would always regret that he did not. But Dylan would not have become the poet he did if he had applied himself to the daily academic grind, and he knew this from an early age. Perhaps, at some level, D.J. did too. By the time Dylan left school, in July 1931, he was hardly attending any classes. As Dan Jones, his best friend, noted, Dylan's final months were a 'transitional period' in which no one was even sure whether Dylan was still a pupil at the school or not.[2]

Poetry and Drama

School was vital to Dylan Thomas's poetic development in several crucial, extra-curricular ways. Most obviously, it gave him his first outlet and audience for his poems. Within three months of starting school, his 'The Song of the Mischievous Dog' had appeared in the December 1925 issue of *Swansea Grammar School Magazine*. Although light verse, it is skilful and amusing (and prophetic, too, in its use of the disruptive mongrel, canine persona that would reappear as the 'dog among the fairies' of 'Altarwise by owl-light' and in the title of *A Portrait of the Artist as a Young Dog*). Poems, essays and stories followed at regular intervals, with, as Constantine Fitzgibbon shrewdly noted, the poems falling into two distinct categories, serious and comic, anticipating the main strands of Dylan's later writing.[3] More impressively, they achieved success beyond school. The poem 'His Requiem' was published in the *Western Mail* on 14 January 1927; Florrie and D.J. were so proud that they refused to let Dylan cash the ten shilling contributors' cheque. In February 1927 'The Second Best' appeared in the *Boy's*

Own Paper, an all-UK publication. In October 1929 two lines from a poem Dylan had submitted to a national competition were quoted in *Everyman* magazine. His supremacy in English was acknowledged at school: an article in *Swansea Grammar School Magazine* titled 'Things We Cannot Credit' included 'That D.M.T. should mispronounce a word'.[4] By 1929 Dylan was the sub-editor of the magazine, and for three issues in 1930–31, his last year at school, he was its sole editor. His involvement, along with the other early successes, fostered his confidence in his poetic ability and helped him to grow into the role of poet.

Dylan also joined extra-curricular groups. He was secretary of the debating society and a member of the drama society, founding the Reading Circle as a spin-off from it. The drama society was by far the most important of the three groups. It staged productions in the summer term, and Dylan had a substantial part in the production in 1929 of John Drinkwater's *Abraham Lincoln*, played the lead in Drinkwater's *Oliver Cromwell* in 1930 and took the central role of Roberts, the strike leader, in John Galsworthy's *Strife* in 1931. His acting was often praised; a reviewer of *Strife* noted that there were times when he seemed to 'lack the coarseness and toughness of fibre necessary' for the character of Roberts, but that he 'is too good . . . to make a hash of any part and he successfully survived an ordeal that would make heavy demands upon a mature and experienced actor'.[5] For all that there could be a certain woodenness and orotundity about his performances – occasionally mentioned during his BBC career later – Dylan was a versatile and impressive actor of near-professional standard. Briefly, in his late teens, he considered joining a repertory group and making a career in the theatre.

In the four years before he left Swansea Thomas was increasingly involved in local amateur dramatics. While still at school, he was accepted by the local YMCA Junior Players in 1931, and acted in six plays in 1931–2; he also directed a play and learned about stage lighting. When he left school, in the summer of 1931, he followed Nancy into the Swansea Little Theatre, the best of the local groups. It held to a high standard; a production might require a month's rehearsal over several evenings a week, often at weekends, and each play would run for several nights, or even a week. Dylan acted in thirteen productions between November 1931 and April 1934, usually in important if not lead roles – he was still a junior – including *Hay Fever*, *The Beaux' Stratagem*, *The Way of the World* and *Richard II*. The company also toured South Wales Valleys towns and participated in drama festivals and competitions, the prize money from which was essential to keep it solvent.[6]

The Little Theatre was also about people. Dylan's friends Wynford Vaughan-Thomas and Vera and Evelyn Phillips were members, and Fred Janes and Tom Warner were involved with painting sets and supplying music. It organized social activities, giving Dylan licence to drink under-age in pubs with cast members, meet members of the opposite sex and travel beyond the confines of Swansea. But while it was a crucial part of becoming an adult, like everything else in his life it was subordinated to his poetry. He was occasionally erratic in his commitment, being in the habit of leaving the theatre for a swift pint between his entrances, like a few others in the troupe, so it is no surprise that he was asked to leave in April 1934, just after a period in which the Little Theatre was intensely

The Swansea Little Theatre cast for Noël Coward's *Hay Fever*, 1932. Dylan Thomas (foreground, lying down) played Simon Bliss.

involved in festivals – nine between October 1933 and March 1934 – at a time when, as his notebooks show, his poetry was undergoing its most intensive phase of development. By April 1934, in any case, he knew his first collection would be published and that he was about to begin his career as a poet.

Even so, engagement with the theatre over these formative years helped to fuel the poems in *18 Poems*. In a general sense, it stimulated an interest in poetic drama; and in particular the influence of Jacobean tragedy can hardly be underestimated. In the autumn of 1931, when Thomas's poetry took a darker turn, it adopted the imagery and rhythms, and occasionally the iambic pentameters, of Shakespeare and Webster. The poem 'Never to reach the oblivious dark' of October 1931, for instance, is the first of many variations on Hamlet's 'To be, or not to be' speech, desirous of 'sweet blankness', oblivion, even suicide, but afraid that death will not offer it.[7] 'Out of the sighs', dated June 1932, also sounds like the musings of a tragic hero, albeit a modern anti-hero who knows he has lost before he has begun: 'After such fighting as the weakest know/ There's more than dying.'[8] More broadly, the immersion in theatre shaped the way Thomas's poetry became dramatic, setting up and orchestrating conflicts within its lyric forms. But, as ever, tragedy and comedy went hand in hand. His acting work also encouraged him to write such light-hearted skits as the self-critical 'Spajma and Salnady or Who Shot the Emu?', included in a letter to Pamela Hansford Johnson.[9] They are the first signs of a taste for scriptwriting that was later to flower in his radio and film work. And in terms of self-development, it is clear that Dylan's theatre-related activity boosted the skills he would use to overcome his essential shyness, fostering his performative, chameleonic side and gift for mimicry, and arming him with a front with which to charm and disarm the world.

Daniel Jones

In his school years Dylan learned little from his teachers, much from D.J.'s library and his extra-curricular activities, but most of all from his best friend, Daniel Jenkyn Jones. They had met in the first-year class at school, to which Dan, who was twenty months older, had been mis-assigned. Dylan would later fictionalize his first meeting with 'a strange boy, whom I had not yet heard approach, [who] pushed me down the bank' in his story 'The Fight', of 1938:

> We walked home together. I admired his bloody nose. He said that my eye was like a poached egg, only black.
> 'I've never seen such a lot of blood,' I said.
> He said I had the best black eye in Wales, perhaps it was the best black eye in Europe; he bet Tunney never had a black eye like that.
> 'And there's blood all over your shirt.'
> 'Sometimes I bleed in dollops,' he said.
> On Walter's Road we passed a group of high school girls, and I cocked my cap and hoped my eye was as big as a bluebag, and he walked with his coat flung open to show the bloodstains.[10]

The encounter is set four years after its actual date (they met when they were ten and eleven, but in the story they are fourteen and fifteen). This allows Thomas to balance the immature behaviour of the two proto-artists with sufficiently convincing signs of genuine creative ability. In truth, Jones was indeed exceptionally gifted – a polymath and prodigy who did write novels and compose music in his early teens, like the Dan Jenkyns of the story (in 'The Fight' he performs his 'twentieth sonata' to the Dylan character before casually bidding him farewell, adding that he has 'to finish a string trio tonight').[11] In their youth, then, it was Dan who was most likely to be seen as the school *wünderkind*, rather than the apparent slacker Dylan. Despite writing fluently himself, however, and being the elder of the two, Jones acknowledged Thomas's superiority in poetry from the very start.[12]

By opening the story with a fight, which swiftly turns to friendship when an adult intervenes, then becomes a deliciously amusing account of precocity, Thomas manages to fuse his young dog and aesthete sides. He differed from the more self-contained and aloof

Dan in having a need to rebel, enjoying escapades with 'his gang' of friends on the Prom and in the cinema, mixing with the 'roughs' as much as with the 'academics'.[13] 'The Fight' is a tale of literal and symbolic blood-brotherhood, and in it Thomas pays tribute to Jones's role in his development by featuring his home, 'Warmley', in Sketty, a mile up the road from Dylan's. Larger than 5 Cwmdonkin Drive, it was both more comfortably bourgeois and more easy-going, with an artistic atmosphere; Dan's father was a musician and raconteur, his mother a singer and embroidery artist, and Jim, his older brother, a musician and jazz fan. Dylan soon became a regular visitor.

The essence of their friendship was a mixture of artistic endeavour, serious play and youthful slapstick. They did what other boys their age would do: went to the cinema (horror films were a particular favourite), played cards, read comics, mock-fenced, argued, smoked furtively and speculated about sex. But there were few barriers between this kind of fun and creativity; indeed, the two were inti-mately linked. Dylan and Dan improvised music, occasionally involving other friends, such as Tom Warner, also a musician. 'Warmley' was well provided with the necessary resources; Dylan might vamp chords D.J. had taught him on the Jones's piano, or play the cello; Dan, an accomplished pianist, might play the piano himself or accompany Dylan on a range of other instruments, from violin to saucepan lids, an old motor horn, whistles or a coal scuttle.

The results lacked cohesion, but Jones was surely right to claim that they were 'never trite'.[14] Their creations were ascribed to imag-inary *Goon Show*-like characters, such as M. R. ('Max') Tonenbach (composer of 'Four horizontal Christmas carols', Op. 181), X. Q. Xumm and the Reverend Alexander Percy (the first man to crawl from London to Brighton on all fours). With Warner's help they fitted up a speaker to a rejigged gramophone and, calling themselves the WBC (Warmley Broadcasting Corporation), used it to transmit their music to other rooms in the house. On one occasion they tricked Dan's father; sat in the living room, listening to what he thought was a recital on the wireless, Dan's father was actually hearing his son's increasingly wild version of Beethoven's *Hammerklavier* sonata.

That such inventive clowning prefigured Dylan's later involvement in radio seems clear enough.

As a musician and composer, Dan introduced Dylan to modern music (Bartok, Berg, Hindemith) and to Surrealism, since he owned copies of the Surrealist journal *transition*.[15] As well as work by French Surrealist poets, *transition* was then serializing work by James Joyce, Thomas's favourite modern writer, as *Work in Progress* (Thomas would buy two instalments of what became *Finnegans Wake* as gifts to himself for Christmas 1933).[16] With his knowledge of modern culture, Dan was the first person to really understand what his friend was attempting in his poetry. In 'The Fight', 'he listen[s] wisely, like a boy aged a hundred, with his head on one side', as the Dylan character recites his poems.[17] They played word games, and fetishized certain words and phrases: 'everything at one time was "little" or "white"; and sometimes an adjective became funny in almost any connection: "innumerable bananas", "wilful moccasin", "a certain Mrs Protheroe".'[18] As well as judging each other's efforts, Dylan and Dan collaborated on writing lyrics, each writing alternate lines, by an imaginary poet named Walter Bram (as in Stoker; but *bram* is also Welsh for 'fart').

Thomas's style at the time was described by Jones as 'bafflingly inconsistent . . . fragile, furious, laconic, massive, delicate, incanta-tory, cool, flinty, violent, Chinese, Greek and shocking'. But, as Jones added, 'These word games, and even the most facetious of our collaborations, had a serious experimental purpose, and there is no doubt that they played a part in Dylan's early poetic development.'[19] Given the exposure to *transition*, the influence of Dada and Surrealist techniques is highly likely. What survives of this material reveals astonishing and dogged invention, a faint echo – juvenile and provincial, but perceptible – of Guillaume Apollinaire, Salvador Dalí, Luis Buñuel and Max Ernst. Two more aspects of this creative play can be noted. First, its interdisciplinary nature; literature, music and visual art were all involved, and this, too, looked forward to the catholicity of Thomas's adult work. Second, the contrast between literature as a sacred text, received from his father, and literature as a medium in which to experiment, as fostered by Dan (revealingly,

Dan disliked D.J., and described Dylan's relationship with him as 'very strained').[20]

By the time Thomas had left school and begun to work for the *South Wales Daily Post*, in September 1931, Jones was studying for his degree. He was an irregular attender of the gatherings at the Kardomah Café in town, where local artists, writers and their friends used to meet, and at the writing group that met at 5 Cwmdonkin Drive and the homes of other of Dylan's friends during his remaining time in Swansea. In 1934 the Jones family moved to Harrow, where Dylan visited Dan in June 1935 not long after he, too, had moved to the capital. Gradually, inevitably perhaps, their paths diverged. After the war, Jones settled back in Swansea and Dylan would meet him when he visited from London or Laugharne. But the intensity of their boyhood relationship was specific to its time and place, as Thomas lamented even as he memorialized it in a long letter from Ireland written to Dan later in the summer of 1935. Its sheer verve could never be repeated and it became part of an ideal past.[21] Whenever Dylan and Dan met thereafter, they would revert to the comic routines and games of their adolescence.

'Imitations of anything'?

Like all beginner writers, Dylan Thomas's poetry in his early school years was utterly imitative:

> I wrote endless imitations, though I never thought them to be imitations but, rather, wonderfully original things, like eggs laid by tigers. They were imitations of anything I happened to be reading at the time: Sir Thomas Browne, [Thomas] de Quincey, Henry Newbolt, the Ballads, [William] Blake, Baroness Orczy, [Christopher] Marlowe, Chums, the Imagists, the Bible, [Edgar Allan] Poe, [John] Keats, [D. H.] Lawrence, Anon., and Shakespeare. . . . they ranged from writers of school-boy adventure yarns to incomparable and inimitable masters like Blake.[22]

Sustained immersion in these led Thomas to a mastery of conventional verse by his early teens: comic, sentimental, war elegies, love poems, nature poems. When he was fourteen or so, he sent a batch of such poems to the poet and critic Robert Graves for his opinion. Graves later noted, 'I wrote back to say that they were irreproachable, but that he would eventually learn to dislike them. Even experts would have been deceived by the virtuosity of Dylan Thomas's conventional and wholly artificial early poems.'[23] Whether or not Thomas was acting on Graves's implicit advice, by this time he was already signalling his dissatisfaction with the kind of poetry he was known for by his family, friends and schoolmates.

One aspect of this was a kind of self-subversion, flirting with shame; a response born of the insecurity that was the flip-side of his confidence in his gifts, and which would create many of his problems in later life. In this case, it was a matter of trivial but telling acts of plagiarism. 'His Requiem', the poem published under his name in the *Western Mail* in 1927, was, in fact, by a poet named Lillian Gard, and had already appeared in the *Boy's Own Paper* in 1923. Revealingly, the 'Dylan' narrator of 'The Fight' refers to this poem, the real Dylan, as it were, fictionally drawing attention to the theft:

> A poem I had printed in the 'Wales Today' column of the *Western Mail* was pasted on the mirror to make me blush, but the shame of the poem had died. Across the poem I had written with a stolen quill and in flourishes: 'Homer Nods'. I was always waiting for the opportunity to bring someone into my bedroom – 'Come into my den; excuse the untidiness, take a chair. No! not that one, it's broken' – and force him to see the poem accidentally. 'I put it there to make me blush'. But nobody ever came in except my mother.[24]

In the famous boat-stealing scene in Wordsworth's *Prelude*, the young poet-to-be is pursued day and night by the spectre of a mountain that looms over him in silent rebuke. This passage, however, reveals an unguilty Thomas who flaunts, without quite revealing, what he did. 'Stolen quill' refers to a real quill in the fiction, stolen for the purpose of writing on the poem, but behind it lies a metaphorical theft in the real world of another poet's work; self-mirroring reflexivity indeed. It is another example of a lie that requires more lies in order to preserve the integrity of the original fib. In addition, in 1929 Dylan had submitted a poem, 'Sometimes', to the *Swansea Grammar School Magazine*. The real author was one Thomas S. Jones, and it had been cribbed from *Arthur Mee's Children's Encyclopaedia*. The magazine's editor, E. F. McInerny, recognized it and told D.J., who allegedly commented: 'After this, everything he writes is suspect.' McInerny's take was shrewder: it was, he wrote, Dylan, 'in an anti-social, devil-may-care mood, like a secret agent fingering a false and superfluous moustache'.[25] 'Superfluous' since, as McInerny understood, the theft was entirely unnecessary. The poets plagiarized in both cases were third-rate; Thomas, even at fifteen, could do much better himself. In this sense it was cocking a snook at authority of various kinds (to compound the joke, 'Thomas S. Jones', as Dylan surely saw, fortuitously combined the surnames of Dylan Thomas and Daniel Jones). To press the semi-hidden point home, in the April 1930 issue of *Swansea Grammar School Magazine*, of which he was now co-editor, Thomas published a pastiche of Yeats entitled 'In Borrowed Plumes'.

Yet while this behaviour was clearly a prank, it can also be seen as stemming from his desperation to impress. Dylan knew D.J. felt let down by his lack of academic effort. Publication of verse in national outlets – the *Western Mail* in particular – would have been a way of pleasing his stern father and justifying his defection. It is also worth noting that Thomas's mature poetry is notable for the impression it gives of simultaneous originality and familiarity; we often have the feeling when reading it that it is murmurous with other voices just beyond the horizon of identification. In the mid-1930s he would charge himself with self-parody, and in poems written towards the end of his life he invokes other writers' styles, Hardy and Yeats in particular.

The second, far more significant response to dissatisfaction with his own facility was creative, and would be the making of Dylan as a poet. In his essay 'Modern Poetry', published in the *Swansea Grammar School Magazine* in December 1929, he reveals an awareness not only of Georgian poetry, which was considered 'modern' by conservative popular taste, but of genuinely modern Imagist and Modernist poetry. Soon afterwards he began a conscious effort to remake himself as a Modernist poet. Starting on 27 April 1930, at the age of fifteen-and-a-half, he began to fair-copy the results into a series of school exercise books, dating each entry as if keeping a logbook of his development. The rejection of the polished verse style and the onset of the notebook poems were not concurrent; he continued writing in the earlier style for some time after he began writing the second. Only a few friends knew of the new, secret poems, and one of them, Percy Smart, noted:

> He was writing at the time some delightful light verse, sparkling, bright and clear, but he was of course already producing verse of a kind which many people can't understand, and I remember asking him why he did it: what was the point of writing 'privately' in this way. But he couldn't really understand the question: he wrote, he said, what was in him, and it was really quite irrelevant whether anyone else ever read it.[26]

The first notebook is inscribed 'Poems mainly in free verse' – a statement of intent, because free verse was the main criterion by which Modernist poetry was popularly defined. The contrast between even the earliest notebook poems, in flexible metres and irregular rhyme, and the *Swansea Grammar School Magazine* verse is striking. The first two notebooks show Dylan responding imaginatively to Imagist and post-Imagist poetry by the likes of Sacheverell and Edith Sitwell, Richard Aldington, H.D. and Ezra Pound, as he strove to develop a genuinely contemporary voice. The bulk of the poems, as one would expect of a boy in his mid-teens, are apprentice work: fluent, interesting to the scholar, but of no great value in themselves. In early 1933, however, in N3, a critical mass – of theme, of personal and public pressure and, above all, of form – was arrived at. Then, from September 1934, in the newly begun N4, we find the sudden explosive take-off into the original style of *18 Poems*. To arrive there, Dylan Thomas had to get out into the world – and reach more deeply within himself.

The world of work

In July 1931, having failed his exams, Thomas left school, and two months later entered the world of work. His contacts – his father and other teachers – helped him to find a job at the *South Wales Daily Post*, where he worked until December 1932. He was joining other former Grammar School pupils, many of them friends, such as Wynford Vaughan-Thomas. Soon he was sent out to report on minor stories. In *Return Journey* he mockingly presents his younger self as 'two-typewriter Thomas, the ace news-dick', and describes how he tried to act and dress the part, with bohemian additions – tweeds, loud checks, a pork-pie hat 'with a peacock feather', 'a conscious Woodbine'.[27] In *Return Journey* he caricatures a typical dull day in and out of the office:

> Let's have a dekko at your note-book. 'Called at British Legion: Nothing. Called at Hospital: One broken leg. Auction at the Metropole. Ring Mr Beynon *re* Gymanfa Ganu. Lunch: Pint and pasty at the Singleton with Mrs Giles. Bazaar at Bethesda Chapel. Chimney on fire Tontine Street. Walters Road Sunday School Outing. Rehearsal of the *Mikado* at Skewen' – all front page stuff.[28]

Although he had no shorthand, Thomas seems to have been an adequate reporter, and tales of his incompetence fall largely into the reprobate myth category. But he certainly did not live up to the 'newshawk slouch' he says he adopted. As with school, the job at the *Post* was mainly about what happened at an angle to any official expectations and duties. In 'Old Garbo', the story in *A Portrait of the Artist as a Young Dog* devoted to this period, the Dylan character looks forward to the supremely 'male moment' of being taken on a tour of the pubs and dives of the seamy dockside area of the Strand by Freddie Farr, a veteran reporter.[29] At first he revels in the colour and camaraderie of his surroundings, but he is unable to handle his drink, falls down, is sick and has to leave his substitute father ('Mr Farr, no father', as graffiti in the toilets of the *Post* building has it) and return home early.[30] The intended initiation rite is a mess, and does not lead to any symbolic transference of authority or attainment of poise and maturity. Similarly, it was soon recognized at the *Post* that Thomas's temperament and talents unsuited him for the daily grind; when possible he was diverted into feature writing, usually for the *Post*'s sister paper, the *Herald of Wales*. It was here that his most notable work as a journalist, a series of six articles on 'The Poets of Swansea', appeared between January and June 1932.

What is most remarkable about this historical survey is its thoroughness, balance and clarity; in a word, its professionalism. Although they are all minor figures, Walter Savage Landor apart, Thomas gives each poet his serious attention and respect, and it is clear that a good deal of research and thought has gone into each article. For the most part he kept his own ambitions out of the pieces, but at times they show through. W. H. Davies, who is not a Swansea poet but is 'the most gifted Welsh poet writing in English today', is criticized in passing for his limited scope; he has 'preferred to follow in the line of hedgerow poets' and failed to make his poetry 'a stepping place for the poor children of darkness to reach a saner world where the cancer of our warped generation is no more than a pleasant itch'.[31] It is hardly a manifesto, but Thomas is sizing up the opposition. In the last section he offers something that might be: 'Only a great writer can give this absurd country, full of green fields and chimney stacks, beauty and disease, the loveliness of the villages and the smoke-ridden horror of the towns, its full value and recognition.'

But feature-article writers are a luxury in an economic recession and it is likely that the management of the *Post* felt Thomas might not pull his weight in the long term. He left, by mutual agreement, on 11 December 1932. The next day he told Percy Smart that he had been offered and turned down a five-year contract, repeating the story to another friend, Trevor Hughes, in February 1933, adding what was perhaps the most compelling reason of all: 'what I feared was the slow but sure stamping out of individuality, the gradual contentment with life as it was, so much per week, so much for this, so much for that, so much left over for drink and cigarettes.'[32] Whether or not the story of the contract was true, it was true that Dylan couldn't square the routine with his writing. As with school, he took from it what he needed and moved on. A year before, he had told Hughes: 'I am at the most transitional period now. Whatever talents I possess may suddenly diminish or may suddenly increase.'[33] His prediction was premature: 1933 was to be the turning point, not 1932.

The Kardomah Gang

Working for the *Post* had opened Thomas's eyes to the broader layers of Swansea society, from aldermanic banquets to the dole queues, just as the Little Theatre was taking him out beyond it to the valley towns. His intellectual horizons were widening, too. The Kardomah Café, near the offices of the *Post*, was the social centre of Swansea, where journalists often lunched or drank coffee. In the summer of 1932 Thomas's former schoolfriend Charlie Fisher joined him at the *Post*, and they began to take their breaks and meet in the Kardomah on Saturdays. Others who joined them included Dan Jones, now at Swansea University, who might bring his own friends, including Tom Warner, Thornley Jones, another composer, the teacher Mabley Owen, and the painter Fred Janes. Janes, who would make three portraits of Thomas, had just won a scholarship to the Royal Academy Schools in London on the strength of a portrait of a fellow student at Swansea School of Art, Mervyn Levy, Dylan's friend from their days at Mrs Hole's dame school. It is too often forgotten that Thomas was one of a golden generation of Swansea 'poets, painters, musicians in their beginnings'.[34] The 'Passer-By' in *Return Journey* recalls 'the old Kardomah days' they enjoyed, and Thomas himself, in some detail:

he wasn't a reporter then, he'd just left the grammar school. Him
and Charlie Fisher . . . and Tom Warner and Fred Janes, drinking
coffee-dashes and arguing the toss [about] Music and poetry and
painting and politics. Einstein and Epstein, Stravinsky and Greta
Garbo, death and religion, Picasso and girls . . . Communism,
symbolism, Bradman, Braque, the Watch Committee, free love,
free beer, murder, Michelangelo, ping-pong, ambition, Sibelius
and girls . . . they talked about Augustus John, Emil Jannings,
Carnera, Dracula, Amy Johnson, trial marriage, pocket-money,
the Welsh sea, the London stars, King Kong, anarchy, darts,
T. S. Eliot, and girls.[35]

This group of friends, which (despite the 'girls' refrain) could
include women, such as Thomas's friends Vera and Evelyn Phillips,
also met to bond and verbally spar weekly in one another's homes
– money being short – as well as in cafés and pubs. Evelyn, who had
first encountered Dylan as a 'skinny little chap' with 'this beautiful
voice' on a summer holiday in Gower, is the likely dedicatee of
'The force that through the green fuse drives the flower', and the
Phillips family home in Bryn y Mor Crescent in the Uplands was as
welcoming as 'Warmley'.[36] (She was to move to London at around
the same time as Thomas, and both she and Vera remained his
friends for many years.[37]) In short, it was an intense and buoyant
cultural milieu in which Dylan was first among equals, an outstand-
ing but not a dominant member. When considering his alleged lack
of interest in any subject but English, it is this broader, sustaining
context of discussion groups, like-minded friends, theatre, film,
books and journalism that must be kept in mind.

Several strains of imagery in Thomas's early poetry derive from
a wide-ranging intellectual curiosity that is usually buried in their
complex textures. Some will be discussed in Chapter Three; here we
will simply take as one example the ancient Egyptian imagery that
features in several early poems, and can be traced back to the public
interest in the subject following the discovery of Tutankhamun's
tomb in 1922, possibly augmented by a mummy on display in
Swansea Museum ('the museum, which should have been *in a*

museum', as Thomas described it).[38] The title of his poem 'My world is pyramid' reflects his use of such imagery to symbolize stifling, four-square stasis, a deathly embalming in familial, spiritual and emotional as well as physical senses. One ancient Egyptian belief was that, after death, the *ka* (life-spirit) is weighed by the god Anubis against Ma'at, the feather of truth and harmony; it is admitted to bliss if they balance, and fed to Ammit, the crocodile-headed Devourer of Souls, if not. In the poetry this surfaces several times in the phrase 'death's feather', alluding not just to ancient Egypt, but to placing a feather on someone's lips to see whether they were dead, the slang phrase 'you could have knocked me down with a feather', the First World War practice of handing white feathers to young men not in uniform in an attempt to shame them into joining up, and John Donne's *Devotions* ('There is scarce any thing that hath not killed some body: a hair, a feather hath done it').[39] Each usage taps into an existential fear – of war, or death – and, along with the immediate, surrealistic frisson, reverberates in a multilayered and richly meaningful way.

After leaving the *Post*, Thomas was able to organize his days around his writing (and contributions to the Little Theatre), establishing a loose pattern that would hardly change for the rest of his life, and which he would try to maintain wherever he lived. It involved writing and reading in the mornings, a drink and lunch, perhaps with friends, more writing in the afternoon, and evenings given over to socializing. Such days were often interspersed with long, solitary walks, to Mumbles, or into Gower, often lasting several hours. He relied on the indulgence of his family, who did not push him to find another job, and financed his social life as well as his domestic upkeep. There is no doubt that, in a house shared by two young frustrated adults and their ageing parents, the atmosphere was less harmonious than it had been. Nancy's letters to Haydn Taylor record the tension and arguments that could break out, although it is possible that she exaggerated D.J.'s temper, Florrie's prying and Dylan's drunkenness and petty thefts in order to hasten her marriage, which finally took place in May 1933 and was followed by a move to the London suburbs in Surrey.

A contributory factor to the complex and sometimes fractious circumstances that attended Thomas's arrival at maturity, as a man and as a writer, was the economic, social and political climate of the time. The Great Depression that followed the Wall Street Crash began just as Thomas was finding his way in the adult world; paradoxically, his mental horizons were expanding just at the moment of maximum external constraint. Although Swansea escaped relatively lightly by comparison with much of industrial South Wales, a quarter of its workforce were on the dole by 1932. Unsurprisingly, Thomas and his contemporaries were broadly socialist or anarchist in outlook. Accounts of his time at the *Post* tend to focus on amusing and colourful details, as he often did himself, such as his shock at the sight of a body in the morgue, the pomposity of an official function or the thrill of slumming it in dockside dives.[40] But this is to simplify, even trivialize, his response to the larger, very uncolourful panorama of human waste that unfolded in the early 1930s, and the radical response to it his work represents. It is true that in the *Portrait* stories and radio broadcasts, Swansea is often presented in amusing and realist terms. But these works came later, and their relatively straightforward treatment of Swansea was not that which fed the process poems and stories, his most original writings, and the work with which he would first make his name.

Swansea and the Anglo-Welsh mongrel

It is well known that Swansea, an industrial port town with a population of 170,000 in 1914, was as crucial to the formation of Dylan Thomas's sensibility as, say, Dublin to James Joyce's. What is less well understood is that its influence on his early, most groundbreaking work had more to do with its divided, borderline character, as embodied in its location and history, than with its surface appearance. Towards the end of the eighteenth century Swansea had briefly been a fashionable resort, a potential Welsh Brighton or Bognor. But it simultaneously witnessed the beginnings of large-scale industry with the development of copper-smelting, tinplate and metal manufacture in the Tawe Valley. The town could have gone in either of two directions at this point, but decisions made by its leading citizens meant that it took the industrial route. By the mid-nineteenth century Swansea was 'Copperopolis', the world's largest producer of copper, hub of a global network for the transhipment of ore and its finished products. Swansea's metal magnates became plutocratically rich, while the Tawe Valley, poisoned by metallic fumes and spoil, became one of the most blighted and polluted places on the planet. The town was starkly divided between a wealthy and spacious western side – where the rich and middle classes lived, with parks, a botanic garden, a county cricket ground, beaches and pleasant suburbs, such as Uplands and Sketty – and the poorer, deprived working-class areas by the docks or inland, cramped up the Tawe Valley to the east and north.

As the most economically developed town in Wales in the early nineteenth century, Swansea was the national centre for the arts, science and technology – it had the first Welsh scientific society, art college and museum – and it remained, until eclipsed by Cardiff in the 1860s, Wales's largest population centre. By the early twentieth century it was still a confident place, with a lively and well-integrated regional centre, past its Victorian heyday but able to live off the fat of past glories; it remained a busy port, with a market, a metal exchange, two active theatres, two large flagship department stores, a brand-new Guildhall, a college of the University of Wales, a football team, numerous cinemas, several newspapers, a complex political culture and a varied artistic life (albeit stifled at times by philistinism). But its distinctiveness came from the contrast between its location – Landor had likened Swansea Bay to the Bay of Naples – and its grimy, industrial *raison d'être* (what Thomas meant when he described it as 'an ugly, lovely town'), as well as from other qualities that pointed up this basic contrast. Swansea was fundamentally a border-zone, end-of-the-line place, somewhat out on a limb, lying on and across a series of boundaries. It was, to start with, at the furthest western edge of the South Wales industrial belt; immediately beyond it lay rural Carmarthenshire. In the 1920s and '30s it was also on the western-most boundary between anglophone Wales and Welsh-speaking Wales. Last, but not least, it lay on the elemental border between land and sea. All this meant that it was a place where contradictory forces met, overlapped, conflicted and, sometimes, fused.

The process poetry and prose derive their power from Thomas's own hybrid and hyphenated status as Anglo-Welsh, and the border-crossing qualities he drew from Swansea and his family background, which contained those qualities in terms of language, class, geographical attachment and genealogy. In Thomas's work, identity is always at least double, as the title of the poem 'I, in my intricate image' proclaims. Even his recurring image for himself as a dog may be said to allude to this mongrel, in-between nature, and his work is characterized by its confrontation with, and violent yoking together of, paradoxical extremes: death and life, flesh and machine, sickness and health, land and sea, the molecular and the cosmic, belief and unbelief. These polar opposites (and 'poles' and the geographic Poles often appear in the work), accentuated by the Depression, matched and confirmed those Thomas found in himself, divided as he was between the 'rough' boy and the elite artist. It is in this profound and radically divided sense that in his most groundbreaking work he is a 'Swansea poet'.

3

The Rimbaud of Cwmdonkin Drive: The Poetics of Process, 1933–4

Dylan Thomas was a writer who reinvented himself on several occasions. By far the most important of these reinventions occurred between April and October 1933. It was during this six-month period that the years of precocious preparation, of interesting but as yet undistinguished poetry, would finally pay off with the breakthrough into a powerfully original and remarkably mature poetic style – in the form of what is known as 'process' poetry – and his recognition as the leading poet of his generation.

After leaving the *Post* at the end of 1932 Thomas established a routine, casual-seeming, but immersive in reading and writing. Depending on which letter of the time one reads, it took various forms, but generally involved late rising, a newspaper (the Thomases took the *Daily Telegraph*) and other, more eclectic reading ('translations out of the Greek or the Film Pictorial, a new novel from Smith's, a new book of criticism, or an old favourite like Grimm or George Herbert, anything in the world so long as it is printed'), writing, a lunchtime pint, a walk, and more writing and reading before going out for a drink in the evening.[1] The routine was to vary little for the rest of his life, although at this period his evenings might also involve Little Theatre activity, discussion with friends or a film. 'Not a very British day,' as he summed up one account: 'too much thinkin', too much talkin', too much alcohol.'[2] Despite his insouciant tone, he was anxious, and sometimes showed it; he had given up a job, and gambled on making a life as a writer, but was keenly aware that he had achieved very little to date. His friends were already moving on. Daniel Jones was now at university, and usually too busy to spend much time with him. Dylan's two main correspondents, Percy Smart and Trevor Hughes, had jobs in London. A plan to work freelance for the Northcliffe Press, owners of the *Post*, soon collapsed. The title of his only article for them, in January 1933, 'Genius and Madness Akin in World of Art', is painfully close to Nancy's descriptions of Dylan in letters of the time to Haydn as 'rushing & raving like a tormented thing'.[3]

High Modernism's New Country

Dylan Thomas's impasse as a writer in early 1933 was connected to a larger one in the literary world. The economic and social crisis of the times had radicalized young writers and intellectuals; capitalism was in crisis, while the USSR, with its planned economy, seemed unscathed. But their natural role models in the previous Modernist generation – Yeats, Lawrence, Eliot and Pound – were reactionaries, and lacking in relevance to a generation that, by 1932, felt itself to be threatened by the spectre of a new world war with the rise of fascism in Europe.

The style that emerged as a result, variously dubbed 'New Country' or 'Pylon' poetry, rejected Modernism's formal concerns – embodied in its irregular verse forms, collage techniques and typographical high jinks – as individualistic and self-indulgent. The aim of its practitioners was to diagnose social ills, comment on them and offer solutions to the crisis. This demanded, they felt, a plain style and collective effort. Experiment was shunned in favour of discursive syntax, rhyme and stanza-forms rifled from English poetry's traditional back catalogue. Out went anguished brooding, mythic structures and symbolic profundity; in came collaborative projects, instructive allegory and sociological surfaces. The leading exponents of the new style were Louis MacNeice, Cecil Day-Lewis and Stephen Spender, with W. H. Auden as their leader, and their work was showcased in two anthologies edited by Michael Roberts, *New Signatures* (1932) and *New Country* (1933).

'MacSpaunday', as they were collectively known, would dominate British poetry until 1939. The positions they adopted in their writing and personal lives were influenced by Marxist and Freudian doctrines; capitalist irrationality had to be replaced by economic planning, bourgeois neuroses to be swept away by a brusque emotional hygiene. Day-Lewis and Spender would briefly join the Communist Party and try to write verse propaganda.

Thomas shared MacSpaunday's revolutionary-apocalyptic outlook and, to a lesser degree, the solutions they proposed. But he distrusted their tactics and differed in his response. In part this stemmed from differences of temperament, nationality and social standing. His lower middle-class, grammar-school, Welsh world was not that of the upper middle-class, public-school, Oxbridge MacSpaunday poets. Thomas saw that MacSpaunday's revolt into plain style was at some level a guilty disavowal of their privileged origins, origins he did not share. He felt their radicalism was 'bogus', and was suspicious of collectivity; all well and good if you had behind you centuries of English poetic tradition and a social assurance from which readers might intuit the ego you were subordinating to the collective effort, but less easy if, as a Welsh anglophone writer, your sense of selfhood and its specific Welsh contexts had never found literary expression before.[4] In addition, Thomas found New Country poetry itself to be cerebral and dogmatic, wilfully neglectful of the relish of language as a medium that he felt was essential to poetry, and he was disinclined to abandon the densities of Modernism for a clarity that seemed shallow and propagandistic.[5]

As a result, his initial response to New Country, in late 1932, involved an uneasy blend of his own subjective, brooding style with their political themes, using Eliot's free, irregularly rhymed verse rather than traditional forms. 'Before the gas fades', of February 1933, is a good example. It tells of 'the century's trap' about to 'snap round your middle', a state that 'falls to bits', the horrors of 'Man's manmade sparetime' – unemployment – and thoughts of suicide. But it does not offer analysis or propose solutions. Thomas is pessimistic about the future, envisaging messy outcomes: 'flesh will perish, and blood/ Run down the world's gutters.'[6] Although gloomy and shapeless, and written in a style he was to abandon, it reminds us that some elements of the early verse would remain constant in his work – among them, its physicality and expressionism. He would acknowledge the dangers of solipsism in 1933 and 1934, in such poems as 'Ears in the turrets hear' and 'Especially when the October wind', but he felt that good poetry ruled out a group mentality, and should not look up to a leader figure. The trouble with 'Before the gas' is that it melds two styles passively, and is turbid and unfocused as a result. Dylan avoids being preachy or *parti pris* in it, but at the cost of a lack of energy or vision.

Bert Trick

As so often in Dylan Thomas's life, the person he most needed at a given moment now appeared on the scene. Thomas Taig, a university English lecturer and fellow Little Theatre member, suggested that he show his work to Bert Trick, a left-wing Swansea Labour Party councillor with literary interests. It was probably in late 1932 that Thomas first visited Trick at the grocery shop he owned and lived above on Glanbrydan Avenue, just a few hundred yards from Cwmdonkin Drive. Trick was instantly impressed. Thomas, in turn, found Trick an invaluable interlocutor, passionate about literature and politics; a married man in his thirties, he was grounded and more worldly-wise than Dylan's contemporaries. They began to hold twice-weekly meetings with other writer friends, and Glanbrydan Avenue became a 'plebeian version of Dan Jones's Warmley', in Paul Ferris's phrase.[7]

Trick's beliefs were an amalgam of pacifism, Christianity and socialism. Thomas met him at a time of intense political ferment, following the defection of the Labour Party leader Ramsay MacDonald to the National Government in 1931, and the Party's shift leftwards under the influence of the Independent Labour Party (ILP) and the Socialist League. Trick's beliefs resembled those of George Lansbury, the pacifist, Christian socialist leader of the ILP, for whom Christ was a socialist revolutionary before his time (Lansbury – roughly speaking, a 1930s equivalent of Jeremy Corbyn – was leader of the Labour Party from 1932 to 1935). In August 1934 Thomas wrote on behalf of himself and Trick to Ithel Davies of the

Bert Trick, the 'communist grocer', outside his shop on Glanbrydan Avenue, Swansea, 1930s.

No More War Movement, seeking to enrol 'not just as nominal members but as active propagandists', and he would stick to his pacifist beliefs throughout the Second World War.[8] On religion, Thomas was more radical than Trick, critical of formal congregations and dogma, satirizing them in such short stories as 'The Enemies' and 'The Holy Six'. Even so, it is highly likely that Trick sparked Thomas's interest in the Unitarianism espoused by his great-uncle Gwilym Marles.

The core principles of Unitarianism strongly resemble the monism and pantheism that are central to what would become Thomas's process style. It dispenses with most Christian dogma, rejecting original sin, the Last Judgement (and thus hell and eternal damnation), miracles, the Trinity, the Virgin birth, predestination and the absolute authority of scripture. Crucially, it also rejects the doctrine of atonement, believing that Christ was neither divine, nor the son of God except in a metaphorical sense. Instead, it stresses our essential unity with God, as the primary power of the universe, teaching that all humans are born in possession of a spark of divinity and the potential to achieve Christ-like perfection. Christ himself is viewed not as the son of God, but rather as a human being who realized humanity's divine promise. Thomas did not believe in a personal God or the afterlife, but he identified passionately with the humble, the oppressed and the downtrodden, believed there was a spiritual dimension to existence, and felt that the divine existed in a metaphorical sense: 'God is the country of the spirit, and each of us is given a little holding of ground in that country . . . to explore,' as he put it.[9] He would use biblical material as a resonant shorthand, a set of commonly understood archetypes, for exploring this spiritual 'ground'.

Trick drew a firm link between Thomas's spiritual beliefs and the politics he now imparted; Dylan, he said, 'was far out on the left . . . He believed in the freedom of man to be man, that he shouldn't be oppressed by his fellows, that every man had the stamp of divinity in him, and anything that prevented that divinity having full play was an evil thing.'[10] And, just as Trick became 'intoxicated with words' under Thomas's tutelage, so did Thomas absorb Trick's knowledge of Marxism and local politics, into which he was now drawn. The Socialist League envisaged socialism occurring through the bringing of the commanding heights of the economy into public ownership, adding that if the democratic will to do so were thwarted by the ruling classes, an Enabling Act, passed by Parliament and backed by the Party and the masses, should be used to enforce change.[11] These were Thomas's politics, as he would set them out in letters to Pamela Hansford Johnson, and while past biographers have tended to dismiss them as incoherent, they were logical, consistent and widely held in the Labour movement at the time.[12] Similarly, in 1934–5 Thomas espoused a revolutionary, Christian-tinged socialism in letters and articles to the *Swansea and West Wales Guardian*, a paper set up and co-edited by Trick to circumvent the right-wing, Beaverbrook-owned *Swansea Evening Post*. It was also with Trick and another friend, the radical priest Leon Atkin, that he joined a 3,000-strong audience at Swansea's Plaza cinema addressed by Oswald Mosley in July 1934. Thomas was sitting beside Atkin, who triggered the uproar that ended the fascist rally, and a few days later wrote his most overtly political poem, 'The hand that signed the paper', dedicating it to Trick. Marxism also had an impact on Thomas's emerging process style in the form of the triad of thesis, antithesis and synthesis, which Marx adapted from Hegel. This is an essentially conflictual model of historical progress that he saw had its literary equivalent in William Blake's belief that 'Without Contraries is no Progression'. Conflict and debate structure the poems he began to write in mid-1933, and shape the triadic form of 'I see the boys of summer' and 'All all and all', the statement poems chosen to open and close *18 Poems*.

Dylan would affectionately but somewhat offhandedly describe Bert Trick as 'a communist grocer' in whose kitchen they had 'threatened the annihilation of the ruling classes over sandwiches and jelly and blancmange'.[13] But he would also make clear that Trick 'gave my rebelliousness a direction', and there is no doubt that Trick gifted the dynamic sense of the world he needed in order to shed his poetic torpor.[14] A decade later, when New Country poets were abandoning their socialist principles, Thomas stuck firmly to his; he was consistently outspoken in his denunciation of individual exploiters and cruel or violent behaviour, vehemently defended the NHS and, as his communist friend Jack Lindsay noted, 'signed the Stockholm Peace Petition [and] the Rosenberg Petition, and actively supported the Authors' World Peace Appeal'.[15]

'And death shall have no dominion'

As Trick noted, 'what made Dylan tick' was a belief that 'man is the creature and creator of his own world, and that means there's frustration *and* commitment . . . [man] must attempt to penetrate the eternal mystery and, being finite, he must accept defeat' (our emphasis).[16] This tension between frustration and commitment, between pessimism and exaltation, is at the heart of the poem that marks Thomas's first step towards his process style, 'And death shall have no dominion'. It was appropriate, therefore, that Trick should have been responsible for it when, in early April 1933, he proposed that he and Dylan compete to see who could write the best poem on the subject of immortality.

'And death' is one of Thomas's best-known poems, and its resounding refrain, adapted from St Paul's Epistle to the Romans, is seen as attesting to a belief in the afterlife. Yet it is deeply ambiguous. In its first version, the 'soul' is mentioned in the opening stanza, and a fourth stanza declares that, after death, souls can 'never be dust'.[17] This version, which endorses a Christian belief in the afterlife, is the one published in May 1933. But before he included it in *Twenty-Five Poems* (1936), he removed the word 'soul' and deleted the fourth stanza entirely. Its final lines now read:

> Though they be mad and dead as nails,
> Heads of the characters hammer through daisies;
> Break in the sun till the sun breaks down,
> And death shall have no dominion.[18]

The defiant assertion of the afterlife remains, in the refrain; but the 'soul', through which we survive death, has vanished, and the lines preceding the last repetition of the refrain derive from slang terms that are dismissive of soul and afterlife, 'dead as a doornail' and 'pushing up the daisies'. 'Heads' decomposing to 'hammer through daisies' is a vitalist vision of the body's decomposition into its constituent molecules and their absorption back into the vegetable and animal life cycle, but death shall have no dominion over my carbon atoms is cold comfort to anyone who expects wings, white robes and a reunion with the dear departed. And while 'till the sun breaks down' is a hyperbolic way of saying eternity, as Thomas knew, it had recently been discovered that stars have a life cycle and do indeed 'break down' and die.

In other words, the poem has been deliberately rendered paradoxical and ambiguous. Rhetorically and emotionally, it still endorses St Paul's promise, and this is how it is usually understood (it is often read at funerals), but its intellectual sense runs counter to it. What is most significant, however, is that there is no attempt to resolve the contradiction: both readings coexist without one being allowed to cancel out the other. What Thomas has done becomes clearer if we imagine the same poem as written by a MacSpaunday poet. In that case, the religious message would have been ironically framed by an atheistic viewpoint. Thomas's preference for open-ended paradox over ironic resolution reflects simultaneous commitment and frustration – his conviction that, whether or not one believes in an afterlife, it will never be possible to definitively prove or disprove, and that this should lead us to distrust hyper-rationalist claims to explain away the mysteries of the universe. It is this realm of unknowability, rather than belief in the afterlife as such, that constitutes the metaphysical, spiritual dimension of human existence for him. In political terms, the preservation of stark antinomies reflects his rejection of the bourgeois liberalism, with its willingness to compromise with the powers that be, that lurked beneath the radicalism of the MacSpaunday poets.

Unpacking the fruitful potential of this ambiguity, and the full implications of 'And death shall have no dominion', from daisy roots to supernovae, would take Thomas some months. Its immediate, and most important, lesson lay in being the first notebook poem to use regular metre, stanza form, rhyme and refrain. This may have been a nod to Trick, who wrote in a more old-fashioned style, or simply because Thomas did not take their competition very seriously. Whatever the case, it was easily the most successful poem he had ever written, despite going against the grain of three years of his effort to cultivate Modernist irregularity. The issue now was one of him realizing why this was so, and exactly how to respond to it.

Dylan certainly understood the poem's effectiveness. He sent it to *New English Review*, where it appeared on 18 May, his first poem to be published in a national journal. But it took a little longer for him to grasp how much its success owed to its conservative form. This is apparent from the fact that, after writing it, he reverted to irregular verse. He then switched briefly to stanza form, then back again. N3 records a three-month tussle between the two principles. Then, on 15 July, he wrote, '"Find meat on bones that soon have none"', a rhyming poem in regular stanzas. With its message that we should surrender to universal cycles ('the maggot that no man can kill'), and that opposition to them is hubristic ('the reason's wrong'), it was another step towards the process vision.[19] As Dylan would explain in October that year, 'I have defended form in my recent letters and spat me of the sprawling formlessness of Ezra Pound's performing Yanks and others.'[20] N3 ends, revealingly, on 16 August, with a run of three stanza-based poems.

Metaphysical Modernism: the 'process' style

The crystallization of the process style took place in a home atmosphere that had grown notably calmer. Nancy had left Cwmdonkin Drive in May and Thomas now often relaxed by visiting the Tricks' weekend bungalow in Gower. He was reading criticism by T. S. Eliot and William Empson on the Metaphysical poets – John Donne, George Herbert, Andrew Marvell – which construed them as Modernists before their time. Eliot's and Empson's advocacy of Donne, whose poetry conveyed religious intensity and a deep sense of mortality through clotted syntax and a lavish use of rhetorical devices, was particularly important to Thomas. Empson, his near-contemporary, had recently published *Seven Types of Ambiguity* (1930), in which the full complexity of such poetry was unravelled for the first time. Thomas had read poems by Empson which were effectively a Modernist updating of the Metaphysical style, and it is likely that he read this critical work too.

Over the summer of 1933 Dylan Thomas felt his way carefully towards a Modernist Metaphysical poetry of his own by devising ways to replicate Modernism's leaps of tone, imagistic juxtapositions and verbal richness within the traditional stanza forms, rhyme schemes and standard syntax of New Country verse, adding to both a Blakean religiosity. His version of Metaphysical Modernism differed from Empson's in its greater dynamism, visceral imagery, gallows humour and emphasis – through alliteration and other devices – on the medium of poetry itself, language. Confident that he was on the right track, on 7 July he entered 'Praise to the architects' in N3, ironically dismissing MacSpaunday: 'A pinch of Auden is a lion's feast.'[21]

Pamela Hansford Johnson and the *Sunday Referee*

Buoyed by the publication of 'And death', Dylan had sent more
poems to national journals. In July he visited London, and at
Bert Trick's suggestion met John Middleton Murry, the founder
of the *Adelphi*, a pacifist and socialist journal with a preference for
Romantic poetic styles, in the Chelsea flat of Richard Rees, *Adelphi*'s
current editor. Rees, who was impressed by his work, took 'No man
believes, who, when a star falls shot', a recent poem in regular stanza
form, for publication in the September 1933 issue. 'No man believes'
exemplifies another aspect of the emerging style, namely the use of
the double negative to create a qualified positive statement. Mean-
while, Rees sent some of Thomas's poems to Herbert Read, a leading
art historian, critic and champion of Surrealism, to pass on to Eliot.
Dylan Thomas, then, was already making ripples in poetry circles in
London a year before he moved there. At this point, however, another
new friend appeared who, along with Trick, would act as a foil to his
energy and midwife to the emerging style.

'That sanity be kept', a still-inert blend of personal brooding and
MacSpaunday-style social commentary, written in irregular, Eliotic
metre, had appeared in another London journal, the *Sunday Referee*,
on 3 September 1933. It attracted the notice of the *Referee*'s star poetry
contributor of the moment, Pamela Hansford Johnson, and she wrote
to Thomas.[22] He replied, so beginning an intense, detailed correspon-
dence that would last for a year and a half and takes up more than a
hundred pages in the *Collected Letters*. More than any other source,
Thomas's letters to Johnson reveal his thinking while he worked out
his new style, as his growing personal involvement with her led him
to define his work against her own more conventional verse. With
his first letter to her he enclosed 'Before I knocked', dated 6 September
1933 in N4.[23] It was his most accomplished poem so far, and the first
to be wholly in the process style.

'Before I knocked' usefully helps to define the 'process' style.
It is, first and foremost, a 'metaphysic' poem, as Thomas called it.[24]
Second, as with '"Find meat on bones"' and 'No man believes', its
regular form acts to powerfully compress its material. Third, it traces

the inner workings of the body, which it links to cosmic cycles, reflected in the pantheistic kinship of the unborn Jesus with forces and substances that embody flux and mutability: dew, water, seas, wind, snow, hail. The verse is reinforced by a strong iambic pulse, which mimics bodily rhythms – of the blood, breathing, sex and so on – while onomatopoeia and alliteration draw attention to the poem's materiality; its own linguistic body. Finally, there is the wordplay, most striking in the use of 'doublecrossed' in the final line:

> You who bow down at cross and altar,
> Remember me and pity Him
> Who took my flesh and bone for armour
> And doublecrossed my mother's womb.[25]

Puns in Thomas's work often link inside and outside worlds, the abstract and the material, and this is a famous instance, brilliantly condensing the poem's conflicts and raising them to a new pitch: Jesus 'doublecrossed' his mother's womb literally, by entering it as the Holy Spirit and exiting it as Jesus; metaphorically, since Mary was ignorant of God's purpose and was tricked by him; and in narrative terms, since Jesus will die on the cross.[26] Given his Unitarian heritage, it is worth noting that Thomas's iconoclasm here exceeds anything any Christian denomination would tolerate, as he identifies his life with that of Jesus, and elsewhere in these poems sets himself up as demiurge. This Jesus is the victim of a 'doublecross' by God, in the spirit of Blake's rejection of the Old Testament Yahweh as a patriarchal tyrant and understanding of Satan as romantic rebel. It is no coincidence, then, that in the letter accompanying the poem Thomas told Johnson that 'I am in the path of Blake, but so far behind him that only the wings on his heels are in sight.'[27]

Process

'Process' is not a term Dylan Thomas himself ever used of his work, but it aptly sums up the style he evolved in the summer and autumn of 1933. It was first applied by the critic David Aivaz in 1945, and later popularized by another critic, Ralph Maud, in his pioneering study *Entrances to Dylan Thomas* of 1963. Aivaz adopted it from the poem 'A process in the weather of the heart' and Maud applied it to the body-centred poems of Thomas's first two collections, although a process poetic may be said to underpin all of Thomas's poetry from this point on. Maud's description of how it works emphasizes the dialectical movement of poems via a series of opposites. In 'I see the boys of summer in their ruin', for example, these are initiated with the terms 'summer' and 'ruin' in the opening line. They give rise to new terms that produce a new pair of opposites – and so on. The triad thesis > antithesis > synthesis is a structural principle for the poem as a whole, which is in three parts: in the first the 'boys' are denounced for squandering their 'promise', in the second they speak to defend themselves, and a final section is made up of lines with no clearly defined speaker, seeming to offer closure but in reality radically ambiguous and open-ended.

'A process in the weather of the heart' is revealing in a different way, giving as it does a more stripped-down blueprint for the vision behind such poetry:

A process in the weather of the heart
Turns damp to dry; the golden shot
Storms in the freezing tomb.
A weather in the quarter of the veins
Turns night to day; blood in their suns
Lights up the living worm.

A process in the eye forewarns
The bones of blindness; and the womb
Drives in a death as life leaks out.[28]

What this reveals, as Aivaz puts it, is that 'Process is unity in nature, its direction is the cyclical return; the force that drives it is the generative energy in natural things.'[29] Organic creation and destruction are simultaneous aspects of the force, such that death and life not only imply each other, but are essentially the same. We are not merely born to die, or even to know we are dying as we live; conception is itself a death, 'the golden shot' of semen 'storms' the 'freezing tomb' of the womb, the eye always signals its coming 'blindness' in age and death. Whatever denies process, whether in art, life or faith, is illusory.

'Process', then, involves an uncompromising focus on first and last things, biological, cosmic and philosophical-religious, and links all objects and events: body and cosmos, atom and galaxy, creation and apocalypse. It is pantheist and monist, supercharged by an awareness of Einsteinian cosmology, post-Darwinian biology and Freudian psychoanalysis, and understands that the seemingly stable universe is in a state of ceaseless flux.[30] Solid matter is mostly inter-atomic void, time is relative, our emotions are functions of hormonal chemicals and our egos are unstable contingent assemblages, bullied by the superego and the id. Appearances are always deceptive, and the one certainty is that there is no certainty. Agreeing with Blake again, Thomas's process poetry assumes that 'you . . . believe a lie/ When you see with, not through the eye', and this sense of deep reality accounts for the paucity in the early poems of recognizable social contexts of the kind found in New Country poetry.[31] Poems are synthetic and summatory, not epiphanic or anecdotal.

In the strictly defined 'process' poems of 1933–6, the negative aspect of the force is to the fore. In 'A process in the weather of the heart', a death is forcefully 'driven in' to the womb, but new life manages only to 'leak out' of it.[32] The embryo dies in being born, elbowing others into the grave; their deaths are, in turn, births into the life of decomposing matter as they re-enter the natural cycle. In these poems – and in such short stories as 'The Visitor' – what is ordinarily drawn out and therefore overlooked in existence is horrifyingly compressed and vividly apparent, as if in some hyper-accelerated time-lapse film. It is this violent and grotesque aspect that distinguishes Thomas's 'process' from Romantic pantheism or idealism.

Bodies, Sex and Repression

Thomas's explication of the effects of process is fixated on the human body. In part this is because bodies were what were most threatened by impending war. They were also neglected by MacSpaunday; 'the emotional appeal in Auden wouldn't raise the corresponding emotion in a tick,' Thomas informed Glyn Jones in March 1934, insinuating poetic anaemia and bodilessness.[33] Moreover, bodies link us intimately to the universe, and are to be understood as microcosms, the processes in one translating those in the other. A new life is a new universe, ontogenesis is cosmogenesis. In the same letter to Jones, Thomas explained: 'My own obscurity is quite an unfashionable one, based, as it is, on a preconceived symbolism derived . . . from the cosmic significance of the human anatomy.'[34] Defending his grim anatomical imagery of gristle, cancers, skin, bone, blood, semen and wombs to Johnson a few months later, he would claim:

> The greatest description I know of our 'earthiness' is to be found in John Donne's Devotions, where he describes man as earth of the earth, his body earth, his hair a wild shrub growing out of the land. All thoughts and actions emanate from the body. Therefore the description of a thought or action – however abstruse it may be – can be beaten home by bringing it onto a physical level. Every idea, intuitive or intellectual, can be imaged and translated in terms of the body, its flesh, skin, blood, sinews, veins, glands, organs, cells, or senses. Through my small, bonebound island I have learnt all I know, experienced all, sensed all.[35]

But bodies were also central to Thomas because the puritan society he grew up in repressed them, adolescent bodies in particular. This is why the early poems steam with sex; they are frank, as never before in English poetry, about masturbation, for example, its 'urchin hungers' 'rehearsed upon a raw-edged nerve'.[36] Writing about sex, Thomas inevitably came up against his own inexperience, and his biologism can seem reductive. Yet its fatalism accurately reflects the sense of impending doom of a generation who felt they were being led to the slaughter. And while he shared some of the prejudices of his era, his attitudes to gender and sex were broadly progressive. He viewed 'sin' as a social construct, condemned 'the medieval laws' that 'dictated compulsory virginity' at a time when the body was ripest for sex and advocated open sexual relationships from puberty onwards – adding, shrewdly, that 'often the opportunity [for sex] comes too late', producing lust, sadism and inhibition.[37]

This aspect of Thomas's writing is most apparent in the short stories of 1933–4, written alongside the early process poems. They owe much to the example of Caradoc Evans, the first Anglo-Welsh Modernist writer, whose savage satires of religious hypocrisy, misogyny and sexual perversion in *My Country* (1915) had made him 'the most hated man in Wales' to nationalists and the religious-minded. Thomas's own calculatedly caricatural depictions of an imaginary Jarvis Valley go further than Evans's, being spiced with paganism, witchcraft, miscegenation, incest and plague. They concern themselves more openly than the poems with lust and sadism, and show a serious attempt to understand its origins. The best, such as 'The Orchards' and 'A Prospect of the Sea', are narratives of male sexual (and authorial) insecurity and initiation by more powerful and knowing, but unattainable, female figures. Others are in a less visionary, more realist, vein. In 'The Vest', for example, a man who has humiliated and murdered a woman wanders in torment through a town centre. Increasingly hemmed in, he finds himself in a bar, where, climactically, he pulls out and brandishes a blood-soaked vest, horrifying and silencing a group of women drinkers.

These stories explore and expose not only hypocrisy and extreme states of mind, such as insanity, which had always fascinated Thomas, but patriarchy's use of a misogynistic double standard, setting women up as pure and innocent while simultaneously punishing them for arousing male desire. This is clearest in 'The Mouse and the Woman', in which a writer conjures a real, naked woman into existence, enjoys her innocent love, but slowly comes to feel that it is sinful. He blames a 'devil' for his creation, but it is clear

The 'Red Notebook' (with 'Danger Don'ts' on the back cover) containing several early short stories.

that the 'uncleanness' he attributes to the woman stems from his own repression.[38] Even so, he kills her off, and the cruelty and self-denial of his act drive him mad. The protagonist of 'The Mouse and the Woman' has a memory of a performance of Sophocles' *Electra* that Thomas himself had seen in July 1933, so the story is, at one level, an attempt to understand the impact of puritanism on himself. With considerable insight, given his youthfulness, Thomas frames and probes his own sexual anxieties and locates the roots of sexual violence in male weakness and fear of the other: 'when he hurt her it was to hide his pain', we are told of the protagonist of 'The Vest'.[39]

In the poems, sex is more abstract, part of the creative-destructive workings of process. It is a hormonal fatality ('daft with the drug smoking in a girl') with little more than reproduction as its aim.[40] Such fatalism can, of course, easily take misogynistic form: sex as a lure by which women ensnare men, a reworking of the Fall. But Thomas generally avoids this. Although sex is viewed in threatening terms, arising from his adolescent fears – as a 'plague' or the 'grief' of post-coital sadness, disease or an unwanted child – women and men are both equally its victims. If anything, as he suggests in 'A grief ago', their more central biological role in the cycles of process gives women a better understanding of these cycles than men.

Wales, the Gothic and Ghostly Fathers

From 1932 onwards Dylan Thomas's poetry acquired a dark, Jacobean tinge. The process poems and stories of 1933–6 not only intensified this trend, but did so to a consciously exaggerated degree, immersed as they were in sickness, death, funerary practices and decay. Indeed, in a striking and revealing image, Thomas described the poems as being born from a monstrous process of charnel reconstruction:

> I believe in writing poetry from the flesh, and generally, from dead flesh. So many modern poets take the living flesh as their object, and, by their clever dissecting, turn it into a carcass. I prefer to take the dead flesh, and, by any positivity of faith that is in me, build up a living flesh from it.[41]

The Frankenstein-like labour he describes here confirms the importance of the gothic material apparent in the welter of references in his poems and stories to vampires, ghosts, doubles, shades, mummies and so on. Throughout, the early poems radiate a morbid atmosphere, their celebratory and positive aspects always inseparable from their darker properties. As we have seen, the first poem of his first collection explores the idea that the 'boys of summer' are 'in their ruin', always in the process of themselves becoming 'the dark deniers'.[42] Crucially, by drawing on the gothic genre to this extent, Thomas was able to explore his liminal, in-between origins and to reinforce the emphasis of his process poetic on the biological bases of existence. It also gave him a way of stylistically challenging the hyper-rationality and dogmatism of the MacSpaunday poets, though not in a merely irrational or ahistorical manner; the anxiety concerning boundary transgression that gothic writing feeds off reflects growing concerns about modernity and an impending world war during the mid-1930s. But it also gave Thomas a way of dealing with the fact that he was creating the Modernist lyric in Wales from scratch. For, as the critic Tony Conran has pointed out, 'Modernism in Wales is most at home with the grotesque . . . the nightmare of monstrosity underlies the middle-class rejection of the *buchedd* [rural way of life, culture], the sense of being suffocated by its hypocrisy and narrowness.'[43] Far from being gratuitous or callow, as some have argued, the gothic and grotesque in Thomas's early work function as a way of dealing with the distortions that Non-conformist repression had bred in the national psyche. Aspects of that 'nightmare' had already been broached by Caradoc Evans, but in Thomas they became more lurid and phantasmagorical, as befitted a younger, urban writer who had largely escaped their effects. The ontogenetic aspect of the poems is not just about creating the self, then, nor is their cosmogenetic aspect simply about imagining the birth of a universe within and from the body. Both are intimately linked with Thomas's creation of an Anglo-Welsh Modernist poetry that had not hitherto existed.

This morbidity suddenly took a personal turn in late August 1933, when, during a routine visit to his dentist, D. J. Thomas was found to be suffering from a cancerous lesion in his mouth. He was given just five years to live, and immediately took time off work. The family rallied round, with D.J.'s new son-in-law Haydn driving him to London for treatment (this involved the painful, but ultimately effective, insertion of radium-tipped needles into the tumour). Dylan was deeply shocked. His immediate poetic response was a poem titled 'Take the needles and the knives', and the episode may well have triggered his final leap into the process style. He had begun a fresh notebook, N4, on 23 August by dedicating it 'To others caught Between [Twixt] black and white', and now his own father was caught between the most terrifying antinomies of all.

Thomas continually incorporates threatened fathers into his poems, and it is probably no coincidence that 'Before I knocked', his first true process poem, and one about a father and son, dates from a few days after he learned of D.J.'s illness. It was already a trend, however; '"Find meat on bones"' pre-dates 'Before I knocked', which would be followed by 'I fellowed sleep' and 'Do you not father me?', both of which deal with the subject. But although personal in one sense, these poems are not so much autobiographical as explo-rations of the father–son relationship in terms that have a broader application. The generational antagonisms in such relationships are explored in 'I see the boys of summer', which takes the form of an argument between a paternal authority figure who takes the 'boys' to task in part one, the retort of the boys in part two and the arrival at an end-stopped armed truce in the final section, in which father and son swap roles and meet: 'I am the man your father was . . . O see the poles are kissing as they cross.'[44]

Dylan respected, admired and loved his father, despite D.J.'s undemonstrative and austere nature, and other poems seek to unravel his tangle of feelings towards the man who had inspired him to become a poet, but whom he had now, perhaps guiltily, eclipsed. To tackle his predicament Thomas made himself something of a Freudian exemplar in these poems, using elements of Freud's Oedipal family romance to dramatize it, though without endorsing Freud in any doctrinal way. This had a literary dimension, since the poems' father figures often appear in Shakespearean guise – that is, in terms of D.J.'s favourite writer, the one he had used to induct Dylan into poetry as a child. The identities adopted include those of Ferdinand, Alonso and Prospero from *The Tempest*, and old and young Hamlet. In 'When once the twilight locks', for example, the Dylan-identified 'creature' briefly enjoys a 'sabbath with the sun' before regressing and 'drown[ing] his father's magics in a dream' (a 'redhaired cancer' appears immediately afterwards). Roles are reversed and complicated, as in dreams, but the primary emotion is fear and guilt that through 'sleep' the usurping speaker may do what Prospero does when he 'abjures' his 'magic' and hurls his book of spells into the sea. The dying father will be replaced by the son, who fears this death will destroy the magic of poetry.

The references to *Hamlet* are more poignant still. One occurs in part three of 'I, in my intricate image', where it is combined with another to *The Tempest*. A ghostly teacher with his 'pointed ferrule' (for use at the classroom blackboard) leads to the narrator described as 'five-fathomed Hamlet on his father's coral,/ Thrusting the tom-thumb vision up the iron mile' – Thomas as T(h)om(as) Thumb.[45] A more direct expression of guilt at usurping the father occurs in 'I fellowed sleep', which concludes with the lines, 'An old, mad man still climbing in his ghost,/ My father's ghost is climbing in the rain.'[46] In reading *The Interpretation of Dreams*, Thomas would have noted Freud's observation that

> *Hamlet* has its roots in the same soil as *Oedipus Rex*, except that in *Oedipus Rex* the child's wishful fantasy that underlies it is brought into the open and realized as it would be in a dream. In *Hamlet* it remains repressed; and – just as in the case of a neurosis – we only learn of its existence from its inhibiting consequences.[47]

Language

Dark, visceral and often morbid though the work of late 1933 and 1934 was, few would describe it as depressing. As Empson said, it paradoxically manages to 'convey a sickened loathing which somehow at once (within the phrase) enforces a welcome for the eternal necessities of the world'.[48] Unlike in the poetry of early 1933, pessimism finds voice in a verbal exuberance that is tonic and raises it to the level of tragedy, and the nature of this exuberance is the last aspect of the 'process' poetic we need to consider here. For it is, above all, Dylan Thomas's ability to 'bend the iron of English', as the critic Karl Shapiro put it, that continues to give these poems their enduring appeal and significance.[49] This is because, in revolutionizing his poetic style thematically in 1933, Thomas also transformed it linguistically. If everything in the universe is subject to process, he reasoned, language cannot be used instrumentally, standing above process to describe it. That would be a false objectivity. Since everything in the universe is subject to process, language must also embody this even as it describes and dramatizes it. So it is that in N4 Thomas's poems started to become increasingly playful, multilayered and risk-taking in a linguistic sense. It was, in effect, a second phase of the harnessing of his writing to a process poetic and philosophy.

Some of its elements have already been noted. As the deployment of 'doublecrossed' in 'Before I knocked' shows, in late 1933 the poems came to evolve more and more out of forms of serious wordplay.

Complex puns are increasingly common; capable of signifying in several directions simultaneously, they embody the everything-in-potential, all-happening-at-once character of process. Similar effects could be achieved, Thomas found, by delaying the main verb, heaping up comma-spliced, appositive clauses, so that several events 'hang', grammatically and temporally, again replicating the effects of simultaneity and interconnectedness, and suspending, folding and dissolving the linear succession of events that standard syntax demands. Single words alone, in this verbal universe, could encapsulate the paradoxes of process. 'Seedy', in 'I see the boys of summer', for example, has a literal meaning of 'full of seed, prime'; yet its slang sense of down-at-heel, past it, points in the opposite direction, destruction and creation 'within the phrase'. In these poems there are many such words: 'lime' (fruit, but also quicklime), 'grain' (both seed and inorganic particle), 'wax' (as in 'waxen' dead flesh, but also 'to grow'). 'Worm' is almost always a grave-worm, but it can also be the penis and the forefinger bent for writing. The last line of 'The force that through the green fuse' brilliantly matches all three of these senses with three for 'sheet', as winding-sheet, bedsheet and the sheet of paper on which the poem is being written: 'And I am dumb to tell the lover's tomb/ How at my sheet goes the same crooked worm.' Rarely has so much meaning been so richly condensed in so few words.[50] Nor is that all; 'worm' is also a kind of mechanical gear, alerting us to the fact that in the process world the archaic is fused with the technological, in a series of cybernetic collocations – 'chemic blood', 'girdered nerve', 'motor muscle' and 'petrol face'. The fear of biological determinism is not reactionary, but rather reflects the same anxiety about subjugation to Fordist and scientific regimes of control that are found in Aldous Huxley's *Brave New World* (1932) and Charlie Chaplin's *Modern Times* (1936).

What Aivaz calls Thomas's 'generative method' bears on how he wrote his poems. One of his few consistently expressed statements on poetry was that it should work 'from words', rather than 'towards' them.[51] For a reader, this means having to be alert to the way puns, wordplay and rhetorical devices offer threads to be followed, and to be prepared to help create the poem by tuning into its devices. In compositional terms it meant that rather than starting out with a preconceived theme or anecdote and finding the words to express it, the poet begins with verbal material that seems inherently interesting, and sees where it leads them.[52] This is why most of Thomas's early poems have no title. They are always about process, and are objects that exemplify language which is subject to process, so there is no need for one; certainly, the poet should not try to impose a fixed meaning on the poem at its outset (later Thomas poems do have titles, as he became less insistent on this point). Freed from attachment to a set theme, the linguistic material takes the lead, although the poet is consciously involved in the hard labour of deciding what works and what does not.

The result is poems often driven by unashamed wordplay, which we read by tracing the transition from image to image via their puns, double meanings, twisted and refurbished clichés, lapsed meanings truffled from the OED, coinages and composite words, pronouns with double antecedents, and wide-ranging registers and vocabularies: slang, abstract, cant, formal. In general terms there is a tendency to transform states of being (nouns) into processes (verbs). Thomas spoke of 'a constant building up and breaking down' of several images derived from a 'central seed, which is itself constructive and destructive at the same time'; crucially, this takes place 'within my imposed formal limits', which are tightly set, the obstacles being what enforces and enables the high level of verbal inventiveness.[53] (This is another reason, of course, why the subject of Thomas's poems is often also its own genesis.) The slipperiness of words, deplored by many writers, was a quality he prized, revelling in the mismatch between words and things, and in surplus meaning – that 'capsized' in 'Once it was the colour of saying', say, could mean 'tilted' and 'the size of a cap', and conjure up (since writing is one of the subjects) 'fools*cap*' *sized* paper. It is this that gives his writing its liberatory frisson, since it continually reveals to us that language, by which we try to define reality, is inherently perverse and playful, and cannot fully define anything.

The early process poems pit a deep biological determinism against an electrifying verbal performance that is thereby charged with melancholia and a lavish, self-spending energy. Sexually dynamic, their universe is 'frighteningly active and alive'.[54] As a result, death itself appears not so much as a negation but as an equally dynamic force. In a strict sense, the poems are repetitive, since they are a series of re-embodiments of the process theme. Repetition is their theme – or, rather, it is the impossibility of *exact* repetition, and their recapitulations, in ever-varying forms, celebrates the beauty of polysemy. They are, however, undeniably difficult to read. As Thomas told Charlie Fisher, 'I like things that are difficult to write and difficult to understand, I like "redeeming the contraries" with secretive images; I like contradicting my images, saying two things at once in one word, two in four words and one in six.'[55] And because process is all-pervasive, there is no padding, no place where the reader can take it easy. 'I've always disliked the weak line,' Thomas would later tell Vernon Watkins. 'I admit that readers of complicated poetry need a breather now and then, but I don't think the poetry should give it them. When they want one, they should take it and then go on.'[56]

Not all the poems are negative or fatalistic, in any case. Several conclude positively. 'Our eunuch dreams', for example, ends with the hope that the 'red-eyed earth' – the revolutionary masses – will overthrow the 'Welshing rich' whose power rests on repression and illusion: 'our shots shall smack/ The image from the plates . . . And who remain shall flower as they love.'[57] It is the most MacSpaunday moment in Thomas's work. This positivity may have a willed quality, as in the last line of 'If I were tickled by the rub of love', 'Man be my metaphor'. It is a reminder that Thomas is 'master of the ambiguous climax', summing up the tendency to despair and celebrate in a single line.[58] But it is telling that while he opened *18 Poems* with the doom-laden and sardonic 'I see the boys of summer', he closed it with a new poem he sent to Johnson in July 1934, 'All all and all', to end on an unusually upbeat, collective note of sexual liberation and socialist vision: 'Flower flower the people's fusion . . . Flower, flower, all all and all'.[59]

Towards *18 Poems* . . .

Between 'Before I knocked', dated 6 September 1933, and 'If I were tickled', the last poem in N4, dated 30 April 1934, Dylan Thomas had written 35 poems. About a dozen were masterpieces; he was still just nineteen-and-a-half. In a single year he had, in the 'smug darkness of a provincial town' (as he rather ungratefully called it), fashioned a coherent, visionary poetic, against the grain of the reigning metropolitan style, and produced a string of Modernist Metaphysical poems of Keatsian richness and intensity.[60] Indeed, it was arguably precisely the 'darkness' and distance from London, together with his hybrid qualities, that had enabled him to do this. Despite his youth, the poetry, rooted in the body, with a cosmic sweep, had a mythic, timeless authority that transcended the specific anxieties from which it arose. And, for all its gothic-grotesque qualities, its 'taste for violence', its energy was revivifying. Far from being regarded as apolitical, it was felt by many to be at least as relevant as New Country verse to the turbulent times.[61]

As Thomas turned to the practicalities of a possible writing career in London, and as his poems became still more complex in the spring of 1934, their output slackened. But his career momentum was building. On 14 March the BBC journal *The Listener* published 'Light breaks where no sun shines', leading to letters of enquiry from Spender, Eliot and Geoffrey Grigson, the last of whom asked him to submit poems to *New Verse*. There were complaints from some readers of *The Listener* about obscenity, but he relished the fuss. 'The little smut hounds thought I was writing a copulatory anthem,' he told Johnson, when 'in reality, of course, it was a metaphysical image of rain.'[62] On 22 April the editor of the *Sunday Referee*, Victor Neuburg, announced that the Poets' Corner prize for the best poem of 1933 had gone to 'The force that through the green fuse', which the *Referee* had published the previous October. It meant the *Referee* would part-fund a first collection of poems the following year, in partnership with a trade publisher.

Thomas decided to make all the poems in his first collection process poems from N4, for maximum impact. He discussed its contents over the summer of 1934 with Johnson, sending her new poems as he wrote them. After six months of correspondence their feelings for each other had grown warm, and a romantic relationship had been clinched when he first visited London to stay with her for a weekend in early March. She introduced him to her literary circle, and he spent time looking for jobs and trying to place poems and stories with journals. Within a few days of his return to Swansea, they had declared their love for each other, her diary full of 'darling Dylans', his letters to her beginning 'My dear' and signed off 'Love'. Another visit followed in early April, when he also met Grigson. These forays into London for love and literary contacts led to meetings with Michael Roberts, a follower of Auden who would edit *The Faber Book of Modern Verse* (1936); Janet Adam Smith, who worked for *The Listener*; and the critic and editor Desmond Hawkins.

By now, with the prospect of full-time access to the delights of London and Johnson looming, Swansea seemed increasingly

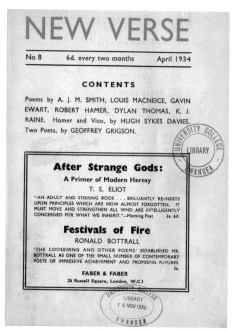

First publication in *New Verse* (of 'Our eunuch dreams'), April 1934.

oppressive. Thomas had vented his frustration at it, and Wales more generally, in his letters to her, exaggerating its backwardness in an attempt to impress and to gee himself up. But at the same time, having become friendly with Glyn Jones, on Whit weekend he travelled deeper into Wales to walk in the area around Llansteffan, where they both had family roots. From Llansteffan they took the ferry to Laugharne, from where he wrote to Johnson, calling it 'the strangest town in Wales'. He was charmed by the place, but his letter to her is 'tortured by every doubt and misgiving' and full of tormented wordplay at the inability of language to convey the reality of the scene before him; he is a 'Symbol Simon' and 'no words can tell you what a hopeless fallen angel of a day it is.'[63]

That the linguistic crisis paralleled an emotional one soon became clear. On the verge of becoming a professional writer, well into his first serious adult relationship, Thomas was panicking. On 27 May he wrote again to Johnson, claiming that on the journey back from Laugharne he had stayed at the home of a former *Post* colleague, been seduced by his fiancée and slept with her for the next three nights. He said he was confessing in the name of honesty, that he still loved and wanted her, and begged forgiveness.

Unsurprisingly, Johnson was deeply hurt, even if she suspected the episode was invented (it seems likely that it was). At the crudest level, it may have been an attempt to get her to have sex before they got married. It may also have been calculated to get her to break the relationship off, out of fear at the kind of domestic set-up that Thomas was intent on escaping at home. Johnson was a middle-class woman who, it was becoming clear, did not fit the bohemian life he had begun to enjoy and was starting to discover could be supported, up to a point, by his new circle. Marriage would mean having to get a job, and the 'squeezing out' of individuality he had feared a year before. Most significant, perhaps, it was an indication of the way that new demands could trigger self-destructive behaviour on Thomas's part, with drink usually acting as the lubricant. Johnson resolved to have no more to do with him; then, soon afterwards, relented.

In mid-June all seemed well again. Thomas was back in London, shuttling between Trevor Hughes in Harrow and Johnson, now living

Dylan Thomas and Pamela Hansford Johnson, autumn 1934.

in Chelsea, and even asking her to marry him. She demurred for the moment. Thomas again did the rounds of his new writer and artist friends. He returned in mid-August, to combine relationship and literary ladder-climbing. Although he hadn't yet brought out a book, he was asked to contribute to John Lehmann's anthology *This Year's Poetry*, while Grigson chose him as one of a handful of poets to answer a questionnaire for the October issue of *New Verse*.[64] On this occasion he remained in London for five weeks; the move there had already occurred in all but name. When he returned home, Johnson, with her mother as chaperone, accompanied him, putting up at a hotel in Mumbles for a week. During that time they made sorties into Gower, and visited Thomas's parents at Cwmdonkin Drive, where they learned that Dylan, who had claimed to be as old as Pamela – 21 – was, in fact, still just nineteen.

Various other milestones were reached over the months before the move on 13 November. In September Thomas published a review in *Adelphi*, and in October he and Glyn Jones made another trip into Wales, to meet Caradoc Evans in Aberystwyth. After tea with Evans, his two young acolytes toured the local pubs, 'drinking to the eternal damnation of the Almighty & the soon-to-be-hoped-for destruction of the tin Bethels'.[65] It was a fittingly symbolic and suitably literary rejection of those aspects of Welsh society that he disliked, but which had inescapably helped to create his poetry, on the eve of leaving it.

For months, Neuburg had been unable to find a trade publisher to partner the *Referee* in publishing *18 Poems*. Impatient, since he had already failed to place it with Cape earlier in the year, Thomas now retrieved the manuscript he had given Neuburg and sent it to Eliot at Faber. His secretary wrote back asking him to 'make no arrangements' for publication until Eliot had read it. But Eliot took his time, too. Finally, in late October, Neuburg persuaded David Archer of the left-wing bookshop Parton Books to act as the *Referee*'s co-publisher. Eager to get *18 Poems* out by the end of the year, Thomas decided not to wait for Eliot's reply, and made his final preparations to move to London, where he could see what Jones would call the 'black bombshell' of his first collection through the press.[66]

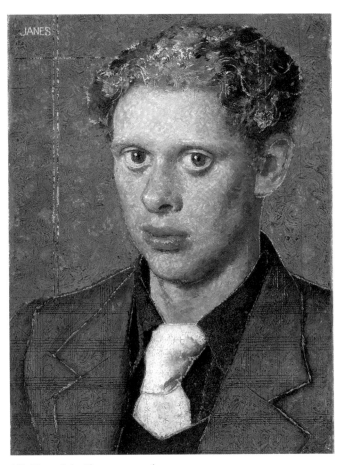

Alfred Janes, *Dylan Thomas*, 1934–5, oil on canvas.

4

The Direction of the Elementary Town: London, Surrealism and Love, 1935–7

In early November 1934 Dylan Thomas left Swansea for London to make his way as a full-time professional writer. Pamela Johnson was on hand to assist as he moved with Fred Janes into a large, sparsely furnished bedsitting room in a house in a run-down part of South Kensington. Mervyn Levy occupied another room on the same premises; it was a little Kardomah beyond Wales. Johnson and her mother donated a table and an iron bedstead, which was upended and covered with a curtain to serve as a wardrobe. Nancy visited and contributed further items to the domestic ménage.[1] Their existence was hand to mouth, but Janes kept the squalor within limits and cooked for them both. Florrie sent Dylan £1 a week for food, and, with D.J., paid her son a visit in the new year.

Thomas saw *18 Poems* through the press on or about 18 December, in a print run of 250 copies, before returning to Swansea for Christmas. By then a final break had occurred with Johnson. Despite their recent closeness, he failed to maintain contact with her and acted in what he admitted some months later was a 'silly & careless' way. His 'rather revolting Bloomsbury fun and games' and self-centredness grieved her, and despite further protestations of his love, the connection fizzled out.[2] Thomas seemed to want the benefits of a relationship without committing himself either to Johnson or to reasonably orderly behaviour. She rightly judged him more dedicated to drink and socializing than to her, and it is clear that the promotion of *18 Poems* and fashioning of a young dog reputation were his priorities.

New places, new friends

Thomas's immediate ports of call on arriving in London were such pubs as the Fitzroy Tavern in Soho, Parton Books and the home of Victor Neuburg and his partner, Runia Tharp (Tharp's first impression was of 'a handsome cherubic youth, crowned with an aura of thunderous power and doom').[3] Over the next year Thomas would meet and mix with members of the literary scene who were younger than the established figures he had already encountered, building a social circle among his contemporaries. Although he made himself known to those who could help him, it is clear that mere public prestige or fashionability was not his prime consideration; he mixed with fellow writers who were laid-back, congenial companions at home in London's literary pub culture. They included the poet and journalist Ruthven Todd; Rayner Heppenstall, a poet, novelist and later BBC editor; and Desmond Hawkins, a reviewer and novelist who edited *Purpose*, *New English Weekly* and fiction for *Criterion*. In such circles his horizons expanded and provincial rough edges were rubbed off; he soon lost his adolescent animus against gay people, for example (if he had ever had one), becoming friendly with a gay couple, the writer and artist Oswell Blakeston and his partner, the painter Max Chapman. Both would claim, convincingly, to have had erotic if not sexual encounters with Thomas, and he shared his humorous, semi-surreal fantasies with Blakeston in particular.

Although the London literary and artistic world was small, Thomas's ability to draw people to him was nevertheless impressive. He soon had a wide circle of friends and acquaintances; as early as February 1935 he was able to name-drop spectacularly in a letter to Bert Trick, mentioning Henry Moore, Willa and Edwin Muir, and Wyndham Lewis.[4] Apart from Stephen Spender, however, he did not meet New Country poets before taking part in a BBC broadcast from Manchester with them in 1938. Shortly after Thomas arrived in London, Geoffrey Grigson introduced him to the poet Norman Cameron, who worked as an advertising copywriter and who became probably Thomas's best friend in the capital. He was certainly the most materially useful, helping him out, as others did, with small gifts of money and the use of his flat. As a result of such generosity Thomas came to spend less and less time living in his digs with Janes and more with Cameron, Grigson and his other new friends.

Although often regarded as disorganized, Thomas was nevertheless energetic and single-minded in going about his business. Janes, attempting to paint his portrait at this time, spoke of Dylan being in and out of their room 'like a cat in a tripe shop', 'tremendously restless', with periods of relative calm punctuated often by 'a furious burst of work'.[5] He had arrived in London armed with a store of poems no writer of his own 'green age' could match – 'The Notebook poems were the ammunition with which he began his assault on London', as Maud notes – and he had a supply of equally striking short stories.[6] From January 1935 onwards he was also able to use *18 Poems* as a calling card. He soon learned how to make the rounds of the literary and artistic circles, initially adopting the stance of a naïf, the small-town boy in the big city; he would always be capable of exuding a disarming air of innocence. He overcame his trepidation by creating an amusing, witty, easy-going persona, channelling his urge to entertain, and used his gifts of mimicry, story-telling and invention to charm and forge his way ahead. Those he met testify to his vividness, warmth, self-debunking modesty and good humour. Soon he became adept at finding friends, a bed for the night, a loan, a drink, a buyer for a poem or story – and surviving.

The style of Thomas's self-promotion bears some study. It was not flamboyant in any obvious, self-advertising way – he was often shy in a new group – although at times he resorted to slapstick, exploiting his resemblance to Harpo Marx, or doing a down-on-all-fours dog-imitation act he had perfected in such Mumbles pubs as The Antelope and The Mermaid back in his Little Theatre days. His taste was more for gossip, wordplay and stories that could be spun out of everyday, humdrum events, the more fantastical the better. One involved an imaginary product called 'night custard', which had a dizzying number of uses, into which he drew Grigson, Cameron and others; these collective, collaborative fantasies might be embellished and added to over weeks or months, ramifying endlessly in pubs, at parties in flats, in drinking clubs, at galleries, over meals in cafés and restaurants, or on walks through the London parks and streets.[7] And, while he was more than capable of memorable pithiness, even Thomas's one-liners usually emerged from rambling narratives; improvisation, missing a too-fixed point, was invariably their real point.

Many of the tales Dylan told were grotesque, comic versions of the material that filled his poems and stories; as Desmond Hawkins observed: 'He had a fund of stories about madness, lunatic asylums, and strange symbolic possessions – usually funny stories, not solemn ones. He had a quick, volatile, chuckling relishing sense of humour. He certainly loved the "Gothic".'[8] If some felt that his charm was facile, they were few at this stage. In any case, most doubters saw that the positives far outweighed the negatives. As everyone he knew also testified, Thomas was a boon companion in being a good listener as well as talker, able to attune himself to others, and make those he was talking to feel as though they, and they alone, were the centre of his attention. It was this empathic gift – 'my everpresent conscience, concealed under a Punch humour', as he would describe it to Henry Treece – that marked him out from other bar-room entertainers.[9]

Reception, retreat and recovery

Reviews of *18 Poems* appeared early in 1935; most, while slightly baffled, were unusually good for a first collection.[10] The best was that by Hawkins, in *Time and Tide*, who understood Thomas's breakthrough in uniting 'Eliot's magical sense of the macabre' and 'Auden's textual firmness' in a new poetry that, for all the surfeit of 'the vocabulary of physiology', '[fused] metaphysical poetry into sensuous terms'.[11] Thomas's PR had largely succeeded; *18 Poems* was a *succès d'estime*, sold well and was reprinted in February 1936. He now had few problems in getting his work published in such leading journals as *New Verse*, *The Listener* and *Criterion*, and began to appear in anthologies, including the most influential of the decade, Michael Roberts's *Faber Book of Modern Verse* (1936). His stories, too, found ready outlets, and 'The Orchards' was included in *The Faber Book of Modern Stories* (1937). Thanks to Grigson he got reviewing work – often of thrillers and whodunnits – for *Bookmen*, *New Verse* and the *Morning Post*. This was a precarious toehold on the ladder of financial solvency, since he could sell the books on after he had reviewed them.

It is important, however, to understand that at no point before 1941 was Dylan Thomas ever able to enjoy even minimal financial security. This was his choice; he was a dedicated full-time writer, with no external means of support, and the demanding nature of his poetry meant that he could not also hold down a day job. On the other hand it should be remembered – particularly when terms like 'sponger' are bandied about – that many of those he mixed with did have financial resources (if not jobs, then remittances, savings, shares and well-off parents) while Thomas himself existed in an era before social security payments, writers' bursaries or credit cards. He lived from hand to mouth, relying on those who were better off, many of whom were happy to support a gifted but impoverished young writer.

Despite the difficulties, Thomas was now established, alongside David Gascoyne, George Barker and a few others, as the leading figure in the post-Auden generation of poets. By March 1935, however, 'The Provincial Rush, or Up-Rimbaud-and-At-'Em approach' to the literary metropolis had taken its toll.[12] The demands of making his way and the attendant socializing and drinking, plus the disintegrating relationship with Pamela Johnson, forced him back to Swansea to recover. It was the first of many such semi-collapses. The first months in London had set a pattern for a relationship with the capital that would continue for the rest of Thomas's life, of oscillation between hectic socializing and seeking work, and retirement to recharge his batteries and, usually, write. He needed the opportunities and thrills only London provided, but he could exist there only in a bravura performative mode, and this led, eventually, to excess and exhaustion. He therefore came to regard London as both alluring and threatening – there are similarities with the cosmic dance of exaltation and despair we find in his poetry, suggesting that these extremes lay within him – and to be wary, even afraid of it, or of what he knew it released in him.

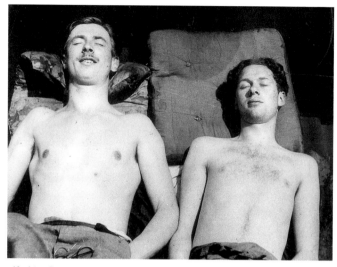

Alfred (Fred) Janes and Dylan Thomas sunbathing on the roof, London, 1935, photograph by William Scott.

This accounts for the ambivalence towards the capital found in the apocalyptic tale 'Prologue to an Adventure', whose protagonist, in an inversion of *Pilgrim's Progress*, has travelled from the heavenly city to the city of destruction; and in *Adventures in the Skin Trade*, in which Samuel Bennet leaves home only to find ever-deeper layers of confusion in the capital as his own layers of selfhood are peeled away. Thomas was only partly joking when he told Richard Church in a letter of 22 June 1936: 'I am about to go into the country again – the only place for me, I think: cities are death.'[13] The same jitteriness crops up in a letter two years later to Vernon Watkins:

> London, city of the restless dead . . . really is an insane city, & filled me with terror. Every pavement drills through your soles to your scalp, and out pops a lamp-post covered in hair. I'm not going to London again for years; its intelligentsia is so hurried in the head that nothing stays there; its glamour smells of goat; there's no difference between good & bad.[14]

The comic self-deprecation with which he dealt with his anxieties was a form of self-mythologizing that helped him to get along, but also harmful because it colluded with attempts to stereotype him (he joked of 'the conventions of Life No. 13' there, 'promiscuity, booze, coloured shirts, too much talk, too little work').[15] Louis MacNeice's review of *18 Poems*, evidently coloured by reports of Thomas's unruly behaviour, had made the tempting but fallacious link between Thomas's unruly social persona and his poetry by describing it as reading 'like a drunk man, speaking wildly but rhythmically', and it was a slur to which many would resort in the years to come, even when the coherent and sober intricacy of the poetry was well known.[16] But in April 1935 this was all in the future; his friends were sympathetic to his symptoms and indulged him. Cameron arranged for him to take a break with his friend A.J.P. Taylor, an Oxford history don, and his wife, Margaret, a wealthy heiress, at their cottage in the village of Disley in Cheshire.[17]

Disley and Donegal

Thomas spent almost a month in Disley – overstaying his welcome, in the opinion of Taylor, who claimed he drank too much of his beer and was 'cruel' for the pleasure he took in teasing his readers (a typical historian's response to Modernist poetry, perhaps: be more prosaic). Taylor's reaction also had much to do with the fact that Margaret, who also wrote poetry, developed a severe crush on Dylan. It was unreciprocated, but after the war it would result in her becoming his main benefactor.

He returned to London in May only to plunge back into a 'ragged life', alarming Grigson and Cameron yet again.[18] They now devised a more radical plan. Grigson was to go with him for a working holiday in a remote part of County Donegal, in the Irish Free State, far from the capital's fleshpots. In July 1935 the pair journeyed to Glen Lough, on Ireland's remote west coast, where they wrote, read, walked, threw stones into the Atlantic, fished, cooked and drank only the odd glass of poitín or Guinness. Dylan grew a gingerish beard. After a fortnight, at the start of August, Grigson left him on his own, continuing to write, 'as lonely as Christ sometimes', as he informed Trick, in a 'wild, unlettered and unfrenchlettered country, too far from Ardara, a village you can't be too far from'.[19] He stayed until the end of August, working hard, sending poems and stories off to journals, but left without paying the grocery bill or the rent on the cottage with the money Grigson had left him.

On his return, Cameron settled the debt, and he and Grigson laid down the law. Dylan was temporarily denied the use of Cameron's flat, and Grigson withdrew the reviewing work for the *Morning Post*. His response was a bout of dissipation that lasted several days, during which he contracted gonorrhoea. This forced his retirement to Swansea, and a long and painful cure, in September. Things were quickly patched up (although he would soon afterwards fall out with Grigson permanently), but the episode highlights the tension within some of his new friendships. There was an unwittingly patronizing side to some of them, which Thomas sensed and resisted by occasionally biting the hand that fed him. The ambivalent attitude towards him is memorably captured in Cameron's poem 'The Dirty Little Accuser', which portrays as a 'crapulous lout' a Thomas figure who smears the sofa, pinches the maid's backside and steals, for which he is evicted; the Accuser's unanswerable response is that 'You and I are all in the same *galère*', which 'checks' the 'righteous jubilation' of the rather superior speaker.[20] Thomas stayed on in Swansea after this episode. Still only twenty years old, over the next few months he was able to catch up with his friends there and consider his next book.

The experimental poet

In Donegal Dylan had filled up the last few pages of N5. This had been his fair-copy notebook since summer 1934 and is a record of his evolution as a poet during and after the move from Swansea to London. What is most revealing about it is that it shows a change of style on the very eve of his move there. Up to the point when he entered 'Seven', 'When, like a running grave', on 26 October 1934, the poems in N5 are in the process style of N4. 'Seven' was the last of the N5 poems to go into *18 Poems*, and was copied into it on the eve of his twentieth birthday. At this moment, as if to emphasize a rupture, he drew a short but emphatic horizontal line under 'Seven', end-stopped with two short vertical strokes – a mark found nowhere else in the notebooks – and entered the date in its fullest form.

The next poem in N5, 'Eight', shows that he had metaphorically and literally drawn a line under a phase in his development, announcing in its shape and apparently impenetrable whimsy a more exploratory style:

> Now,
> Say nay,
> Man dry man,
> Dry lover mine
> The deadrock base and blow the flowered anchor,
> Should he, for centre sake, hop in the dust,
> Forsake, the fool, the hardiness of anger.[21]

It is no accident that 'Eight' ('Now') and the next poem in N5 'Nine' ('How soon the servant sun') have been judged Thomas's most unreadable, nor that the nine poems that follow them include 'I, in my intricate image' and half of 'Altarwise by owl-light', the most ambitious and daunting he ever wrote. (The others include the beautiful and mysteriously quibbling 'A grief ago' and 'Hold hard, these ancient minutes', in which Thomas attempted the verbal equivalent of an abstract painting.) 'I, in my intricate image' and 'Altarwise' are both summary poems, his attempt to take stock of the dizzying advances of the previous year.

These are poems designed to test a reader's interpretative powers to the limit. Technically, they outdo the poems in *18 Poems*. The rhyme scheme of 'I, in my intricate image', for example, end-rhymes vowel + 'l' (for example, 'pinnacle', 'coral', 'spiral') in a regular pattern in 72 of its 108 lines. The imagery, too, reaches a new level of strangeness, and such poems as 'To-day, this insect' and 'Grief thief of time' are harder to construe than the most difficult in *18 Poems*. Syntax is stretched further than ever. Interleaved among the tougher poems

I damp the warlights in your tower dome.
Joy is the knock of dust, Cadaver's shoot
Of bud of Adam through his boxy shift,
Love's twilit nation and the skull of state,
Sin, is your doom.

Everything ends, the tower ending and,
Have with the house of wind, the leaning scene,
Ball of the foot depending from the sun,
Give summer over, the cemented skin,
The actions' end.

All, men my madmen, the unwholesome wind
With whistler's cough contages, time on track
Shapes in a cinder death; love for his trick,
Happy Cadaver's hunger as you take
The kissproof world.

26th October
1934.

A turning point: 'When, like a running grave', entered in N5 the day before Dylan's 20th birthday.

are more straightforward ones, however; the density is not uniform, as it was in *18 Poems*.

'Altarwise', a series of ten inverted Petrarchan sonnets, is the climax of this phase. It has attracted a legion of critics, but they have disagreed on such basic details as who the speakers are and which lines can be attributed to them. All that is certain is that efforts to trace a single, unifying narrative are doomed to failure. Parallels certainly exist to be drawn between the young Dylan Thomas and the poem's 'dog among the fairies', whose nativity is announced in part I, and the life of Jesus. This is followed by a sequence of key points in his growth to maturity: learning to read in III, an encounter with religion in V, crucifixion in VIII, burial in IX, resurrection in X. But the rapid tonal and thematic shifts, from profane to devout, flippant to solemn, and the superabundance of meaning generated by pun, reversible syntax, blurred agents and events, ambiguous punctuation and so on, make this less a poem about some*thing*, or by some*one*, than the vehicle of a 'trickster' principle, driven by an 'outlaw' logic, as the critic Don McKay puts it. It is poetry as a kind of carnivalesque collage, which flaunts its illusion and flamboyance like a series of floats in a parade, 'momentous and momentary'.[22] Little attention would have been paid, of course, were not the music, wit and sheer verbal grandeur of 'Altarwise' so apparent, however murky the narrative.

Twenty-Five Poems and Surrealism

It can be argued that 'Altarwise' and other poems in *Twenty-Five Poems* are post-modernist *avant la lettre*, as has been said of Joyce's *Finnegans Wake*, and Thomas undoubtedly owes much to Joyce. But without dismissing his experimentalism, we should be wary of placing too heavy a burden on such playful writing. He would tell Johnson, 'I'm not an experimentalist and never will be. I write in the only way I can write, & my warped, crabbed & cabinned stuff is not the result of theorizing but of pure incapability to express my needless tortuosities in any other way.'[23] This is tongue-in-cheek, but Thomas was keenly aware of Modernism's innately parodic aspect, and he was fond of mocking its tendency to mythicize itself. In *Twenty-Five Poems* he pushed his style to the verge of self-parody in an effort to see how far it could go, and was bullish in defending himself: 'I'm not sorry that, in ['Altarwise'], I did carry "certain features to their logical conclusion"', he told Glyn Jones. 'It had, I think, to be done; the result had to be, in many of the lines & verses anyway[,] mad parody; and I'm glad that I parodied these features so soon after making them, & that I didn't leave it to anyone else.'[24]

'Now', for example, showcases a seriously playful avant-gardism.
At first glance it seems like a nonsense poem. But once the disguised
main verbs are grasped – 'say', 'mine' and 'forsake', in stanza 1 – it
reads as the soliloquy of a Hamlet-like figure trying to argue himself
into turning his suicidal anger against the outside world. The shape
of the stanza is part of the joke; odd-seeming, it becomes a standard
quatrain if the first four lines are added together to create an iambic
pentameter. But, as Thomas realized almost as soon as he began
to push his style to extremes, there was a limit to how far these
procedures could be taken.

A similar approach characterized Thomas's relationship to
Surrealism. The stories before 1938 often contain surreal imagery
or follow a dream-logic. Thus, in 'The Map of Love' the children
Beth Rib and Reuben move through a map that is organic and alive;
a 'sow-faced woman' appears in 'The Burning Baby'; and in 'The
Orchards' Marlais walks out of his bedroom window across the roofs
of the town to begin his journey westwards. Similar disorientating
mutations of location and image occur in other stories. But it is in the
poems that Surrealism is most evident. It ranges from the brilliant,
Magritte-like image of a 'bearded apple' of 'Incarnate devil' and
'candle in the thighs' of 'Light breaks', to a womb with a 'tongue that
lapped up mud' of 'I make this in a warring absence'.[25] The opening
of 'When, like a running grave' is a high point:

> When, like a running grave, time tracks you down,
> Your calm and cuddled is a scythe of hairs,
> Love in her gear is slowly through the house,
> Up naked stairs, a turtle in a hearse,
> Hauled to the dome,
>
> Comes, like a scissors stalking, tailor age,
> Deliver me.[26]

A running grave, 'stalking' scissors, a 'turtle in a hearse' and
a 'scythe of hairs' – all on a par with Dalí's lobster telephone
or Meret Oppenheim's fur cup and saucer – form a thoroughly

Scenes from *Un chien andalou* (1929; dir. Luis Buñuel), co-written by Salvador Dalí and Luis Buñuel.

surrealistic *mise en scène*. The basic narrative is the death of
love over time ('turtle' as in 'turtle-dove', emblem of true love in
Elizabethan poetry), but Thomas is perfectly aware that the marine
animal will also be evoked, in a manner recalling Buñuel and Dalí's
film *Un chien andalou* (1929). It is no surprise to find in 'I, in my
intricate image' an allusion to the infamous eyeball-slicing scene in
the same film: 'Death instrumental,/ Splitting the long eye open.'[27]

Thomas was heavily involved in the London Surrealist Exhibition
of June 1936 (he is said to have carried a teapot of boiling water and
a cup of string around on a tray, enquiring if visitors wanted it
weak or strong). He was a friend of many of its organizers – David
Gascoyne, George Reavey, Roland Penrose, Stanley William Hayter
and Henry Moore – and of many of the artists, including the famous
'Surrealist Angel', Sheila Legge, who posed for the exhibition's
publicity photographs wearing a meat cage covered with roses over
her head.[28] (After Thomas's death one of those artist friends, Eileen
Agar, memorialized him in a striking biomorphic-surreal portrait.)
On 26 June, after the close of the exhibition, he gave a poetry reading
with Paul Éluard, a leading French Surrealist poet. Years later, in
1950, he played a lead role in a performance of Picasso's Surrealist
play *Le Désir attrapé par le queue* (Desire Caught by the Tail) at the
ICA in London.

Yet Thomas's indebtedness to Surrealism has been muddied
because he sometimes denied it. He was sensitive to charges that
his writing was just an uncontrolled unconscious outpouring, a
charge based on the simplistic conflation of Surrealism with auto-
matic writing. His description of his writing process showed that
he granted the unconscious some agency, and imposed tight formal
confines in the hope that the unbidden and unknown would 'creep,
crawl, flash, or thunder' into a poem.[29] But his Surrealism, like Joyce's
in *Finnegans Wake*, was largely verbal (many of his seemingly surreal
visual effects are better understood as grotesque or gothic, or – as
with the zoomorphic mutations of snail, octopus, turtle, lion, bird
and fish in 'How shall my animal' – deriving from literature, in
this case from the Welsh legend of Taliesin). Another reason for the
denial was pragmatic. In 1935, on Neuburg's recommendation,

J. M. Dent offered to take his second collection – a major advance on the publishing arrangement for *18 Poems*. Thomas's editor at Dent, Richard Church, an old-school Georgian poet, disliked Surrealism intensely. Predictably, he detected it in some poems in the first batch Thomas submitted to him. Church suggested he cut them out and Thomas was worried that he might break their contract if he did not. But he circumvented Church's objections by denying that he even knew what Surrealism was, and hinting he might go elsewhere if he had to drop them. It worked; Church replied, confessing: 'Still cannot understand the meaning of the poems, but in this matter I have decided to put myself aside and let you and the public face each other.'[30] Still, as with experimentalism more generally, it is clear that by 1936 Thomas was beginning to back away from his embrace of Surrealism.

Thomas the experimentalist and Surrealist is most pronounced in *Twenty-Five Poems*, but it is also in many ways his most conservative book. He had wanted to build on the success of *18 Poems* as quickly as possible, and *Twenty-Five Poems* was published on 10 September 1936, less than two years later. It consolidated his reputation, but the haste in getting it out is reflected in its unevenness. After the astonishing creativity of the period between September 1933 and April 1934, Dylan's output of poetry had slowed considerably. When the Dent contract prompted him to think about a second book, in late 1935, he had just ten new poems: those in N5 that had not gone into *18 Poems*, plus two more sonnets in the 'Altarwise' sequence, which now had seven parts.

Aware that he was not producing new poems quickly enough, in December 1935 he started revising earlier notebook poems to bulk out the second book. They were mainly items from N3: 'Why east wind chills', '"Find meat on bones"', 'And death shall have no dominion', 'Ears in the turrets hear', 'Was there a time', 'I have longed to move away' and 'Here in this spring'. There were also two poems from N4 that Thomas had deemed too transparent in style for *18 Poems*: 'The hand that signed the paper' and 'This bread I break'. In the case of another N4 poem, 'Grief, thief of time', Dylan experimented by dropping the comma of the charming but conventional original lyric to induce syntactic contortion, and rewrote the entire poem to make it conform, in his new, radically playful spirit. But none of the other poems he included were as thoroughly rejigged. He even reworked one poem he had already journal-published in two different versions, 'Foster the light'. Alongside this repurposed material, he wrote two new poems ('To-day, this insect' and 'Then was my neophyte'), and the final parts, IX and X, of 'Altarwise', in April–May 1936.

All in all, the gamble to maintain early momentum paid off. Critics were less keen on *Twenty-Five Poems*, and some thought the simpler poems represented a new style when in reality they were fossils (and many preferred these to the denser pieces). Thomas may have been amused by the error. But any confusion was made up for by a rave review by Edith Sitwell in the *Sunday Times* on 15 November 1936.

Sitwell, a leading poet and nationally influential reviewer, had initially proclaimed her dislike of his work, denouncing 'Our eunuch dreams' as 'an appalling affair' in her book, *Aspects of Modern Poetry* (1934). (Unknown to Thomas, at this point he was collateral damage in her feud with *New Verse* and Grigson, still a friend.) But her mind was changed when she read 'A grief ago' in October 1935, and she belatedly gave a good review to *18 Poems* in the *London Mercury* in February 1936. She and Thomas had corresponded in January 1936, and his courting of her paid off handsomely in her *Twenty-Five Poems* review: 'the work of this very young man', she wrote, 'is on a huge scale, both in theme and structurally – his themes are the mystery and holiness of all forms and aspects of life.' She noted the 'danger' posed by the 'difficulty' of the poems, but observed that this did not diminish the 'poignant and moving beauty' of their imagery, and concluded: 'I could not name one poet of this, the youngest generation, who shows so great a promise, and even so great an achievement.'[31] It was vague and fulsome, and Thomas grumbled about some of her interpretations, but it did the trick. The first impression of 750 copies of *Twenty-Five Poems* sold out and was reprinted, and several weeks of debate on modern poetry in the letters pages of the *Sunday Times* ensued. Thomas now had a national reputation and a lifelong staunch supporter in Sitwell, although the connection turned Grigson against him.

Vernon Watkins

In assembling *Twenty-Five Poems* Thomas had enjoyed the help of a new friend, Vernon Watkins, whom he met soon after returning to Swansea in September 1935. Watkins was eight years older than him, a clerk at the town-centre branch of Lloyds who had been educated at Repton and Cambridge. He was a gentle and in some ways unworldly man, a prolific but as yet unpublished poet, complementary in temperament to Thomas. He had suffered a mental breakdown in 1928 and had chosen to live a sheltered and undemanding life dedicated to poetry, which he had decided would not be published until after his death. In his cloistered existence in Pennard, a Gower village, he had been surprised to learn of another Swansea poet when he came across *18 Poems* in a Swansea bookshop in the spring of 1935. Impressed, piqued even, he tracked Thomas down via his uncle David Rees, and they immediately took to each other.[32]

From early October onwards they met two or three times a week, lunching on Wednesdays at the Kardomah. Thomas introduced Watkins to other Kardomah regulars: Fred Janes (now also back in Swansea), Dan Jones, Tom Warner and others. Watkins's extensive knowledge of poetry meant that he could take the place of necessary interlocutor that Pamela Johnson had vacated and Bert Trick could occupy only to a limited degree. Watkins had considerable technical expertise, was obsessed with the poetry of Yeats, could read French, German and Spanish – he introduced Thomas to the work of Federico García Lorca and Rainer Maria Rilke, among others – and possessed a finer-grained sense of what Thomas's writing was about than any previous friend. From 1936 onwards, Dylan would show or send Vernon just about every poem he wrote, for comment, and their letters amount to a textbook on poetic craft. But the most intense period of interaction was between 1936 and 1941; 88 of the 117 pages of the letters to Watkins date from that period, and after it there is a falling away, their correspondence and friendship disrupted by war and family commitments.

Watkins, for all his intense admiration, was not afraid to express his dissenting opinion on some of the poems in *Twenty-Five Poems*. He fully appreciated Thomas's need for density, his uncompromising approach and commitment to poetry, although his tolerance was tested by 'Now' and 'How soon the servant sun', which he told him he should exclude, if only because critics would seize on them at the expense of the better poems: 'Let them have a bone', was Thomas's response. But he persuaded him to include 'And death shall have no dominion' and cut a weak final couplet from 'Should lanterns shine'. And on numerous points of word order, particularly in the poems published in Thomas's third collection, *The Map of Love* (1939), Watkins made suggestions that were taken seriously and sometimes acted on. As with all those whose poetry he was asked to read, Thomas gave Watkins frank, thorough and insightful criticism of his own poems in return. As ever, his commentary on the work of others said much about his own work: 'All the words are lovely,' he said of one of Watkins's poems,

> but they seem so *chosen*, not struck out. I can see the sensitive picking of words, but none of the strong, inevitable pulling that makes a poem an event . . . not a still-life or an experience *put down*, placed, regulated . . . the whole poem seems to come out of the nostalgia of literature . . . I don't ask you for vulgarity, though I miss it; I think I ask you for a little creative destruction, destructive creation.[33]

Thomas's friendship with Watkins lasted throughout his life, but slackened during the war and faded in the late 1940s. Nor was Thomas always careful of the friendship; in 1937 he altered the wording of Watkins's poem 'Grief of the Sea' when he was editing the first issue of *Wales* (as he said, he 'Thowdlerized' it); a furious Watkins tracked down every copy in the local bookshops, altering each one by hand. Worst of all, he failed to turn up as best man for Watkins's wedding in 1944. Gwen Watkins was understandably suspicious of him. Rather harshly, yet with justification, she noted: 'People were important in Dylan's life only as far as they gave him what he needed.'[34] But she softened her judgement in later years. Thomas picked Watkins's brains, borrowed his books and dunned him for small gifts of money. Yet it was he who broke Watkins's self-absorption; without Dylan's encouragement, Vernon might have remained unpublished. Thomas challenged his friend to improve and consistently promoted his work, ensuring that Watkins was published, in 1940, by Faber & Faber. The main bonds between them – a shared obsession with poetry, an Uplands childhood and a taste for wordplay and zany humour – kept them close.

Moving towards marriage

Dylan Thomas spent the first few months of 1936 living in London in his usual hand-to-mouth way, and with the usual result: intense engagement with the literary and social scene, followed by burnout. Yet again Norman Cameron arranged a break, this time with Wyn Henderson, a friend of Oswell Blakeston who ran a guest house in Polgigga, near Land's End in Cornwall. Henderson was a former music-hall musician who had managed Nancy Cunard's press in Paris and trained and worked as a typographer in London before moving to Cornwall after losing her job. She was an energetic and liberated woman with a keen interest in psychosexual theories, and had herself been psychoanalysed. Her intellectual interests were matched by her sexual appetite and a 'shattering succession of lovers', as her son the artist Nigel Henderson put it.[35] But in early April, just before leaving London to travel down to Cornwall, Thomas met Caitlin Macnamara, the woman he was to marry.

Their first brief encounter followed an introduction by the much older Augustus John, a leading artist, whose companion-cum-mistress Caitlin was at the time.[36] She was Irish-French by parentage, a year older than Dylan; intelligent, quick-witted, with cornflower-blue eyes, a rose-pink complexion and shimmering blond-auburn hair, she had worked as a stage dancer and Isadora Duncan-style eurhythmic performer in Paris, where she had lived for a year with an artist boyfriend but failed to make a career (Caitlin's creative frustration was at the root of some of the Thomases' later problems). Like Dylan, she was articulate, had considerable literary ability, dabbled in painting and was more than capable of holding her own in discussion – and in drink. But unlike him she was a genuine bohemian, with a patrician sense of entitlement, while her flamboyance and uninhibitedness, although often attractive, also carried a brazen and even threatening edge.

Caitlin's father, Francis Macnamara, was an Anglo-Irish land-owner from County Clare who had literary pretensions (he was a friend of Yeats and other leading Anglo-Irish writers). He had frittered away his inheritance and abandoned his wife when their children were still small. They had been raised by their mother, Mary ('Yvonne') Macnamara, in rural Hampshire. The domestic set-up was unconventional; Yvonne had a long-standing lesbian relationship with a neighbour, the photographer Nora Summers, and her children grew up with those of John's family, who also lived nearby. John, a notorious philanderer, had exploited this closeness; he had used Caitlin as a model, and at the end of the very first session, forced himself on her sexually. At the time she was just fifteen years old, and she would be his occasional companion and mistress for several years.

Thomas left London for Cornwall, as arranged, on 8 April. Once there, he found Henderson good company and grew to enjoy the surroundings; she kept him out of the local pubs, up to a point, and entertained and irritated him when she held forth on the sexologist Havelock Ellis (whom Dylan dubbed 'Havelick Pelvis') and her own liberated sex life. She would involve Thomas himself in it before he returned to London at the end of May, in a relationship that was warm but brief. Their area of Cornwall was host to a colony of artists and intellectuals, and there were other congenial spirits to meet, including Veronica Sibthorp, with whom Thomas would also have a fling the following year. As he had hoped, he was able to get down to work, finishing 'The Orchards', writing 'Then was my neophyte' and the final two parts of 'Altarwise by owl-light', IX and X, the entombment and resurrection episodes, and revising

'To-day, this insect'. With these poems, *Twenty-Five Poems* was complete. In 'Altarwise' IX, sterility and death are symbolized by ancient Egyptian motifs; but sonnet X features 'winged harbours' and a 'foam-blue channel', in which it may not be fanciful to recognize the rest cure with a lover in the setting of a Cornish seascape.

Dylan returned to London in late May and met Caitlin again; their relationship became a sexual one at this point. After a brief spell in Swansea he was back in London for the International Surrealist Exhibition in mid-June. Yoyo-ing back to Swansea, he negotiated final adjustments to *Twenty-Five Poems* with Church. Then, very likely tipped off by Caitlin that she and John were about to drive through West Wales, staying overnight with the novelist Richard Hughes and his wife Frances in Laugharne en route to Fishguard, Thomas enrolled Fred Janes and his Austin 7 to intercept them. What followed is part of the Dylan and Caitlin myth: the pair spent the next two days together, with Janes and John as bystanders, until John's jealousy – he was incensed by the sight of them in his rear-view mirror 'osculating assiduously' – led him to knock Thomas down in a pub car park and drive off with Caitlin.[37] But it was a pyrrhic victory; the incident pushed Caitlin into ending her relationship with John and promising to marry Dylan.

That would not happen for another year, however. Back in Swansea for the rest of 1936, Dylan and Caitlin repaired the friendship with John and spent the August bank holiday together. Thomas saw *Twenty-Five Poems* through the press on 10 September and his relationship with Caitlin flourished. But there was a long hiatus when Caitlin caught gonorrhoea – not from Dylan – and returned to Ireland to recover for several months. It did not affect their feelings for each other, as his letters show. 'I love you,' he wrote, 'and we'll always keep each other alive. We can never do nothing at all now but that both of us know all about it.' He would add that 'there is . . . a sort of sweet madness about you and me, a sort of mad bewilderment and astonishment oblivious to the Nasties and the Meanies . . . you're the only person from here to Aldebaran and back with whom I'm entirely free; and I think it's because you're as innocent as me.'[38] But for now they had nothing to marry on.

Late in 1936, while Caitlin was in Ireland, Oswell Blakeston introduced Dylan to Emily Holmes Coleman, an American writer living in London, the author of the novel *The Shutter of Snow* (1930).[39] Coleman had lived in Paris and been a contributor to *transition*, and was a friend of the better-known novelists Antonia White and Djuna Barnes. Thomas had read White's work and had reviewed Barnes's recently published *Nightwood* (1936), a Modernist-Gothic masterpiece of obsessional love, describing it enthusiastically if backhandedly as 'one of the three greatest novels ever written by a woman' (he was so smitten that he lifted a word-cluster from it for his poem 'If my head hurt a hair's foot' in 1938, and later included chunks of it in his U.S. reading tours).[40] Emily and Dylan now began an affair that lasted into the spring of 1937. In a sign of his growing reputation, he was invited to talk at Cambridge University in mid-February 1937, and Coleman accompanied him. She felt he was torn between her and Caitlin, but he was open about the fact that he was more in love with Caitlin, and determined to marry her. Coleman admitted later, 'I just wasn't crazy-bohemian enough for him.'[41] The only poem of the period, 'It is the sinner's dust-tongued bell claps me to churches', has been explicated, rather mechanistically, as being 'about' Dylan's recent bout of gonorrhoea. The pun on 'clap' undeniably alludes to it, but as an introductory detail only. As Thomas told Watkins, it was largely 'about churches', understood as a metaphor for bodies in which the ritual of sex is performed. The words that recur are 'time' and 'grief', in a typical linking of sex and death; 'all love's sinners', himself and his lovers, have led to 'the plagued groom and bride/ Who have brought forth the urchin grief.'[42] It would be the last poem in which he treated sex in the negative mode of the early process poems.

This poem may also reflect the way events in Thomas's London life yet again overwhelmed him in early April 1937.[43] He had contracted with Dent to write a book about a journey through Wales and taken up some of the advance money; the plan was to stay with writers he knew, such as Caradoc Evans, and to write up the book when he returned to London. On 6 April, in an attempt to do some of the legwork before Caitlin's return, he took a train from Aberystwyth to Machynlleth 'with a haversack and a flapped cap' and set out walking. But he seems not to have properly organized the tour, and had no resources: 'I'M IN GOD KNOWS WHERE' ran the desperate telegram he sent to Coleman that evening.[44] A few days later he was back in London. There followed an increasingly farcical bout of musical beds, as Caitlin flitted between Hampshire and London, and Thomas flitted between her and (in her absence) Coleman. During these confused weeks, he forgot that he was due to give his first BBC broadcast on 21 April, on *Life and the Modern Poet*, from the Swansea studios. Luckily, his friend and fellow poet John Pudney, who worked at the corporation, helped him to make it from a London studio. But Thomas then failed to produce a copy of his script for the records, permanently blotting his copybook with members of the BBC hierarchy.

Thomas now found himself laid up, recuperating from bronchitis and laryngitis (as so often, illness attributed solely to drinking also involved respiratory illness). But his year of experiment, in living as in poetry, was not quite over. With Caitlin in Hampshire again and nowhere else to go, he spent May in Veronica Sibthorp's London flat. Sibthorp was a fine cook, and had a good sense of humour, a love of word games and a disability that she made light of (she had a prosthetic leg, called 'Gilbert', which she would park on a stool while she hopped around her kitchen).[45] As with Henderson and Coleman, the relationship was an amicable one; she dubbed him 'the Angelic Pig', bathed him daily, and was happy to drink with him. An endearing record of their relationship is contained in a scrapbook in which they doodled and wrote comic, childish and erotic verse ('Poem to Veronica' runs: 'Wherever there's honey there's bees & bears there/ And I'm a bad bee & you're a good bear', scribbled beside a cartoon of a bee in bed with someone, entitled 'Bear in a bed').[46] Yet he made little headway in writing his Welsh journey book, and soon Caitlin was back in town.

Dylan and Caitlin now decided that they had waited long enough. They resolved to get married, even if it meant that Caitlin would have to live with her mother while Thomas returned to Wales to work on his travel book. On 10 June he wrote to D.J. and Florrie from Cornwall, announcing the impending marriage in Penzance Registry Office and requesting money and clean clothes. They tried to stop the marriage, and the effort of trying to get £3 together for the marriage licence dragged things out; but, on 11 July, now with his parents' reluctant blessing ('the two young irresponsibles are bent on their act of supreme folly,' D.J. expostulated to Haydn and Nancy) and a gift of £5 from D.J., they tied the knot.[47]

5

Loving Presences, Warring Absences: Marriage, Wales and War, 1938–41

In early May 1938 Dylan and Caitlin Thomas rented a cottage in Laugharne; its name, appropriately, was 'Eros'. Caitlin soon discovered she was pregnant, and their first child, Llewelyn, would be born in January 1939. The next two years in Laugharne were to be the happiest of their life together. The town had a special appeal for them. Thomas had first visited it with Glyn Jones in 1934, and had been impressed by its laid-back, backwater charms. He and Caitlin had also memorably encountered each other there in the summer of 1936, when he was competing with Augustus John for her favours, as we have seen. Along with the ruins of its Norman castle, the town was distinguished by its town-hall clock tower, its portreeve (for a mayor; a medieval survival) and its scattering of distinguished-looking Georgian town houses, relics of long-vanished prosperity. In 1938, however, it was neither a market town nor port and had no industry or railway station. Its population of a few hundred was clannishly divided, and its leading family were the Williamses, who owned the town's bus company, the electricity generating plant and Brown's Hotel (run by Ivy Williams, who soon became a good friend of Thomas's). It was a 'Little England beyond Wales' – an English-speaking outpost in Welsh-speaking countryside – with eccentric customs, 'sociable' and with 'little law and no respect', as Thomas approvingly told his U.S. publisher, James Laughlin.[1] The hospitable Richard and Frances Hughes still lived in Castle House, in the grounds of the castle, and Thomas's rural hinterland of relatives lay to the east, accessible by ferry across the estuary to Llansteffan. About a mile up the hill from Llansteffan, in

Llanybri, lived the poet Lynette Roberts and her husband, Keidrych Rhys, editor of the recently launched literary journal *Wales*.

After a few months in cramped 'Eros' the Thomases moved to 'Sea View', a larger house nearer the town centre. Despite poverty and disorder – their furniture consisted largely of beer crates and packing cases, and the floors were littered with crushed oyster shells – the contentment marriage brought Dylan is evident from his letters. He and Caitlin settled into the life of the town, making friends, having guests to stay and getting to know the area through visits, walks and picnics. But for the first three months there the stream of poetic productivity Dylan had enjoyed when living at Yvonne Macnamara's house at Blashford dried up. This writer's block was partly the result of the protracted tussle for a new

Caitlin Macnamara, Dylan's future wife, posing on the banks of the River Avon in Hampshire, 1936, photograph by Nora Summers.

style in the wake of his experimental phase. With his prose, however, there was no such difficulty. In his letters and oral performances, over several years, he had already forged a fluent, often comic, prose idiom. It lent itself perfectly to short stories with a broader appeal than his early fiction (which Caitlin dismissed as 'muddled up with surrealism and pornography').[2] Before leaving Blashford in April 1938 he had written 'A Visit to Grandpa's', the first of the tales he would gather in the short-story collection *A Portrait of the Artist as a Young Dog* (1940). Apart from 'An Adventure from a Work in Progress', a final experimental fiction, completed in Laugharne, all his prose would henceforth be in the same comic-realist vein.

A new poetic style

With poetry, the process of readjustment was more problematic. Thomas had written just one poem, 'It is the sinner's dust-tongued bell', between *Twenty-Five Poems* and his marriage; the rest of 1937 was devoted to the long and sporadically brilliant, but always tortuous, 'I make this in a warring absence', which explored the stresses of his marriage to Caitlin. Their volatility meant that rows could flare up easily. Like Caitlin, Dylan was highly sensitive, and capable of losing his temper, but he almost invariably beat a retreat in the face of her wrath, often meekly accepting her verbal (and sometimes physical) abuse. In any case, reconciliation was usually swift. As late as 1952, Ruth Witt-Diamant would claim that the pair were generally happy, their arguments 'backhanded love quarrels'. Whether things were as harmonious by that date as this suggests is debatable, but the evidence certainly bears out Watt-Diamant's other claim that Dylan and Caitlin used arguments as a stimulus to their relationship. It is clear, also, that they would stage quarrels in public to unsettle or amuse others, and themselves.[3] As we have seen, Thomas was constantly acting out different versions of himself and often drew those around him into the performance.

'I make this in a warring absence', however, records the after-math of a serious row, charting a trajectory of punctured male pride, anger, jealousy, metaphorical death and resurrection. The date of its composition suggests that it was begun after a very early falling-out, probably in late summer 1937; certainly, the shock it records seems raw. It is primarily about the 'pride' the speaker has in the world he and his lover have forged for themselves ('pride' occurs nine times in the poem), its sudden collapse, followed by its rebuilding and a rueful recognition that such collapses will recur. Thomas told Desmond Hawkins, 'the stanzas are a catalogue of the contraries, the warring loyalties, the psychological discrepancies, all expressed in physical and/or extra-narrative terms, that go towards making up the "character" of the . . . "beloved" . . . in whose absence, and in the fear of whose future unfaithful absences, I jealously made the poem.'[4]

The poem is notable for its frankness about the abject state to which the male speaker is reduced by the 'warring'. In what may be the most vivid account of deflated cocksureness in English poetry, its speaker finds himself detumescently 'corner-cast, breath's rag, scrawled weed, a vain/ And opium head, crow stalk, puffed, cut, and blown'. In imaginary revenge at her rejection of him, and having walked out on her, he 'make[s] a weapon of an ass's skeleton . . . Cudgel[s] great air, wreck[s] east, and topple[s] sundown.'[5] But he soon realizes that these are absurd, hyperbolic gestures; his defection hurts him, not her, and it is he who topples, 'sprawl[s] to ruin' and undergoes a psychic death and entombment (which is also an en-wombment). In this state he is reminded of the origins of his life in death, and becomes aware that his beloved, for all the imagined violence he has inflicted, 'Walks with no wound'. Here, as in 'A grief ago', and again in 'Into her lying down head', Thomas sees women as proof against masculine pretensions and rage because, in the final analysis, they are more central to the energies by which life and the universe are continually remade. The psychodrama ends in reconciliation, with the beloved imagined as a balm-bringing raincloud. But it is only a temporary truce: 'In the groin's endless coil a man is tangled.' He will inevitably suffer such jealousy again, hence the wryness of the last line's reversal of the opening: 'Yet this I make in a forgiving presence.'[6]

Dylan and Caitlin in Brown's Hotel, Laugharne, 1938–40, photograph by Nora Summers.

After this 'exhauster' of a piece, as he called it, Thomas rewrote five notebook poems at Blashford in the winter and early spring of 1937–8, prior to the move to Laugharne.[7] Four were 'simple poems', not much revised from their originals – they appeared in *Poetry* (Chicago), where they advanced his growing u.s. reputation – while the fifth, 'How shall my animal', was a major work in a new style.[8] It has the verbal richness and force of the best of his previous poetry, but with a quicksilver agility that is new. With the same thoroughness, in March 1938 he completely refashioned an elegy he had written for his aunt Ann in February 1933 (the 'Annie' of the short story 'The Peaches'). 'After the funeral' begins in the satirical register of its original, mocking the hypocrisy of her mourners. Then, in a striking departure, it modulates into a critical portrait of its author, the teenage Dylan, as 'a desolate boy who slits his throat/ In the dark of the coffin and sheds dry leaves'.[9] The callow adolescent who wrote a sterile and unfeeling elegy is rejected, and the focus of the poem is shifted from the mourners to Ann herself, and the contradiction between her narrow religious creed and her generosity, rendered in images of water and greenery. The poem then revises itself again, suddenly alert to the danger of drowning Ann in its own rhetoric.

After this second volte-face, the speaker makes himself Ann's 'bard', subserving her loving-kindness, as he 'call[s] all/ The seas to service' and turns the spaces of her chapel and home into pagan places of worship in the 'ferned and foxy woods', celebrating the cosmic process of death and renewal. Ann and her bard, breath and marble gravestone angel, living and dead, become, by syntactic sleights, interfused:

> These cloud-sopped, marble hands, this monumental
> Argument of the hewn voice, gesture and psalm
> Storm me forever over her grave until
> The stuffed lung of the fox twitch and cry Love
> And the strutting fern lay seeds on the black sill.[10]

Even more than 'How shall my animal', 'After the funeral' marks the arrival of a new poetic style and attitude, empathetic as well as flexible and dynamic.[11]

A new prose style

The impact of the breakthrough into a new prose style and a new poetic style in early 1938 was reflected in the decision Thomas now took to abandon his attempt to publish a collection of the short stories he had written, 24 in all, since 1933. As we have seen, they were almost wilfully anti-realist pieces, born of the same process vision as the poems, and deal in iconoclasm, deviancy and madness. They are more transparent than the poems, and their take on taboo subjects is more provocative; these include incest ('The Burning Baby'), vivisection ('The Lemon'), crucifixion ('The Tree'), sexual violence ('The Dress'), murder ('The Vest'), madness ('The Mouse and the Woman') and interracial sexual magic ('The School for Witches'). While not as far-ranging as the poetry, they are never-theless formidable examples of experimental, expressionist-gothic writing, unlike almost anything being written at the time. The last two stories, 'In the Direction of the Beginning' (1937) and 'An Adventure from a Work in Progress' (1938), are more like prose poems than stories. Both are sea-voyage quests reminiscent of Rimbaud's 'Le bateau ivre' (The Drunken Boat), their protagonists seeking a female archetype who promises some ultimate revelation and consummation. Blatantly sexual, accounts of the workings of desire itself, they also enact the struggle to write, proceeding as they do by verbal play and word association. It is easy to understand why Thomas would have wanted to collect and publish them.

In 1937 he offered his collected stories to Dent, but Church turned them down on the grounds of obscenity. Bypassing his agent, Thomas struck a deal with George Reavey's Europa Press to publish them as *The Burning Baby: 16 Stories*. But after months of keeping Dylan on tenterhooks Reavey told him in February 1938 that the printer refused to handle the book on the same grounds. He was prepared to accept cuts, but Reavey failed to specify what those should be, instead proposing publication by Obelisk, a 'Paris smut press', but on worse terms than those originally agreed.[12] At this Thomas withdrew the book. Perhaps he now felt that a collection of stories in the style of 'A Visit to Grandpa's' was a better commercial prospect; the letter he had sent to Hawkins accompanying that story spoke of the ambition to write a batch of related tales.[13] The fact that he now had to support Caitlin as well as himself must have been a consideration. At the same time, he may also have realized that the early stories might be published in a different format.

The Map of Love

Thomas's poetry drought of summer 1938 ended in September with 'On no work of words', the subject of which was the 'three lean months' of writer's block, comically contrasted with the 'big purse' of his by now bulky body (he had put on 2 stones in weight – 13 kilograms – since the start of the year):

> On no work of words now for three lean months in the bloody
> Belly of the rich year and the big purse of my body
> I bitterly take to task my poverty and craft:

To take to give is all, return what is hungrily given
Puffing the pounds of manna up through the dew to heaven,
The lovely gift of the gab bangs back on a blind shaft.[14]

The lean/excess paradox is enacted in the sixth line, in which
the vocables mirrored on either side of the two central 'b's (in
'gab bangs') – 'g', 'ft', 'a' and 'l' – mimic the refusal of his prayer
for inspiration, while ingeniously belying that refusal. The phrase
'currencies of the marked breath' in the third stanza alerts us to a
series of mordant puns – on 'marks', 'pounds', 'purse', 'treasures',
'expensive', 'count' – involving the money that he and Caitlin so
sorely lacked. More broadly, 'On no work of words' affirms that
artists have a duty to make a return on the gifts the world has
lavished on them in creations of their own. As in 'After the funeral'
a positive rather than a negative emphasis is given to process. In
addition, while it confronts large issues of life and death, 'On no
work of words' clearly benefits, like 'After the funeral', from a
new level of self-awareness and a specific biographical source.

The more emotionally open quality of the poetry Thomas
now wrote was the result of marriage and impending fatherhood
as well as the stylistic dead end he had reached by 1937. There
is a tendency to attribute a writer's change of style to purely
personal and social events, and to ignore the internal logic of
aesthetic development that is often at some distance from these.
Still, it is undeniable that Dylan Thomas's poems now reflected
his personal circumstances to a greater degree. This is nowhere
more apparent than in two poems of fatherhood (and mother-
hood) written in late 1938 and early 1939. '"If my head hurt hair's
foot"' imagines a colloquy between a mother and her unborn child,
in which the child selflessly asks its mother to 'rage me back to the
making-house' if s/he hurts her during labour. The mother, equally
selflessly, tells the child that she would not 'change my tears or your
iron head', even for the heaven of 'Christ's dazzling bed/ Of nacreous
sleep among particles and charms'.[15] In an even more unorthodox
trope, 'A saint about to fall' imagines the travails of the child poised
to leave its 'father's house' in sperm form, then cuts from conception

to its birth, as the child is welcomed by its mother 'in my house
in the mud/ Of the crotch of the squawking shores' of Laugharne.
Despite their subject-matter, however, neither poem could be
described as sentimental; both are full of foreboding for the world
the child has entered, with 'A saint about to fall' warning the child
that '[T]he skull of the earth' is 'barbed with a war of burning brains
and hair' and asking it to 'wail' among the 'herods' in protest.[16]

The poem that alludes to the change in style most clearly in
autobiographical terms is 'Once it was the colour of saying', in which
Thomas contemplates his childhood as 'the Rimbaud of Cwmdonkin
Drive', as he self-deprecatingly put it elsewhere, 'soak[ing] my table'
with ink as he wrote poems on the 'uglier side of a hill', Cwmdonkin
Drive, but now accepting that he must 'undo' the 'gentle seaslides of
saying' he once pursued so single-mindedly:

> When I whistled with mitching boys through a reservoir park
> Where at night we stoned the cold and cuckoo
> Lovers in the dirt of their leafy beds,
> The shade of their trees was a word of many shades
> And a lamp of lightning for the poor in the dark;
> Now my saying shall be my undoing,
> And every stone I wind off like a reel.[17]

If, in his early teens, words had been valued for their 'shades', and
used heedless of their immediate everyday contexts, like the stones
he and other 'mitching boys' threw at the lovers in the bushes of
Cwmdonkin Park, he will now 'wind' them 'off' more carefully, with
the 'stones' (poems), 'like a reel', as he angles for a more considered
catch.

Despite his recent steady productivity, by 1939 Thomas again
found himself in the position of lacking sufficient poems for a new
collection. To bulk out the sixteen he had written since *Twenty-Five
Poems* he decided to include in it some of the stories that had been
earmarked for *The Burning Baby*. The result, *The Map of Love* (1939),
was another intriguingly hybrid book, whose first part reflects
the partial shift in poetic style, while the second part is made up

of seven of the early stories. He had wanted to include more, but five – including 'A Prospect of the Sea', which he thought the best – were vetoed (Church felt it had 'unwarrantable moments of sensuality'). The book's title was that of one of the 'unviolent' stories that made the cut, 'The Tree', 'The Enemies', 'The Dress', 'The Visitor', 'The Orchards' and 'The Mouse and the Woman' being the others.[18]

Wales and *Wales*

The late 1930s was a period of resurgent cultural nationalism and regionalism in the component parts of the United Kingdom. One of the factors that made Laugharne attractive to Dylan Thomas in 1938 was that, for the first time, a self-sufficient anglophone literary culture – that is, one that did not require writers to be based in London – had begun to emerge in Wales. It was an expression of the depth of talent in what is known today as 'the First Flowering' of Anglo-Welsh literature. Dylan Thomas is its best-known figure, but it included many other outstanding writers.[19] Swansea and southwest Wales was an epicentre of activity, with Thomas in Laugharne, Watkins in Swansea, and Rhys and Roberts in Llanybri. This anglophone flowering was paralleled by one in Welsh-language literature, and – despite the strictures of Saunders Lewis, the leading Welsh-language author and leader of Plaid Cymru (who declared that Thomas 'belongs to the English') – there was significant convergence between the two groups.[20] It was in this atmosphere of burgeoning cultural self-confidence and a joining of forces that Keidrych Rhys had started *Wales*, the first Anglo-Welsh literary journal; its inaugural issue, in June 1937, carried one of the Thomas stories that Church had vetoed, 'Prologue to an Adventure', on its front page. *Wales* was joined in 1939 by the *Welsh Review*, edited by Gwyn Jones. A lift-off into national literary autonomy seemed a real possibility at this point. Rhys pitched the idea of a series on Anglo-Welsh poets to the BBC, and Aneirin Talfan Davies, working at the BBC in Cardiff (a Welsh BBC Region was established in 1937), approached Thomas about a broadcast. Early 1939 also saw Dylan liaising with

Thomas Taig to run an Anglo-Welsh poetry and drama programme at the Mercury Theatre in London.

Thomas largely supported Rhys, and even did some editorial work on *Wales*, but he was constitutionally averse to manifestos or belonging to literary groups or movements. He had, in the past, supported the idea of 'Celtic' writing, championing the margins against the centre.[21] But he was wary of Rhys's nationalist agenda: 'I've never understood this racial talk, "his Irish talent", "undoubtedly Scotch inspiration", apart from whisky. Keidrych Rhys [is] a believer in all that stuff about racial inspiration, etc.'[22] But these differences would not have dissolved the Anglo-Welsh literary renaissance; what did was the outbreak of the Second World War in September 1939. The war's impact on a still-fragile cultural formation was disastrous. Writers were scattered by wartime directives and reviewing work dried up. Regionalism would soon reassert itself, and its Welsh poetic apotheosis was *Modern Welsh Poetry* (1944), a splendid Faber anthology edited by Rhys. But by that time *Wales* had limped into oblivion – its later iterations were faint echoes of what had gone before – and many of its contributors, including Thomas, had long since been displaced beyond Wales.

For Thomas and his young family, enjoying professional success and a modicum of stability despite his poverty, the impact of the war was harsh. *The Map of Love* was published on 24 August 1939, overshadowed by the Stalin–Hitler Pact a day before, and Britain's declaration of war on Nazi Germany a few days after it, on 3 September. The plug was pulled on a BBC Welsh Region radio broadcast he was due to give on 6 September, and he would not have another BBC engagement for a year. In the light of the timing, the praise lavished on the book received must have seemed ironic. Desmond Hawkins lauded it in the *Spectator*, as did Cyril Connolly in the *New Statesman* and Herbert Read in *Seven*: 'With this volume', Read wrote,

Mr Thomas quells any reasonable doubts about the quality of his poetic genius . . . there is a variety of rhythm or measure which shows the completest mastery of technical means . . . These poems

Caitlin Thomas and Llewelyn, 1939.

cannot be reviewed; they can only be acclaimed . . . *The Map of Love* . . . contains the most absolute poetry that has been written in our time.

He added, however, 'one can only pray that this poet will not be forced in any way to surrender the subtle course of his genius.'[23] But more pressing concerns were uppermost in people's minds in late 1939. *The Map of Love* had sold just 280 copies by the end of the year, and *A Portrait of the Artist as a Young Dog*, his book of stories in the new prose style, would appear with equally unfortunate timing, just before the Dunkirk crisis, in April 1940.

A Portrait of the Artist as a Young Dog

The timing was doubly unfortunate given that, aside from the tougher poems and tales in *The Map of Love*, both books displayed what became one of the hallmarks of Thomas's mature work, namely its ability to combine textual complexity and wide appeal. *A Portrait*, in particular, is perfect of its kind, even if Thomas dismissed it as a 'potboiler'.[24] Its ten quasi-autobiographical stories, modelled on Joyce's *Dubliners*, focus on episodes in Thomas's Swansea childhood and adolescence and are often brilliantly comic, full of shrewd and subtle observation and, in places, intensely moving. The best stories – 'The Peaches', 'The Fight', 'Who Do You Wish Was With Us?' and 'One Warm Saturday' – are masterpieces, a reminder that Thomas was perhaps the last great poet in English who was also a great short-story writer; but there are very few weak links.

'The Peaches' is far more than the social satire poignantly symbolized by the tinned peaches the narrator's aunt Annie offers the snobbish Mrs Williams, only to be turned down. It unerringly renders the blend of insight and ignorance in the boy's-eye view of the 'insanitary farm' that is its setting, and the complex quirkiness of its inhabitants, and convincingly evokes the full range of his thoughts and emotions – fear, content, confessionalism, curiosity, bafflement and joy in the life of the body – to get under the skin of what it is to be exuberantly young. In 'The Fight', Thomas charts a very different area of the boy's consciousness – his status as preco-cious artist-to-be – but does so through comedy that, again, contains the boy's own sense of fun, within a humorous frame of adult irony.

As the protagonist ages the stories grow darker. In 'Old Garbo', he enters the sordidly alluring realm of alcoholic excess, while mortality looms as the narrator of 'Who Do You Wish Was With Us?' desperately staves off his friend Ray's compulsion to talk about his brother's death. Finally, in 'One Warm Saturday', the narrator finds himself thwarted and 'lost' at night surrounded by the rubble of demolished houses, like the 'never-to-be-forgotten people of the dirty town' – Thomas's own fate, it may be, if he had not moved to London in 1934. The book's title, a laddish revision of Joyce's

A Portrait of the Artist as a Young Man, refers to Thomas's doggish-mongrel persona and the sense in which the stories (usually gently) mock the pretensions of his younger self and Modernism's sanctification of the artist, matching the staged self-reflexiveness of such poems as 'After the funeral' in a comic-realist vein.[25]

The increasing seriousness of the stories of *A Portrait* is mirrored in the way they look ahead to the war, revealing a growing sense of conflict and fear. The boys in 'The Fight', for example, early in the book, glamorize their blood and bruises ('the best blackeye in Europe'), and a fellow pupil's reference to his father fighting in 'Salonika in the war' passes by harmlessly amid the banter, the 'battles [and] sieges' referred to belonging to a merely imaginary realm.[26] Near the end of *A Portrait*, however, in 'Who Do You Wish Was With Us?', Ray and Dylan are trapped on the tidal island of Worm's Head by the incoming tide: 'The slipping stepping stones [are] gone', and the ambiguous figures in the dusk, 'jumping and calling' from the mainland, prefigure Britain's imminent isolation from war-torn Europe.[27] In the same bleak vein, the 'brick-heaps and the broken wood and the dust that had been houses once' in the closing image of 'One Warm Saturday' seem to uncannily anticipate the destruction soon to be visited on British cities, including Swansea, in the Blitz.

War and work

'Yes, terrible, terrible', Dylan began his letter to Desmond Hawkins on the day Britain declared war, adding that his 'chief concern' was 'to keep out of death's way. And no, I don't know what to do either: declare myself a neutral state, or join as a small tank.'[28] To Glyn Jones on 11 September he wrote, 'I want to get something out of the war, & put very little in (certainly not my one & only body),' mapping the war on to his own surroundings by describing Laugharne as 'a little Danzig'.[29] His flippancy in the face of 'this war trembling over the edge of Laugharne, fill[ing] me with . . . horror & terror & lassitude', was typical of a tendency to deal with serious matters by mocking them, playing down his own fears; but there is no denying

that he found the war profoundly disturbing.[30] Like many on
the political left, he had little trust in a government that had been
appeasing militarism and fascism abroad throughout the decade.
Most, however, accepted the logic that, since a time had finally
come when fascism could be fought, they should be part of it. As
Cecil Day-Lewis put it in 'Where Are the War Poets?', 'It is the logic
of our times . . . that we who lived by honest dreams/ Defend the
bad against the worse.'[31] But Thomas resisted this, unusually, for
some time, on grounds that were moral as well as selfish. Writing
to the art critic and historian Kenneth Clarke, he explained, 'My
great horror's killing.'[32] He tried to persuade fellow writers to sign
a pacifist 'statement of objection' to the war. Some did so; more
demurred. He took issue with Rayner Heppenstall's claim that
writers should accept their generational destiny; it was 'hysterical
and pernicious misreasoning', he told him, that he had to 'undergo
contemporary experience to the uttermost' in order to earn the right
to write about the war: 'Lorca didn't have to be gored before writing
a bullsong.'[33] The supreme duty of the writer was to stay 'upright'
and to write. Thomas framed what he regarded as Heppenstall's
illogicality in a grammar-twisting construction: what will you do,
he demanded, when the government tells you to 'fight not your
enemies'? That is, are you prepared to kill those with whom you
have no personal quarrel? To do so, Thomas felt, required the
dehumanization of an entire population, 'a bewildered, buggered
people', the Germans. Such ethical absolutism was untenable –
Nazism had to be fought – but it was his acute awareness of the
inhumanities this would entail, his refusal to be inured or reconciled
to them, that would give his wartime poems their power.

Dylan considered becoming a conscientious objector, but felt
he could not honestly plead religion, given his lack of orthodox
belief. It was not that he was a physical coward, terrified though
he was by air raids – he described himself as a 'belligerent pacifist'
and sometimes provoked fights in pubs with servicemen who
boasted about their prowess in killing – but he was determined
to avoid combat or munitions work: 'Clocking in, turning a screw,
winding a wheel . . . every cartridge case means one less Jerry . . .

turning and winding and hammering to help kill another stranger, deary me, I'd rather be a poet anyday and live on guile and beer.'[34] Even the Army Medical Corps would mean 'patch[ing] poor buggers up to send them out again into quick insanity and bullets'.[35] Several efforts to find a job in a reserved occupation followed, all unsuccessful. In May 1940 an Army medical in Llandeilo graded him C-3, unfit to fight, on account of an 'unreliable lung'.[36] But this did not mean that he could not be called up to work in some non-combatant unit.

Whatever his military status, it was now imperative to find work. As journals folded under wartime restrictions, the reviewing he had been relying on dried up. In 1938 he had applied for a grant from the Royal Literary Fund, but, despite the backing of T. S. Eliot and other eminent literary figures, he had been turned down because he was not an 'established writer' (sardonically he noted that had he been one he would hardly have needed to apply). A second application also failed, and over the winter of 1938–9 the Thomases were forced to retreat from Laugharne to Yvonne Macnamara's once more. One-off appeals to patrons of the arts, friends and other writers yielded temporary alleviation, and Stephen Spender, Herbert Read and Henry Moore organized a whip-round through *Horizon*, which netted £70, but this did not fix the problem – part of which was, of course, Thomas's improvidence. In the meantime Norman Cameron devised a scheme by which better-off friends could support him through weekly five-shilling donations – a 'Dylan Flotation Fund' – but this, too, fell through. Soon the unpaid bills mounted, and it was 'among dunning and suspicion' that the Thomases left Laugharne once more in April 1940.[37] They returned briefly in the summer and paid off some debts, but in July 1940 a small allowance from Dent, which covered basic expenditure, ended, and they fled again (returning briefly the following summer as guests of Frances Hughes).

In the summer of 1940, leaving Llewelyn with Yvonne, Caitlin and Dylan went to live at the Mansion House, the home of Thomas's friend John Davenport, at Marshfield in Gloucestershire.[38] Davenport held open house for a number of friends that summer, subsidizing a supportive, febrile, bohemian atmosphere of music, drinking, games and the inevitable attendant artistic and sexual rivalries as the Battle of Britain raged overhead. Other members of the entourage included Antonia White and the composers Lennox Berkeley and William Glock. Thomas paid his way by working with Davenport on a satirical novel, *The Death of the King's Canary*, which he had begun some years before with Hawkins. Its plot was loosely related to the kind of activities taking place in the Mansion House, centred as it was on a weekend country-house party thrown to celebrate the appointment (and murder) of a new Poet Laureate, and containing parodies and pastiches of the work of leading poets, from Auden to Thomas himself. These are the only noteworthy parts of what is an underwritten and incoherent work, unpublished until 1976 because of the libel laws. More importantly, however, with Davenport's help, Thomas picked up three temporary script-doctoring jobs for the BBC.

Poetry and violence: *New Apocalypse* and war

It was deeply ironic that, even as his financial plight intensified, Thomas's poetic star was rising more rapidly than ever. In January 1939 Auden had left Britain for the United States, anxious about his absorption by the establishment and the prospect of war. Whether or not this amounted to desertion (his reputation never fully recovered), Auden's move was a graphic illustration of the fact that New Country poetry, with its rationalist diagnoses of the ills of society, had failed in its mission. Its stylistic dominance swiftly evaporated and its flagship journal, Grigson's *New Verse*, also went under. MacSpaunday was swiftly superseded by New Apocalypse poetry, its polar opposite: neo-Romantic, focused on the unconscious and the body, delving into myth, religion, dreams and the extremes of the human condition – birth, death, sex, faith, madness and social collapse.[39] It took its name from the anthology *New Apocalypse* (1939), edited by J. F. Hendry and Henry Treece, two members of a loose grouping of poets that also included G. S. Fraser and Dorian Cooke. They cited Thomas as their chief contemporary inspiration, and had asked him a year before to sign their manifesto. Thomas had refused. But now, like it or not, he was their uncrowned king. In effect, with the New Apocalypse group, contemporary taste – since Hendry and Treece were no younger than Thomas – had caught up with him. He was suddenly a prophet vindicated by events.

The 1940s were to become Dylan Thomas's decade, just as the 1930s had been shared between him and Auden. Thomas's influence and that of the New Apocalypse poets rippled outwards to shape the poetry at the universities and in the burgeoning Regionalist move-ment, its scope and impact increased by a BBC broadcast of 1942 in which Herbert Read aligned poetry with neo-Romanticism in the visual arts.[40] Two more Apocalypse anthologies followed, in 1943 and 1944. The high point of the influence of the style, midway through the decade, as James Keery has argued, would be Thomas's 'arch-apocalyptic' *Deaths and Entrances* (1946).[41] In the meantime, despite his new reputation and influence, Thomas remained harassed by debt and his family condemned to a peripatetic existence between Bishopston, Blashford, Laugharne, London and the houses of various friends as he tried to scrape and beg a living.

The poems Thomas wrote between the autumn of 1939 and mid-1940 reflect the uncertainty, fear and eerie calm of the 'Phony War' period and its immediate aftermath. In May 1940 the German invasion of the Low Countries and France led to the debacle of Dunkirk. The Chamberlain government, guilty of appeasement and a half-hearted prosecution of the war, was replaced by a National Government. Over the summer of 1940 the nation prepared for a German invasion as the Battle of Britain was fought to deny the enemy the aerial dominance they required. Victory bought time, but Britain still stood in isolation against the Germans, who began a night-bombing campaign against British cities that lasted from September 1940 to May 1941.

Thomas's first major war poem, 'There was a saviour', captures the mood of a nation slowly realizing that its leaders had led it to the brink of disaster. It does so by probing the workings of charismatic power, as embodied in the form of a composite father or leader figure – primarily the Christ of organized religion and the European dictators but, by extension, any abusive authority. The 'we' of the poem craves the security such leaders seem to offer, in the manner of a needy child or adolescent. That security is unstable, a paradoxical 'safe unrest', but to gain it, the addressee will 'hide [its] fears' within the saviour's 'murdering breath' and keep silent within the 'tremendous shout' of his rhetoric, tolerating oppression. This murky but memorable poem is, at one level, a critique of those who ignored the suffering caused by the Depression, who 'could not stir/ One lean sigh when we heard/ Greed on man beating near and fire neighbour'. Isolated by self-interest in the past, they suffer the blackout of the Blitz as retribution for their lack of empathy; frozen and alone, they are cut off from their own humanity. Only now, the poem implies, *in extremis*, have they come to learn compassion and at last 'break a giant tear'

> For the drooping of homes
> That did not nurse our bones,
> Brave deaths of only ones but never found,
> Now see, alone in us,
> Our own true strangers' dust
> Ride through the doors of our unentered house.
> Exiled in us we arouse the soft,
> Unclenched, armless, silk and rough love that breaks all rocks.[42]

The unequal-length lines of the final couplet enact the shock and release involved in discovering this estranged generosity, and the last line ends in a succession of eight single-syllable words that enact the outpouring of 'love', which, 'soft' like water, will in time nevertheless prove to be 'rough' in breaking the hardest of all rocks, the heart. As in other war poems, Thomas sets sexual healing and nature's regenerative powers to make good the destruction of war, using Christian allusion and ritual to provide a language capable of articulating its apocalyptic nature.

This religious aspect is present, if less obviously, in the other major poem of this period, 'Deaths and Entrances', written over the summer of 1940. Its title derives from John Donne's last sermon,

'Death's Duell', in which birth is dismissed as an 'entrance' from one 'death', in the dark womb-tomb, to another, in this life. Only death will provide an entrance to real, eternal life. As early as May 1940, Thomas told Watkins that it would be the title poem of his next collection 'because it is all I ever write about or have written about'.[43] In it, he anticipates – 'On almost the incendiary eve' – the deaths to come from the air raids. Tellingly, though, his title alters Donne: 'entrances' are not exactly births, or only metaphorically so. There is also an echo of the 'entrances and exits' of Jaques's 'Seven Ages of Man' speech in *As You Like It*, hinting at the theatrical, unreal aspect of wartime life, in which so many had to play a role allotted to them and don some form of costume. Accordingly, the poem develops the issue of fluid identities touched on in 'There was a saviour'. There is a nightmarish, evasive quality to it, reflecting the 'burning birdman dreams' and invasion fears that Thomas reported having to Watkins, with a deliberate blurring of self and others, combatants and civilians, Luftwaffe pilot and his victims below: 'near' inhabits 'far', 'stranger' 'friend' and 'deaths' 'entrances' at every point.

Signed up by Strand

As Thomas was completing 'Deaths and Entrances', in early September 1940, he travelled down to London about a BBC job. Arriving there, he was caught up in the first big London raid, as life imitated the art of his poem. He described the mingling of the everyday and the apocalyptic in semi-Surrealist terms in a letter to Watkins a week later:

> Guns on the top of Selfridges. A 'plane brought down in Tottenham Court Road. White-faced taxis still trembling through the streets, though & buses going, & even people being shaved. Are you frightened these nights? When I wake up out of burning birdman dreams – they were frying aviators one night in a huge frying pan; it sounds whimsical now, it was appalling then – and hear the sound of bombs & gunfire only a

little way away I'm so relieved I could laugh or cry . . . I get
nightmares like invasions, all successful. (Ink gone)[44]

In the event, he failed to get the BBC job. But on the same visit he
met Donald Taylor, the director of Strand Films. Taylor was a leading
light in the documentary-film movement of the 1930s, and in 1940
Strand was the largest maker of documentary films in the country.
It was under contract with the Ministry of Information, and its
output was largely short propaganda films. Thomas and Taylor
immediately took to each other; Taylor knew his poetry and was
keen to recruit good writers, even if they had no scriptwriting
experience. He agreed to take Thomas on. Unfortunately, the job
would not be available until the following September. Until then, the
Thomases' penury – and other, more serious troubles – continued.

6

Singing in Chains:
Apocalypse and Fame, 1942–7

The early years of the war had been tough ones for Dylan Thomas
and his family. But, matching the fortunes of the nation, his own
were to improve quite dramatically during 1942. In September 1941
he began work at Strand Films, and fitted in as well as Donald
Taylor had hoped; the convivial, flexible teamwork required for
film-making suited him perfectly, and he proved adept at doctoring
scripts and writing them, as well as capable of taking on other roles
if required. Despite his awareness that time spent working in films
was time not spent writing poems – he considered it hack-work, and
Caitlin constantly reminded him of the fact – Thomas nevertheless
enjoyed it. Film people, like journalists, broadcasters and actors, were
the sort of intelligent but not intellectual company he preferred.
And, crucially, the regular income – £8 per week, rising to £10, plus
expenses – put the Thomases on a relatively sound financial footing
for the first time, despite Dylan's and Caitlin's profligate habits.

Still more significantly, in terms of his career and future reputa-
tion, Thomas would begin regular work for the BBC two years later,
in 1943, as an actor, reader and – for the first time – writer. Partly as
a result of the film and broadcasting work, his poetic output dried
up in 1942–3, comic squibs excepted. But in that period he was able
to incubate another change of style, leading to the most productive
poetic period since his Swansea years, in 1944–5. The new poems,
with those written in 1939–41, would make up *Deaths and Entrances*
(1946), the collection that confirmed his status as the leading young
British poet and – with *New Poems* (1943) and *Selected Writings*
(1946) appearing in the United States – give him an international

reputation. Even so, despite relative prosperity, the road to success would be a gruelling one.

The marital and the martial

Leaving Laugharne in 1940 coincided with difficulties in the Thomases' marriage. From its outset, Caitlin could easily trigger Dylan's jealousy, while Dylan himself sometimes took advantage of his London trips to have dalliances (a situation hinted at in the uncollected poem 'The Countryman's Return'). Like other bohemian marriages of the time, it is likely that he and Caitlin had agreed that theirs would be, to some degree, an open one. As is so often the case, however, the liberty – in the early years, at least – was more often exploited by the husband than the wife, for all that Thomas was a rather desultory and ineffectual Don Juan. At Marshfield, frustrated at being left behind so often, and in retaliation, Caitlin had her first serious affair, with William Glock. As she would reveal in her memoir *Leftover Life to Kill* (1957), Thomas was furious when he found out. The affair continued for some time, and Dylan kept his distance from Caitlin for a while after it ended. In December 1940, with the crisis apparently weathered, but scarred, they left Marshfield to continue an itinerant existence that would last until after the war was over.

Although they patched things up, Caitlin's affair had an impact on Thomas's poetry. In 'On a Wedding Anniversary' of July–August 1940, he had described 'the ragged anniversary of two/ Who moved through three years in tune/ Through the singing wards of the marriage house', but who now, under the 'wrong rain' of the bombs, find their 'house' is 'burning' like those bombed in the Blitz.[1] A sense of the interconnectedness of the martial and the marital, of the war as a mirror of events in the marriage and of marriage as a kind of intimate war, suffuses several other poems. The most demanding of these is 'Into her lying down head'. It pre-dates the Glock affair and, like 'I make this in a warring absence', registers an earlier wave of jealousy. Its title – in which the absence of a hyphen gives 'lying' and 'down' a second sense – encapsulates its narrative. Far more

complexly than 'On a Wedding Anniversary', it envisions the
sexual fantasies of the narrator's partner as she dreams beside
him, imagining her 'sighing . . . down/ To a haycock couch'.[2]
Her dream-lover becomes the nation itself: 'Man was the burning
England she was sleep-walking . . . the enamouring island'.
Described as a 'thief of adolescence', he again resembles Augustus
John, and the poem's sympathies shift at this point to the woman
as victim of male predation – even though, as the final stanza sadly
concedes, she is, by nature, bound to attract 'the treading hawk' to
'chirrup [her] bright yolk'.[3]

The same marital–martial imagery recurs in the post-affair
poem 'Love in the asylum' of April 1941, but in a way that reflects
the couple's reconciliation. Marriage is figured as a kind of madness,
and the asylum of the title is a psychiatric ward. But it is also an
asylum as refuge from the greater madness of the war, even if the
poem uses the image of love as a wild beast that 'roar[s] on a chain'
like a bedlamite or wild animal, as in 'On a Wedding Anniversary'.[4]
In January and February 1941, before writing this short lyric, Thomas

Alfred Janes, *Castle Street, Swansea after the Blitz*, 1947, oil on canvas.

had written 'Ballad of the long-legged bait', the longest of all his published poems, in which he worked out his conflicted feelings at length. The narrator's boat 'swims into the six-year weather' of Dylan and Caitlin's relationship; he allows the 'bait' her 'weddings in the waves', but only grudgingly, inserting 'hooks through her lips' and throwing her into 'the swift flood'. This gives a brutal edge to his acceptance that she must be lost in order to return, and the 'thoroughfares of her hair' may 'Lead her prodigal home to his terror,/ The furious ox-killing house of love'. It is a dynamic, no-holds-barred, psychosexual drama, cast in the form of a fishing expedition. Like other poems about their relationship it ends ambivalently, with the fisherman on the threshold of his home, perhaps on the verge of voyaging again to repeat the violent, loving cycle:

> Goodbye, good luck, struck the sun and the moon,
> To the fisherman lost on the land.
> He stands alone at the door of his home,
> With his long-legged heart in his hand.[5]

Wartime film scripts

The sheer momentum and onrush of 'Ballad' – deriving from its fishing-expedition narrative, its intercutting between land, sea and an undersea realm, its contrasts of light and dark, its pictorial qualities – provide a reminder of how intensely cinematic Thomas's poetry can be. It is telling that Vernon Watkins reported that 'it was so much a visual poem that [Thomas] made a coloured picture for it . . . of a woman lying at the bottom of the sea.'[6] Thomas's long-standing passion for film proved invaluable in his scriptwriting labours for Strand from September 1941. An avid cinema-goer since childhood, he already had an extensive knowledge of specific films and of filmic genres, as well as a grasp of the aesthetics of cinema. Filmgoing was a lifelong habit; Mervyn Levy told how, during their early years in London, he and Thomas would go to the newsreel cinemas in the late morning and stay until closing time.[7] Theodora Rosling recalled that she and Thomas used to recite whole chunks of

James Whale's film *The Old Dark House* (1932) to each other, and went regularly to the Classic in the King's Road 'to see any old film which took our fancy. Once we were asked to leave because we sobbed so loudly.'[8]

To begin with, however, Thomas's scope for imaginative engagement was strictly limited. Strand made propaganda films, usually shorts, exclusively for the Ministry of Information (MOI). In 1942 he wrote six of its output of 75 films, all run-of-the-mill pieces, as their titles suggest: *This Is Colour* (about aniline dyes), *New Towns for Old*, *The Battle for Freedom*, *Balloon Site 568* (a recruitment film for women's barrage-balloon teams), CEMA (about the forerunner to the Arts Council) and *Young Farmers*, and he was to write at least ten more Strand scripts in 1943–5. Such work generally cramped Thomas's style, and one of them, *The Battle for Freedom*, parroted the British government's opposition to Indian demands for independence, in contrast to his own anti-imperialist attitudes. (These are clear from his spoof Auden poem 'Brothers Beneath the Skin' in *The Death of the King's Canary*: 'Look, dead man, at this Empire, at this Eastscape of suffering,/ Monocled glaucoma over India's coral strand./ They can hear in twilight Ealing/ The forts fall in Darjeeling/ As the last White Hope is snuffed out in that dark-skinned No-Man's-Land.'[9]) In almost every script, however, he displayed a gift for injecting colloquial dialogue and humour to lift a film above the ruck. He also met deadlines, and was happy to tour with film crews and travel on research missions. When Taylor reorganized and rebranded Strand as Gryphon Films in 1943, Thomas was kept on – unlike several others, including his co-writer Julian Maclaren-Ross.

When he was allowed to exercise his imagination, Thomas did so with gusto. An attack on the Nazi leaders, *These Are the Men* (1943), grafts a satirical voice-over on to footage from Leni Riefenstahl's *Triumph of the Will* (1935), and was much praised. Its most convincing aspect, however, is not the takedown of individual Nazi leaders so much as its lamenting of how they have turned 'man against man', perverting their natural potential, an idea that distantly echoes the sentiments of 'I see the boys of summer'.[10] More impressive still is *Wales: Green Mountain, Black Mountain* (1942), commissioned by the British Council. A lyrical historic-geographic overview of Wales, it sketches past struggles against the English and divisions between rural north and industrial south, which it then subsumes into a vision of present-day unity around the war effort. The evocative text often exceeds its morale-boosting aims, and although Thomas writes against the grain at one point (in praise of the chapels), he is able to make his political inclinations clear. One passage features footage of closing colliery gates, dole queues and people desperately grubbing for coal on spoil-heaps. It had been shot for *Today We Live*, a social-realist documentary film made by Strand Films in 1937, directed by Ruby Grierson and Ralph Bond, partly filmed in Depression-hit South Wales. Thomas accompanies it with an exhortation not to forget the 1930s:

Remember the procession of the old young men
From dole queue to corner and back again . . .
Dragging through the squalor with their hearts like lead
Staring at the hunger and the shut pit-head . . .
It shall never happen again.[11]

As a result of what it saw as a socialist message, the British Council rejected the film as unsuitable to be shown abroad. The MOI, however, had no such qualms, and snapped it up.

Thomas's best wartime film was *Our Country* (1944), directed by John Eldridge and produced by Taylor himself, originally made for distribution in the USSR. Visually as well as textually lyrical throughout, and free of the straining to link north and south, past and present that weakens *Wales: Green Mountain, Black Mountain*, it follows the travels of a recently torpedoed merchant seafarer as he seeks a new berth. His improbably drawn-out and varied itinerary takes in Glasgow, London, Kent, the Fens, Aberdare and Rhondda, Herefordshire, Sheffield (where he meets his girlfriend, a factory worker), the Scottish Highlands and Aberdeen, linking the constituent parts of the Great Britain to symbolically enact wartime national unity. Equally symbolically, the seafarer joins in the life of the local people he encounters: helping with hop- or apple-picking, threshing, visiting a school, socializing at a harvest festival dance and lumberjacking. The flow of the visual narrative is matched by a voice-over reading of Thomas's script, which is largely word-painting but sometimes reaches subtly beyond it; 'the searchlighted night is at war with another darkness', that of Nazism.[12]

Within the seafarer's journey, the musings of the girlfriend, dramatizing her fears of death in an air raid and the resurgence of the life force after it, act as a still, central point, as well as a focus for the urban workers who would have made up the majority of its audience: 'And you were dead as well . . . And then we'd grow alive again, slowly, like blind people creeping out of a cave at the very beginning of the world.'[13] There is also an extended sequence in which African American GIs are shown playing jazz and dancing with white British revellers in what is evidently an attempt to erode racial prejudice. The descriptions of Blitzed London, the pastoral settings and the use of symbols personal to Thomas link the script at numerous points to the wartime poems.[14]

Dylan Thomas's film work is best understood in the context of the leftward political shift in British society during the war years. In response to pressure for reform, the government commissioned the Beveridge Report (1942), which assured the population that after the war there would be no return to the unemployment of the 1930s, and promised a Welfare State. This was aimed at boosting the war effort, and the MOI reflected this aim and the national mood in its film output. Thomas's scripts express that promise of post-war reconstruction and planning, as titles such as 'A City Reborn' make clear. To watch these films is to be reminded of Lord Boothby's quip that 'The Ministry of Information did not win the war, but it certainly won the election for Labour.'[15] Thomas was fully aware of this aspect of his work, but while he was in sympathy with it he could not help but resent his involvement in propaganda work and begrudge the time spent not writing poetry.

Wanderings

During the early war years the need to keep his family safe in the countryside, away from the raids, while he worked in London meant that Thomas had to shuttle to and from the capital constantly. This helped to dissipate a good deal of his earnings in pubs and clubs and taxis before he got home, putting a strain on the family finances and his relationship with Caitlin. She also suspected, rightly, that he was having affairs; he had several brief flings during the war years, and letters relating to a potentially more serious one, with the young Welsh actor Ruth Wynn Owen, survive.[16] Caitlin was, in any case, annoyed at being stuck in cramped rural quarters, with little intellectual stimulation and numerous domestic chores. The situation

'Blaencwm', 'a breeding box in a cabbage valley', 1950s; the two cottages in Llangain part-owned by Florence Thomas, where Dylan wrote 'Fern Hill'.

was exacerbated by being continually on the move; an incomplete list of places they stayed in during the four years after leaving Laugharne includes Marshfield, Talsarn, East Knoyle, Beaconsfield, Bosham, Bishopston, the 'Blaencwm' cottages in Llangain (after D.J. and Florrie moved there from Bishopston in 1943) and New Quay. The greatest and most lasting harm to the family was that, from 1941 onwards, the Thomases placed Llewelyn with his grandmother Yvonne Macnamara in Hampshire; he would not return to the family home until the war ended (and soon after that he would be sent to a boarding school). Only on very rare occasions did Caitlin accompany Dylan on his work trips. However, in July 1942 they did travel to Scotland together. Dylan took the opportunity to visit David Archer, who had moved from London to set up the South Street Art Centre in Glasgow, and Sydney (W.S.) Graham, the best of the New Apocalypse poets and the one whose work owed most to Thomas's own, as well as Hugh MacDiarmid, leader of the Scottish literary revival. In September 1942 Thomas began renting a one-room studio flat in Manresa Terrace in Chelsea, and this became the family's London base for two years, enabling Caitlin to give birth to their second child, Aeronwy, at a Kensington hospital on 3 March 1943. In September 1944 the family moved to New Quay, where they settled for almost a year and where Thomas began writing poetry again.

Poetry: Blitz elegy and the problems of praise

It is likely that the demands of Thomas's film work, as well as a disrupted existence, helped to halt his poetry-writing at the end of 1941. However, it was not simply a case of one kind of work driving out another. During his second great period of poetic productivity, in 1944–5, he was writing more scripts than ever before. Nor was the scriptwriting a necessary discipline, as some have claimed, to achieve his new style; its basic elements were already clear in 1941.[17] A better explanation for the mid-war poetic silence is the relaxation of the threat to the civilian population in 1942–4. This threat had been the basis of the horror and moral outrage Thomas had felt about the war in 1939–41, and had generated his first slew of war poems. With the 'Little Blitz', which began in early 1944 and was soon followed by the terror of the V-weapons, that threat and outrage was renewed, and with it came more poetry.

The nature of the poems of 1944–5 had been heralded by those of the summer of 1941 and 'A dream of winter', finished in early 1942. 'Among Those Killed in the Dawn Raid Was a Man Aged a Hundred' (1941) was Thomas's first elegy for a civilian victim of the Blitz, while the childhood memories of 'Poem in October' (1944) and 'Fern Hill' (1945) are anticipated in 'The hunchback in the park' of 1941. The Second World War was the first major war in which civilians, rather than soldiers, were the primary target of the enemy onslaught, and the bombed city became its iconic image, just as the trenches of the Western Front had for the First World War. Thomas's significance as a wartime poet is that he lived through the Blitz himself and found words that adequately memorialized and dignified those who bore the brunt of it. The difference between the poems of 1939–41 and those of 1944–5 is that the second group can be seen to initiate a larger pastoral vision that would inform Thomas's post-war poems and *Under Milk Wood*.

The change is apparent in the indirectness of the poems of 1944–5 compared with 'Deaths and Entrances' and 'There was a saviour'. War infiltrates them obliquely. The frozen battlefields of the Eastern Front and the Ardennes in 1944 find their correlative in the snowbound countryside of 'A Winter's Tale', in which the hermit-pilgrim achieves transcendence while dying of hypothermia. Equally subtly, behind the images of a figure cast adrift in 'Lie still, sleep becalmed' loom the torpedoed merchant seafarers of the Battle of the Atlantic. More glancingly still, in 'Poem in October' the primary sense of the phrase 'the long dead child sang burning' is the intensity of the speaker's recall of his earlier self.[18] But in a collection that also contains two poems about children burned to death in air raids, this is unavoidably ghosted by a more disturbing, literal sense. War is omnipresent and has infected not only the present and the future but a once-idyllic past. Even an image as innocent-seeming as 'the shadow of my hand' in 'Fern Hill' evokes the famous shadowgraphs cast by bodies vaporized by the blast of the atom bomb (the poem was completed in the same month as the bombings of Hiroshima and Nagasaki), as well as echoing the Anglican Service for the Dead ('he fleeth as it were a shadow').[19]

As in 'Among Those Killed in the Dawn Raid' – in which the final, surreally startling image is of a hundred baby-bearing storks 'perch[ed] on the sun's right hand', one for every year of the dead centenarian's age – the poems of 1944–5 counter the depredations of war with a vision of regeneration in the face of violent, unnatural death.[20] The jealousy and angst of the early wartime poems have gone, and a forgiving and sensually restorative spirit now reigns. It is only out of its 'immortal hospital' that the 'cureless counted body' of the wartime dead, as 'Holy Spring' has it, can be 'soothe[d]', healed and made good.[21] Derek Mahon has noted that the later poems of *Deaths and Entrances* present 'calm mystery [and] quietude' by contrast with the earlier ones.[22] Body and spirit are no longer at war with each other; the religious transfiguration the 'she-bird' brings to the questing hermit of 'A Winter's Tale', to take another example, is a profane miracle, figured in terms of 'mature sexuality':

> And through the thighs of the engulfing bride,
> The woman breasted and the heaven headed
>
>   Bird he was brought low,
> Burning in the bride bed of love, in the whirl-
> Pool at the wanting centre, in the folds
> Of paradise, in the spun bud of the world.
> And she rose with him flowering in her melting snow.[23]

In accordance with their healing function, these poems are ritualistic. The 'legend' of the Bible and its language are the most available and are perforce 'never for a second/ Silent in my service', and Thomas's poem-rituals – conversions, baptisms, visions, prayers, marriages, funerals – must therefore avail themselves of religious rhetoric, whether he is a believer or not.[24] This is reflected in the number of invocations and apostrophes in *Deaths and Entrances*, from 'Holy Spring's 'O/ Out of a bed of love' to 'Fern Hill's 'Oh as

I was young and easy', joyful at the poem's opening, rueful at its close, but nevertheless offering the visible sign of a complete circle, a figure for unity and reconciliation to process.[25] For a similar reason, ritualistic repetition is also common. The words 'sky', 'bird', 'snow', 'log', 'bride', 'bright', 'stars' and 'seed' are repeated in ever-shifting, ever-altering contexts, woven in complex musical patterns, in 'A Winter's Tale', while in 'The conversation of prayers' key terms and phrases, compounded by a criss-crossing rhyme scheme, combine to produce an interlaced, mesmeric verbal texture.[26] This harmonious, ceremonial quality is often manifest in the way the poems appear on the page. 'Poem in October', 'Holy Spring', 'Fern Hill' and 'Vision and Prayer' – its diamond- and hourglass-shaped stanzas are the most elaborate example – are centred on the page, giving them a symmetrical, mandala-like appearance.

But there are continuities between the earlier and later war poems. One is the use of titles derived from public media. As its title makes clear, 'Among Those Killed in the Dawn Raid Was a Man Aged a Hundred' is a newspaper headline (the poem was based on a newspaper article about an air-raid on Hull) and 'Ceremony After a Fire Raid' and 'A Refusal to Mourn the Death, by Fire, of a Child in London' take the form of public declarations. These are Thomas's three major war elegies, and show his awareness that the poems deal not just with the deaths, but also with their reception, and the discourses of state, Church and news media that try to appropriate and co-opt them. For all their religious tenor, these poems are resolutely materialist. Thus, in 'Ceremony', as in 'Among Those Killed', bloodless official spiritual consolation is replaced by the physical kind, with the dead child chiefly (and daringly) mourned for her lost potential progeny, while the final section of the poem is a gigantic birthing of the coming generations that will replace the Blitz dead, imaged as an amniotic tidal wave that douses the fires of the burning city:

Into the organ pipes and steeples
Of the luminous cathedrals,
Into the weathercocks' molten mouths
Rippling in twelve-winded circles,

Into the dead clock burning the hour . . .
The masses of the sea
The masses of the sea under
The masses of the infant-bearing sea
Erupt, fountain, and enter to utter forever
Glory glory glory
The sundering ultimate kingdom of genesis' thunder.[27]

Between this poem of 1944 and Thomas's final elegy, 'A Refusal
to Mourn', of March 1945, the mood gets bleaker, such that 'A Refusal'
may be read as a poem of apology (or palinode) for 'Ceremony',
whose optimistic surging movement Thomas may have regretted,
feeling it was too close to his work for Strand. Opposition is inscribed
in its title and its opening word, 'Never', the latter probably chosen
because it features in Winston Churchill's speeches of June and
September 1940: 'never in the field of human conflict' and 'we will
fight them on the beaches . . . we will never surrender.' The speaker
tells us he will never have the right to mourn the child's death until
he approaches his own and enters the same radical phase of the cycle
of process. To do otherwise is to appropriate the girl's death wrongly,
'murder' her again by adding his voice to those of officialdom heard
'down the stations of the breath' (the girl's last halting breaths, but
also radio stations over which propaganda is transmitted). The child
has entered the London clay, at one with all those who have ever
died, both regally 'robed' and reduced to a molecular level:

Deep with the first dead lies London's daughter
Robed in the long friends,
The grains beyond age, the dark veins of the mother,
Secret by the unmourning water
Of the riding Thames.
After the first death, there is no other.[28]

Yet if the Thames is 'unmourning' it is also 'riding' – a word that
has sexual, regenerative connotations in Thomas's work – while
'grains' signifies inanimate mineral particle and organic seed

promising rebirth. The resounding final line, then, is profoundly ambivalent. In its most obvious sense it proclaims that there will be no Last Judgement, no 'second death' in which the dead are irrevocably divided into the saved and the damned; the afterlife and judgement were notions Thomas found particularly abhorrent. This assumes that the child has found peace, even a kind of eternal life, perhaps, in the processual round. But in a more negative sense the line also foregrounds the fact of our personal extinction; after death there is nothing else, no 'other'. This reading would seem to be strengthened by the comma after 'death', deliberately obtrusive in a poem that otherwise notably lacks punctuation. Its effect is to weaken the link between 'death' and 'other', and undermine a positive interpretation.

One reason for this may lie in the circumstances of the poem's composition. Its first draft is dated November 1944, and in it the images of a water droplet and an ear of corn simply symbolize the cosmic cycle in natural terms. But the draft is incomplete, and the poem was revised and finished in March 1945. Between those dates, in January 1945, the Red Army had liberated Auschwitz. Thomas was good friends with the émigré Polish-Jewish artist Jankel Adler who had heard of the horrors of the Nazi death camps (Adler at one point performed a mock ceremony in a Fitzrovia pub making Dylan an 'honorary Jew' because of his sympathy for the plight of European Jewry).[29] In the final version of the poem, what had been 'the round/ Eye of the sea drop' and 'white drop/ Of a snow flake's field' have become 'the round Zion of the water bead/ And the synagogue of the ear of corn'.[30] Perhaps because it is so well hidden in plain sight, before 2013 only one critic spotted the allusions, albeit glancing and discreet, to the Holocaust.[31] The subject is one that many non-Jewish poets have felt compelled to address, even as they are aware of the dangers of tackling it. Thomas's tact in this regard, for a poet sometimes given little credit for it, is remarkable.

Deaths and Entrances was published on 7 February 1946 and sold out in its initial print run of 3,000 copies within a month. It was widely reviewed, and in overwhelmingly positive terms. The book's mixture of Blitz elegy, pastoral, mature love lyric and self-reflexive nostalgia matched the nation's post-war mood of exhaustion and hope on the eve of the social revolution ushered in by the Labour Party election victory of May 1945. But it was not the only or even the most important reason for the celebrity status Thomas suddenly achieved in 1946. To understand that, we must look at the story of his involvement with the BBC.

Running away to the BBC

Dylan Thomas had already contributed to BBC broadcasts in 1937, 1938, 1941 and 1942, and doctored three scripts for them in 1940. But he became more than an ad hoc presence only in 1943, when Aneirin Talfan Davies commissioned a script for a series on writers' memories of childhood. *Reminiscences of Childhood*, his first through-written BBC feature, was broadcast in February 1943 and printed in *The Listener*. 'There was immediate recognition that Thomas had hit the right note,' as Ralph Maud observed, but no immediate rush for more scripts.[32] The next commission was *Quite Early One Morning* in 1944, a vivid evocation of morning-waking and walking through New Quay, delving into the dreams of the townspeople, and including characters destined to reappear in *Under Milk Wood*. In 1945 Thomas re-broadcast it, and rewrote and re-broadcast *Reminiscences of Childhood*, plus *Memories of Christmas* (a new work that, augmented by a *Picture Post* article of 1947, became *A Child's Christmas in Wales*, one of his most popular radio works, in 1950). All three share the digressive form and wry nostalgic humour that were to be the hallmarks of his work in the radio feature genre.

Although he wrote just one BBC script of his own in 1945, Thomas contributed to ten other programmes that year, including one on his own poetry. His literary fame, and the BBC's creation of the Third Programme in 1946, a station devoted to culture, led to an exponential increase in radio work in 1946, when he wrote no fewer than thirteen scripts (reading or acting in eleven of them), and acted or read in a further 37 broadcasts. Two of his scripts, *The Londoner* and *Margate: Past and Present*, were complex half-hour drama features, and important steps along the road to *Under Milk Wood*.[33]

After *Deaths and Entrances* was published in February 1946, Thomas was one of the readers at a Wigmore Hall event before the royal family in May. That month he also presented *On Reading Poetry Aloud* on the Home Service. *Poets on Poetry* followed on the Light Service on 18 June, and *Poems of Wonder*, also on the Home Service, on 14 July. The quantity and high-profile nature of the broadcasts over that year made Thomas a radio personality and amplified by several orders of magnitude the fame he had accrued from his purely literary publications. Jack Lindsay recalled a poetry reading with Thomas in Bayswater in early 1946 with 'only the usual small audience', and another, just a few months later, 'at which there was an overflowing and rapturous audience of young people'.[34]

After 1946 the quantity of Thomas's BBC contributions slackened, but they remained sufficient to reinforce and expand his reputation. In 1947 he wrote just three scripts, but one was *Return Journey*, his best before *Under Milk Wood*. Its origins lay in his visit to the devastated centre of Swansea in late February 1941, just days after three nights of bombing, in which 230 people had been killed and much of the town centre reduced to rubble. He and Caitlin encountered Bert Trick beside the 'blackened mound' of what had been a pub on the corner of Union Street and Oxford Street. Trick recalled, 'Dylan said, "Our Swansea has died", and by God he was right. The pubs and familiar places we knew had gone for all time.'[35] The central, very simple conceit of the piece is the returning narrator's search for his own younger self, now vanished, like pre-war Swansea. He is tracked from a town-centre bar back into the past, via conversations between reporters in the vanished Three Lamps pub, a passer-by's memories of conversations in the Kardomah, a minister's memories of him in Ralph the Books bookshop, those of a former schoolmaster and a seafront promenader, and finally those of the park-keeper in Cwmdonkin Park.

While humour is dominant for most of the piece, the mood of *Return Journey* – like that of *A Portrait* – is ultimately elegiac, even sombre. The park-keeper's comment, near its close, that 'I think he was happy all the time' serves only to intensify the sense of lost innocence, underscored by the intoning of the names of the war dead on Swansea Grammar School's Roll of Honour board. The twist at the end is that the earlier self is discovered to be like them, 'Dead . . . Dead . . . Dead . . . Dead . . . Dead . . . Dead'.[36] As in 'Fern Hill' and 'Poem in October', it is not only the pre-war self, but the very concept of childhood and innocence that has been destroyed. Genuine loss counters the nostalgia inherent in the material, offering pathos without lachrymosity, to make it a moving and lasting work that testifies to the continuing aftershocks of the Second World War.

Thomas contributed to 23 more programmes, and broadcast 'A Visit to Grandpa's' in 1947, followed by a similar number in 1948 (and just one script). The contributions dropped to single figures between 1949 and 1952 (he was touring the USA in 1950 and 1952), but picked up in 1953, when, despite the U.S. tours, he contributed to fifteen programmes, made two television broadcasts, and wrote and read four new scripts, as well as delivering the now largely complete manuscript of *Under Milk Wood* to the BBC producer Douglas Cleverdon. In all, between 1943 and 1953 Thomas contributed to or wrote a total of 154 programmes, an average of just over one a month.

Dylan Thomas's timing in his work for the BBC was as fortuitous as for almost everything else in his career. He had a sure grasp of the possibilities of radio as a medium from the start and his radio scripts are distinguished by their variety, their eagerness to entertain and their avoidance of anything null or padded. Language switches from the florid to the conversational, a poetic phrase or wordplay is counterpointed by sharply observed detail, sentences are frequently distended, building comic tension (how far can it go out on a digressive limb, the listener feels, and still retrieve itself; how will it ever get back down to grammatical earth?). Brief quotations, lists and snatches of verse break the flow, mixing up the rhythm. Delving into memory, they amusingly concede and parade uncertainties about its accuracy ('I can never remember whether it snowed for six days and six nights when I was twelve or whether it snowed for twelve days and twelve nights when I was six'). The humorous self-qualification and self-questioning create

a persona at once engagingly vulnerable and bantering.[37] There are
marked elements of fantasy, ranging from whimsy to the surreal
('What would you say if you saw a hippo coming down Terrace Road
. . . Iron-flanked and bellowing he-hippos clanked and blundered
and battered through the scudding snow towards us').[38] The chief
stylistic model is Dickens, a novelist whose work Thomas continu-
ally re-read – *A Child's Christmas in Wales* is a homage to Dickens's
creation of Christmas, among other things. Offsetting what might
otherwise become too schmaltzy, Thomas's radio works often
display an element of voyeurism; this mimics the situation of the
radio listener, bonding listener and narrator. In *Quite Early One
Morning* the narrator enters the dreams of the town's sleepers;
a similar eavesdropping figure, Captain Cat, would become the
basic structural principle of *Under Milk Wood*.

Trauma into pastoral

The trouble with 'running away to the BBC', as Thomas described
it, was that the work was bitty and necessitated both travel and,
invariably, the pubs, clubs and socializing that were an organic
part of the London literary scene. Nor would it – no matter how
much or how well he might perform – ever land him the permanent
post that might have given him security. His occasional slip-ups –
lapses that might have been tolerated had he been less of an outsider
– triggered an innate prejudice in the ranks of the corporation
which helped to keep him off the permanent payroll; eventually
he would be employed on a contractual, piecework footing.
(This only exacerbated problems, of course, since it meant that
Thomas eventually began to ask for advances, which he spent
before completing the work he was contracted to do.)

In the summer of 1944 the Thomases gave up their London flat
and, after some months in cramped lodgings in Llangain with D.J.
and Florrie, moved to 'Majoda', a holiday chalet near New Quay
on the Cardiganshire coast. Dylan's old friend Vera Phillips, now
Vera Killick – she had married William Killick, an officer in the
Royal Engineers, earlier in the war – was living in the neighbouring

chalet with her baby daughter.[39] In Llangain Thomas had started writing poetry again, and it continued after the move. It was the flowering of a new mellifluous, pastoral style, and would produce many of his greatest poems. At the same time, his path to the pastoral calm and comedy of his later work had been hard-won (one of the painful paradoxes of Dylan's final years is the stark contrast between the anxiety that could overwhelm him and the serenity and good humour of his writing). Trauma was transmuted, rather than evaded. As the critic David Daiches cautioned, writing of the later work, 'Thomas did not rush towards the celebration of unity of all life and all time which later became an important theme of comfort to him: he moved to it through disillusion and experiment.'[40] But in London his behaviour had been growing more erratic as the war dragged on. There were several excesses, usually involving drink and favourite watering holes, such as the Gargoyle Club. Most were of a harmless, victimless kind – pratfalls and drunken escapades – but some were more serious. The worst, and the most symptomatic of his loss of direction, was his failure to turn up as best man for Vernon Watkins's wedding in London on 2 October 1944. Thomas was silent for more than three weeks afterwards, eventually sending the note of apology he said he'd scribbled on the train back to Wales on the Watkinses wedding day, with a covering letter dated 28 October apologizing for forgetting to post the apology. Gwen Watkins did not believe the story, guessing that Dylan had received a fee the day before, gone drinking and simply forgotten his obligation.[41] She was probably right. And, as was increasingly the case, the fibs had not arisen from a love of fabrication. At the heart of the lapse – as Watkins herself later saw – was the anxiety, the level of psychological disorder, such actions bespoke.

Worse was to come. In May 1945 Thomas was badly shaken by a shooting incident. William Killick, on leave after several gruelling months of undercover combat in Yugoslavia, had just returned to New Quay. He felt his wife was being sponged off by the Thomases. One evening, annoyed at being ignored by Thomas and his visiting film-industry friends in a pub in New Quay, he began an argument, directing antisemitic remarks at Fanya Fisher, a Jewish member of the group. There was a scuffle between him and Thomas, and Killick was asked to leave the pub. But after closing time he followed Thomas back to his bungalow, drunkenly fired several shots into it from an illegally held Sten gun, and threatened those inside – including a baby – with a hand grenade. Thomas calmed Killick down, but not before someone had alerted the police. A court case followed some months later, in which Killick, still a serving officer, was acquitted of attempted murder. The Thomases, who had not pressed charges, immediately left New Quay for Llangain. They never saw Vera or William Killick again. At Llangain, in September, Thomas completed 'Fern Hill' and 'In my craft or sullen art', the final additions to *Deaths and Entrances*, and the family was back in London by the end of 1945. But the incident had realized his worst nightmares, and while he never alluded to it in his writing it added to the burden of his psychological distress.

The demands of Thomas's lifestyle and wartime strain eventually caught up with him. On 10 March 1946 he admitted himself to St Stephen's Hospital in Chelsea, complaining of vomiting blood. He stayed for five days, but no physical cause for his condition was found; the doctor examining him scribbled 'Anxiety' on his notes and gave him sedatives, while a psychiatrist diagnosed 'reactive depression' and a 'hypercritical attitude'.[42] Margaret Taylor now came to his rescue, taking on the role of patron that she would maintain until the end of his life. In August 1946 she arranged for the Thomases to move to her home at Holywell Ford, in the grounds of Magdalen College, Oxford. It was not a wholly satis-factory arrangement – Caitlin had to indulge Taylor as a benefactor, while resenting her charity and adoration of her husband – but by 1947 she had found the Thomases a house in South Leigh, just outside Oxford itself, which she bought and rented to them.

In Oxford, Thomas made just a few friends among the university dons – the Rimbaud scholar Enid Starkie was one – but he became something of a draw on his expeditions into Oxford for students interested in poetry. In informal pub gatherings he introduced a new generation of undergraduate poets to the work of such u.s. poets as Theodore Roethke, John Crowe Ransom, Richard Wilbur, John

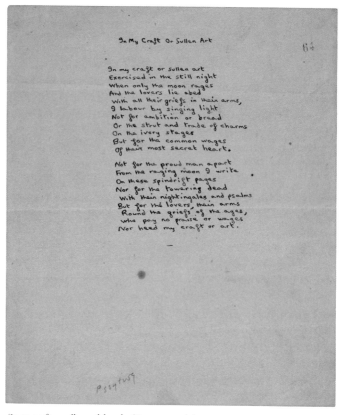

'In my craft or sullen art', handwritten manuscript.

Berryman and Robert Lowell. He also travelled abroad for the first time. Leaving Llewelyn and Aeronwy with relatives, he and Caitlin flew to Ireland for two weeks in the summer of 1946 with their friends Bill and Helen McAlpine. From April to August 1947, following some string-pulling by Edith Sitwell, the British Council paid for the Thomases to visit Italy for four months. There, in a villa in the hills above Florence, he finished his first post-war poem, 'In country sleep'.

On returning to South Leigh, Thomas moved his parents there so that he and Caitlin – although this largely meant Caitlin – could look after them. The market for propaganda films had ended abruptly with the war, but Thomas had been able to use his experience with Strand to get work writing feature-film scripts for Stratford Films and Gainsborough Films. This would be his most important source of income until 1949. He wrote scripts for three films that made it to the screen – *No Room at the Inn*, *The Three Weird Sisters* and *Me and My Bike* in 1948 – and several that did not (at least during his lifetime). The best of these, *The Doctor and the Devils* (eventually released in 1985), was a treatment of the tale of the nineteenth-century Edinburgh body-snatchers William Burke and William Hare. Thomas's detailed, highly readable treatment drew heavily on gothic tales, Dickens and Robert Louis Stevenson's *Dr Jekyll and Mr Hyde* and is characterized by his sympathy for society's victims, exploring the use of noble ends to justify criminal means. One reason it remained unmade was that in 1948 the British film industry went into recession. For Dylan the consequences were dire, since it brought his most lucrative income stream – he had been paid up to £1,000 per script – to an abrupt halt.

The problems that had beset him in the war years did not, therefore, end in 1945. Settling in Oxfordshire stabilized his situation, but still entailed a draining oscillation between the countryside and the capital, and its cycles of excess and recuperation. Even so, in the mid- and late 1940s he was writing prolifically for film and radio, making a start on *Under Milk Wood*. There was a year-and-a-half hiatus in his writing of poetry after September 1945, but before he left for Italy in April 1947 he conceived an ambitious poetic project entitled *In Country Heaven*, and slowly began to fulfil it. An incomplete draft of the title poem, intended eventually to introduce its component parts, was written in March–April 1947, with 'In country sleep' planned as its first section.[43]

Back from Italy in September 1947, then, Thomas faced mixed prospects. He had work, but most of it was BBC piecework and hack work on film scripts. He wanted something more permanent that would also allow him the time to write poetry. Since 1945 he had been asking American friends, such as Oscar Williams and James Laughlin, about an invitation to tour the United States, or to work there on a university writing programme or as a writer in residence. He had good reason to hope for success. By the mid-1940s there was substantial transatlantic interest in his writing. Three U.S. editions of his work had appeared, he had a following among many younger U.S. poets and his work was seen as exemplary by the New Critics who dominated U.S. academia. Kenneth Rexroth's anthology *The New British Poets*, published in January 1949 by New Directions, Thomas's U.S. publishers, made the case for Thomas as 'the greatest phenomenon in contemporary [British] poetry'. Rexroth's enthusiasm is revealing in a double sense. On the one hand, his U.S. vantage point allowed him to be more appreciative of and shrewder about Thomas than almost any British commentator (he noted with approval Dylan's Welsh, class and religious dimensions as they did not). On the other hand, his enthusiasm now seems rather ominous in its emphasis on Thomas's alleged 'primitivism'.[44] Nevertheless, it was intelligent advocacy, and a sign of a rapidly growing reputation in the United States. If Thomas was more prone to sickness after the war than before, more harassed by personal problems and more angst-ridden about his (and the world's) future, there was still good reason for him to be broadly optimistic. His reputation was nearing its zenith, and new prospects, in poetry and his writing more generally, were beginning to open up.

7

Against the Dying of the Light:
Pastoral and America, 1948–53

Riding the wave of his fame, Dylan Thomas in the latter half of the 1940s seemed, to all appearances, 'brandy and ripe in [his] bright, brass prime'.[1] His BBC work slackened off from its high point in 1946 but remained steady, and his film script work lasted until 1949. *Under Milk Wood*, begun in New Quay, progressed at South Leigh. But, wishing to put more distance between himself and the distractions of London, Thomas had for some time been thinking of returning to Wales. In May 1949, with Margaret Taylor's financial support, he and the family moved into the Boat House, a fisherman's cottage built against the cliff on the outskirts of Laugharne, with sweeping views of the Taf estuary.[2] Dylan and Caitlin were returning to the place where they had been happiest together before the war. For Dylan it was also a return to a more settled, productive way of life. Over the summer of 1949 he took up the projected *In Country Heaven* sequence again, returning to it when he had time free from his U.S. tours, which began in February 1950. In early 1952 he published a chapbook of the seven poems he had written since 1947 as *In Country Sleep*, in a U.S.-only edition, an interim version of *In Country Heaven*. On 10 November that year, the seven new poems, together with those of his first four collections, and prefixed by the virtuoso verse 'Prologue', were published as his *Collected Poems 1934–1952*. For Philip Toynbee, reviewing it in *The Observer*, it was proof of Thomas's status as 'the greatest living poet' in the language, and it went on to win the Foyles Poetry Prize for 1952.[3] Thomas's reputation was now at its peak, even if there were already mutterings of dissent from one or two of the young writers who would form the Movement, a plain-style group of writers who consciously defined themselves against Thomas and the histrionics for which it was felt he stood. And while F. R. Leavis and his academic epigones displayed their disdain in the periodical *Scrutiny*, Henry Treece's critical study, *Dylan Thomas: 'Dog Among the Fairies'*, had appeared in 1949 – a remarkable accolade for a poet who was only 35 years old.[4]

There were several publications by Thomas, some lucrative, right up to the last year of his life. His first spoken-word LP had appeared from Caedmon Records in the United States in April 1952.[5] His film script *The Doctor and the Devils* was published in book form in March 1953. In May 1953 *Under Milk Wood* received its first public reading, and a BBC broadcast and publication of the book were projected. In May 1953 Thomas was offered $750 for the U.S. serialization rights, and up to $2,000 for the U.S. publication rights, for *Adventures in the Skin Trade*. Meanwhile, the trips to Ireland and Italy were followed by a brief visit to Prague in 1948 and a five-week stay in Iran in early 1951, researching a film script.[6] These widening horizons matched a growing foreign interest in his writing. This worked both ways; one result of his own receptivity to other literatures was an enthusiastic review he wrote for *The Observer* in July

The Boat House, Laugharne, on its 'breakneck of rocks', 1950s.

1952 of Amos Tutuola's novel *The Palm-Wine Drinkard*, a seminal intervention which would be credited by several African writers with helping to put West African writing on the map of world literature. Interest overseas was most obvious in the response to Thomas's U.S. reading tours of 1950, 1952 and 1953, which were met with acclaim. Yet it was during the fourth U.S. tour – the second of 1953 – on 9 November, that Dylan Thomas died in New York City. He was just 39 years old and seemingly at the height of his powers. Grief, followed by prolonged mourning at his passing, was sincere and near-universal.

There is a temptation, in tracing the last years of Thomas's life, to view them through the lens of his premature demise; to soften the blow of it, as it were, by attempting to discover some kind of fatedness in it, some kind of foreshadowing in his later writings. This is understandable and is given substance by the acute problems disguised by his success. His health was poor – by this stage he was obese and wheezy, prone to lung infections, a heavy smoker and drinker, and possibly suffering from gout. His marriage was under strain as never before, and he embarked on two serious extramarital affairs during his first and third U.S. tours. His family had grown – a third child, Colm, was born in July 1949 – and with it his financial troubles. Work on feature films had dried up, and he was unable to complete radio adaptations for the BBC of *The Plain-Dealer* and *Peer Gynt* that might have substituted for it. He was also being pursued for unpaid income tax and National Insurance contributions.[7] Near the end of his life there was a succession of deaths of several people close to him: his father, D.J. Thomas, in December 1952; of Marged Stepney-Howard, a woman who had promised to become a new patron, in January 1953; and of his sister Nancy in April 1953. These events have led some to detect in the elegiac tenor of the later poems – particularly an unfinished 'Elegy' for D.J. and 'Do not go gentle into that good night' – a world-weariness, or even a death wish (the flip-side of which is the view of Thomas hounded to an early grave by a philistine world).[8]

There is a grain of truth in this view; Dylan Thomas may not have tried to kill himself, but he did not strive as hard as he might have done to stay alive. Yet to allow that his death was willed or inevitable goes against what we know of the facts, and risks swallowing the romantic myth of the doomed poet that was part of his self-performance – even if we allow that that performance, carried too far, and misunderstood, undeniably played its part in his death. All the most reliable accounts, including that of his GP, show that in Laugharne, where Thomas spent the most time during his final years, his life was unintoxicated, humdrum and relatively productive; and, while he was clearly anxious and ill when he set off for New York in October 1953, his prospects were improving and he had every intention of enjoying them.[9]

In Country Heaven and Cold War pastoral

After returning from Italy in September 1947, Thomas wrote no more poetry for the remainder of his time in Oxfordshire. The start of 1948 was spent in dealing with a family crisis; Florrie broke her leg at Blaencwm, and arrangements to help her and D.J. had to be made. Thomas went to Blaencwm, and Nancy (who during the war had divorced Haydn Taylor and married Gordon Summersby, an Army officer) travelled from Brixham in Devon, where she was living, to help look after D.J.[10] Once Florrie was out of hospital, Thomas – again with Margaret Taylor's assistance – rented another house in South Leigh so that his parents, who were now too frail to fend for themselves, could live nearby. But their demands became a source of friction between him and Caitlin, on whom most of them devolved. In June the family was struck with measles and Caitlin decamped with the children to Blashford. During 1947 and 1948, as we have seen, Thomas spent most of his time writing film scripts, but in early 1949 his main employer, Gainsborough, folded.

The mood of serenity that pervades most of the work he wrote after 1944 stems from the fact that it is in the elegiac pastoral mode prefigured in 1941 and realized in 1944–5 in 'Poem in October', 'A Winter's Tale' and 'Fern Hill'. 'Pastoral' is used here in its literary critical sense to describe writing that treats complex subjects in

Colm, Llewelyn and Aeronwy Thomas, c. 1951.

ways that seem simple, as well as in its usual, bucolic sense. In stylistic terms, for example, we find what seems to be the rather simple repetition of certain words and phrases ('green' and 'golden', say, in 'Fern Hill'). But on closer examination, we find that the contexts in which these occur are continually shifting, altering their senses. Complexity lies more on a poem's surface than in Thomas's earlier poems, extensive and visible rather than intensive and concealed.

The pastoral turn, as we have seen, was in part an attempt to recall and lament the loss of personal innocence, and human innocence more generally, in the face of wartime barbarism, sustained by fear of annihilation as a result of the nuclear stand-off between the United States and the USSR. Thomas was sceptical of Cold War rhetoric – in a letter to Oscar Williams he described liberty as 'what Our Side gives to people after it has napalmed them' – and his letters often echo the paranoid times, usually with similar self-protective flippancy, as when he described an unproductive period as 'two months when there was nothing in my head but a little Nagasaki, all low and hot', but sometimes with genuine anguish, as on the occasion of the execution of Julius and Ethel Rosenberg in June 1953.[11] But even in rural west Wales there was no escape; explosions from a missile-testing range that had recently sprung up a few miles along the coast at Pendine were often audible in Laugharne.

The pastoral mode was underpinned by a new, holistic, positive vision of process in the natural world. The fierce charnel-house simultaneity of the early process vision had yielded to an acceptance of the natural cycle of procreation, birth, growth, decline and death, exemplified by regenerative nature – albeit that nature, too, is marked by a rapacity and violence that the human world in some ways mimics. As noted in the previous chapter, *In Country Heaven* was the poetic structure in which the interaction between these forces was to be explored. In a broadcast of 25 September 1950, Thomas explained how it would include 'In country sleep' and the more recently completed 'Over Sir John's hill' and 'In the White Giant's Thigh', and sketched its rationale:

> The godhead, the author . . . the beginning Word . . . – he, on top of a hill in heaven, weeps whenever, outside that state of being called his country, one of his worlds drops dead . . . And when he weeps, light and his tears glide down together . . . So, at the beginning of the projected poem, he weeps, and Country Heaven is suddenly dark. Bushes and owls blow out like sparks. And the countrymen of heaven crouch all together under the hedges and . . . surmise which world . . . has gone for ever. And this time, spreads the heavenly hedgerow rumour, it is the earth. The earth has killed itself . . . insanity has blown it rotten . . . And, one by one, these heavenly hedgerow-men, who once were of earth, tell one another . . . what they remember . . . what they know in their edenie hearts, of that self-killed place . . . The poem is made of these tellings. And the poem becomes, at last, an affirmation of the beautiful and terrible worth of the earth. It grows into a praise of what is and what could be on this lump in the skies. It is a poem about happiness.
>
> The remembered tellings . . . are not all told as though they are remembered; the poem will not be a series of poems in the present tense. The memory, in all tenses, can look towards the future, can caution and admonish. The rememberer may live

himself back into active participation in the remembered scene, adventure, or spiritual condition.[12]

The blend of pastoral, secular religiosity, sci-fi and anticipatory memory is typical of the fluid generic mix of Thomas's later writing. Haunting it is the threat of nuclear annihilation; its centrality was signalled by the 'Prologue' to *Collected Poems*, an apocalyptic pastoral poem of great technical intricacy that foresees the flood of 'molten fear' in the 'cities of nine/ days' night whose towers will catch/ in the religious wind/ like stalks of tall, dry straw'.[13]

Yet *In Country Heaven* is also 'about happiness', and the 'Prologue' presents Thomas as a Noah whose poetry ark saves the creatures of the countryside round about from destruction. Despite (and because of) the threatened extinction of all sentient beings that inhabit it, the planet continues to have a 'beautiful' as well as a 'terrible' worth, and it is the unnerving blend of these that constitutes the sublime in these later poems. Nor is knowledge of the *In Country Heaven* scheme necessary for enjoyment of the individual poems, which stand alone. Yet their celebration of nature is given greater poignancy if we are aware that it is being made possible as a knowingly idealized, post-atomic memory. They reflect the impossible conditions of their existence by dramatizing a desire to believe and the impossibility of believing.

'Over Sir John's hill', written in the summer of 1949, exemplifies this. A Laugharne poem, it depicts and meditates on the view of the Towy estuary and the hill beyond that Thomas had from his writing shed. The intricacy of form so marked in many of the poems in *Deaths and Entrances* reaches a still more virtuosic pitch in this majestic quasi-ode.[14] The scenario it outlines – of the hill as it 'dons', judge-like, 'a black cap of jack-/ Daws' in sentencing the 'small birds' to their executioner, the 'hawk on fire' on the 'halter height', and of hawk and prey eliciting 'All praise' as part of the natural cycle – is both fanciful and fatalistically Darwinian. It is also obliquely charged with menace for its 'young Aesop' poet-observer; the hawk is like a fighter jet with a 'viperish fuse' hanging, bomb-like, 'under the brand/ Wing', while God, as 'In country sleep' puts it, is erased by the 'whirlwind silence' of the atom bomb. The poet identifies with the 'elegiac fisherbird', the heron, which seems to stand apart from this 'wrangling', and is said to 'grieve' – a word that chimes with 'grave' in the final stanza. There, 'grave' also means '*en*grave', referring to the writing of the poem as a memorial for 'the souls of the slain birds sailing', characteristically fusing creation and extinction.

'Over Sir John's hill' is typical of the later poems in its blend of lushly rendered pastoral detail and complex self-referencing to poetry and the creative process. Rather than being nature poems as such, they are about the conditions of possibility of such poems, exposing human presumption in anthropomorphizing nature (the poet identifies with the 'grieving' heron, but in truth it 'stabs' as rapaciously as the hawk) while succumbing to that very impulse. Yet the sensuous rendering of the natural world is a reminder that, however sophisticated the poem, nature is, after all, 'holy', wholly itself, and does not require translation into human terms to have value.

Thomas's paradoxical pastoral is apparent in a non-topographical way in his next two poems, 'Lament' and 'Do not go gentle into that good night'. Composed in early 1951, they form a complementary pair, drafted at times on the same worksheets. The first is 'coarse and violent . . . a crotchety poem, worked quite hard at between the willies', as Thomas punningly told Marguerite Caetani, who published them in her journal, *Botteghe Oscure*.[15] 'Lament' is a deathbed repentance poem that does not repent so much as regret. A caricatural womanizer looks back over his life, from 'springtailed tom' and 'hillocky bull' to 'crumpled horn', and with his last words regrets the constraints of age and a 'sunday wife' in lines that are themselves constrained: 'Chastity prays for me, piety sings,/ Innocence sweetens my last black breath,/ Modesty hides my thighs in her wings,/ And all the deadly virtues plague my death!'[16] It is a crude, comic poem that mocks its 'old ram rod' phallic stereotypes, not to mention depictions of Thomas himself, as much as it does repressive puritanism, but manages also to celebrate a lust for life. In several of its details, as well as its use of stereotypes, it echoes *Under Milk Wood*.

'Do not go gentle' is a more serious affair, famously sent to Marguerite Caetani in May 1951 with a letter explaining: 'The only person I can't show the little enclosed poem to is, of course, my father, who doesn't know he's dying.'[17] A dutiful son, Thomas had moved Florrie and D.J. to Laugharne soon after his own move there, to a house called 'Pelican', opposite Brown's Hotel, where he visited them daily. The poem is another lament, expressing the wish that the now declining D.J. might reassert his truculent temperament and atheistic cast of mind. As Thomas explained, D.J. 'grew soft and gentle at the last', but he 'hadn't wanted him to change'.[18] Yet the poem's ostensible message of resistance is counterpointed and resisted by its rhythms, which lull and soothe, as if to help the dying man on his way to a 'good' death, and it asks for the benediction that can be granted only by those who have resigned themselves to death. The most notable technical feature is the poem's demanding villanelle form, in which two lines alternate as endings to each three-line stanza before they meet as the concluding couplet, with only one other rhyme for the lines between. Thomas sings in his metrical chains in order to express powerful emotion without being overwhelmed by it, and his genius lay in devising two equally memorable repeat lines – 'Do not go gentle into that good night,/ Rage, rage, against the dying of the light' – to bind the poem together. Like 'Lament', 'Do not go gentle' is a pastoral insofar as its simple, repetitious form is charged with complex, contradictory feeling: the appeal to a severe but beloved father to 'curse, bless me', blessing by cursing, where 'bless' carries something of the French sense of *blesser*, to wound.

In the summer of 1949 Thomas began another long poem, 'In the White Giant's Thigh'. The 'giant' is the figure of a man carved into the chalk of a hillside at Cerne Abbas in Dorset, not far from Blashford, and the poem's origin was a local legend that women who were unable to conceive would do so if they made love within the perimeter of the giant's 'thigh' (a euphemism for its 26-foot-/ 8-metre-long phallus).

The poem's version of pastoral is implicit in its opening lines:

Through throats where many rivers meet, the curlews cry,
Under the conceiving moon, on the high, chalk hill,

And there this night I walk in the white giant's thigh
Where barren as boulders women lie longing still

To labour and love, though they lay down long ago.[19]

At first, it seems that a contrast is being established between sea and inland hillside, Welsh Laugharne (where the River Towy meets the Taf and Gwendraeth in the 'throat' of a three-pronged estuary) and English hillside. Yet the giant was (until very recently) believed to

'Do not go gentle into that good night', handwritten manuscript.

be a pre-Roman, Celtic creation, while Laugharne, as we have seen, was a 'little England beyond Wales'. The same playful undoing of fixed identities applies even to the curlews, a bird that spends the winter in river estuaries but migrates to upland heaths in the spring and therefore inhabits both zones of the poem. Stereotypes and solid identities, dwelt on in much of Thomas's late work, are shown to be fluid, and to deconstruct themselves, shaping the poem as a whole. With its 'wains tonned' with hay, 'ox roasting sun' and 'butter fat goosegirls', its landscapes resemble Breughel the Elder's pano-ramic, carnivalesque depictions of peasant life, tinged with Thomas Hardy's sense of bygone rural communities. But there is more to it than mere rustic utopia or idealized past; the poem becomes a moving, proto-feminist threnody, in which the spirits of the child-less women actively 'clasp' the poet to their 'grains' in a vigorously sexual way, speaking through him as he accepts their invitation to lie with them and let them use him as their mouthpiece: 'Now curlew cry me down to kiss the mouths of their dust'. The poem is his response to their yearning to conceive, and 'the dust' of the women, immediately repeated, opens the final section in which it is regener-ated, 'swing[ing] to and fro', until they 'hold [him] hard' and teach him the 'evergreen' 'love' that is the unstoppable force of process. 'No longer grieved', they continue to love their 'hale dead' former lovers as fiercely as before, 'daughters of darkness' who, with insurrectionary energy, 'flame like Fawkes fires still'.[20] The 'fires' are ominous, too, echoing the atomic conflagrations of other late poems, but more mutedly, and the general effect is defiant and invigorating.

If the 'midlife' it refers to is taken literally, Thomas's penultimate completed poem, 'Poem on his birthday', was begun around the time of his 35th birthday, in October 1949, soon after 'In the White Giant's Thigh', although it would not be completed until late summer 1951. Thomas could not, therefore, include it in his *In Country Heaven* broadcast of 1950, although it may well have been intended for the sequence. If so, its register is keyed several notches up from the other late poems, the strain of composition reflected in the way it 'sings towards anguish'.[21] As in 'Over Sir John's hill', the natural world's cycle of birth and death and that of humanity run in parallel, but

The Cerne Abbas Giant, Dorset.

with more emphasis on 'the logical progress of death' in Thomas's own life, and on atomic extinction, as he observes himself in the third person wandering a bare shore that is the Towy estuary, but also one on the far side of death. The language of faith is repurposed to endorse an 'always true' *concept* of a heaven (rather than the actual one posited by religion) and a 'fabulous, dear God' ('fabulous' in the slang sense of 'very good', but literally a fable, hence untrue). Ultimately the future will be freed by love and death, but before then a 'rocketing wind will blow/ The bones out of the hills'.[22] Two-thirds of the way in, Thomas switches to a first-person 'I' in order to 'count my blessings aloud', the greatest being that 'the closer I move/ To death', the more the world 'spin[s] its morning of praise'. The split in the poem between third person 'he' and first person 'I' embodies the difficulty of conceptualizing the way 'ruin' and imminent extinction exist within the urge to praise the natural world. This is presented as unresolved in the contradictory final images, as the poet 'sail[s] out to die' – the seasons grow 'greener at berry brown/ Fall', spring is in autumn,

and angelic cockle-pickers stand on 'fiery islands' that are both
dazzling mudflats and the semi-vaporized islands (Bikini, Enewetak,
Montebello) of the Pacific test ranges.[23]

Under Milk Wood

Under Milk Wood, the other major work of Thomas's final years,
is a radio feature, or 'play for voices' as he subtitled it, in a pastoral
mode similar to that of the late poems (the first use of the name
'Milk Wood' occurs in a worksheet for 'In the White Giant's Thigh').
It is an impressionistic narrative of the doings of one spring day in
the life of the Welsh seaside town of Llareggub, an idealized Arcadia
or utopia ('utopia', from the Latin, means 'no-place', and 'Llareggub',
a spoof Welsh name that Thomas had first used in his story 'The
Burning Baby' in 1934, reads 'Buggerall' backwards, and so means
much the same). The basic premise went back many years; he had
spoken of writing a 24-hour, day-in-the-life work to Bert Trick as
early as 1933, and in 1939 he told Richard Hughes that the people
of Laugharne needed 'a play about Laugharne characters'.[24] Two
wartime pub poems set in New Quay, 'Dear Tommy, please' and
'Sooner than you can water milk', anticipate some of its themes,
and Thomas seems to have begun sketching it while he was living
in New Quay – probably as a spin-off from the poem that concludes
Quite Early One Morning, since his friend Dan Davin heard Thomas
recite a series of comic-satiric verses in the same vein in 1945.[25] The
idea was to create a comedy of humours based on life as Thomas
had experienced it in Laugharne and New Quay, drawing on the
inhabitants' eccentricities and obsessions. As originally related to
Hughes and Constantine Fitzgibbon in 1943 and 1944, these would
be brought to light as the result of a government attempt to certify
Llareggub insane, although over the course of the play it would be
shown to be an island of sanity in a mad, hell-bent world (he told
Fitzgibbon that Llareggub would be considered so dangerous that
the government would propose to surround it with a barbed-wire
fence, like a concentration camp).[26] Thomas took further steps
along the road to Llareggub with other features, such as *Return*

Journey, and his letters show that he was thinking of this proto-*Under Milk Wood* in Italy in the summer of 1947.[27]

Once back in South Leigh from Italy, Thomas probably tinkered with *Under Milk Wood* in between writing film scripts. His own works aside, its literary antecedents can be found in Edgar Lee Masters's *Spoon River Anthology* (1915), a sequence of poems in which the dead in the churchyard of a Midwestern town describe their former lives, and from which a critique of small-town puritanical repression and hypocrisy emerges – one readily transferable to a Welsh context. Others include Sherwood Anderson's more genial *Winesburg, Ohio* (1919), Thornton Wilder's *Our Town* (1938), the stories of T. F. Powys (referenced in an *Under Milk Wood*-like context in Thomas's talk 'How to Begin a Story' in 1946) and such Thomas Hardy poems as 'Voices from Things Growing in a Churchyard'. But there were also models offered by contemporary radio, among them the comedy series *ITMA* (*It's That Man Again*), which ran until 1949. *Under Milk Wood*'s semi-surreal flavour also invites comparison with *The Goon Show* (1951–60), while its day-in-the-life-of format recalls soap opera, which also relies on

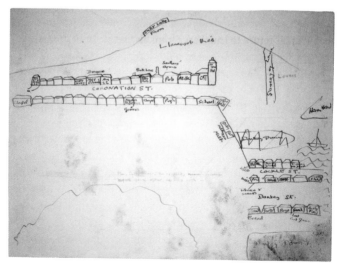

Dylan Thomas's sketch map of Llareggub for *Under Milk Wood*, 1951.

a fixed location and two-dimensional characters; *The Archers* had begun broadcasting in 1950.

The working title for *Under Milk Wood* was 'The Town That Was Mad'; it was at this stage that Thomas gave an informal, private recital of sections of it to fellow writers in Prague, in March 1949. Accounts show that after material much like the first half of the play as it now stands, Llareggub would be put on trial in its Town Hall, its inhabitants quizzed by an official prosecutor from London and defended by Captain Cat in his capacity as town spokesperson. The inhabitants of Llareggub crowd into the courtroom to witness the proceedings, only to learn that their attempt to defend themselves is to no avail; the town is judged mad and sentenced to be cordoned off. Rather than being dismayed, however, the townsfolk have heard such discouraging things about the world beyond that they declare their alleged insanity to be preferable, and happily embrace their fate.

The courtroom-drama format may have arisen from the sense that a more ambitious successor to *Return Journey* should have a more formal structure. But by mid-1949 the courtroom part remained undeveloped. Although Thomas gave his literary agent David Higham to understand that it was nearly finished in September that year, his return to Laugharne from his first U.S. tour in May had meant a return to finishing and polishing the poems begun the summer before, and he got no further with *Under Milk Wood*. In October, however, he was able to send Douglas Cleverdon at the BBC the first 39 pages of 'The Town That Was Mad'. A rethink now took place, since it was clear that the format was holding the play back. It was decided that he should continue the play in the episodic, comic-surreal, pastoral style of its first part. But there was no immediate follow-up to this. In the summer of 1951 it was being referred to as 'Llareggub Hill'; the title reflects the change of approach, but the section of *Under Milk Wood* sent to *Botteghe Oscure* that October was still only a shortened version of the opening section of a year before. It was not, in fact, until 1953, when a reading of *Under Milk Wood* became a requirement of the third U.S. tour, that Dylan would – almost – complete it.

The enduring popularity of *Under Milk Wood* lies in its humour, linguistic exuberance and challenge to authority and social propriety. In a conservative post-war climate the play's gusto and exuberance were particularly tonic, and it retains much of its gently subversive charge. The threat of an over-administered, hyper-regulated society still exists, and so does a delight in seeing people push back against it. It helps that the energy *Under Milk Wood* recruits is a blend of archaic and modern popular cultures. Llareggub has Rabelaisian folk roots in the medieval Land of Cockaigne, and its cast are standard comic types: the insubordinate servant, the milk-watering milkman, the butcher who adulterates his meat, the postman who steams open the post, the boarding-house landlady of such 'scrupulous & godlike tidiness' that 'the only boarder good enough for her in the end' is death.[28] It is a version of the world turned upside-down. Yet its one-liners and exchanges, as in the opening interplay between Captain Cat and the drowned sailors, are indebted – albeit with a surreal, poetic twist – to the quickfire exchanges of twentieth-century radio and film, from the Marx Brothers onwards, while its voyeurism and bawdy ('It's organ organ all the time with him') are kin to contemporary saucy seaside postcards and end-of-the-pier comedians, and prefigure the *Carry On* films of the late 1950s.[29]

The play's subversiveness is generated by, but contrasts with, its many symmetries. On the one hand, *Under Milk Wood* can be viewed as an extended hymn to the energy whose workings Thomas delineated two decades before in 'The force that through the green fuse', embodying it in a softer, communal form on one sunny, erotically charged 'May-milk' day. On the other, the forces in it are static and schematic, and knowingly so. Llareggub is a 'place of love', to use Mary Ann Sailors's phrase, but it is so precisely because the darker aspects of erotic passion have been eliminated. The couples in the play are frozen in paradoxical ways (the realist point being that many relationships are frozen, of course, if rarely so amusingly). The affair between Mog Edwards and Myfanwy Price, for example, is epistolary only and will never be consummated; they live 'happily apart from one another', feigning frustration but preferring deferment.[30] Mr and Mrs Pugh relish their mutual antagonism, and, as

Thomas observed, would be lost if they did not have it. The sexual attraction between Gossamer Beynon and Sinbad Sailors will remain unconsummated because of class and cultural differences that – although neither regards these as a genuine obstacle ('I don't care if he *does* drop his aitches, so long as he's all cucumber and hooves') – nevertheless prevent them from declaring their passion.[31] The complexity of adult identities and relationships is also displaced by embodying the attributes of a single partner within a pair of stereotypes: the 'sacklike & jolly' Mrs Dai Bread One and 'gypsy slatternly' sexy Mrs Dai Bread Two, for instance.[32]

The most important divide in the play is that of its title: between the relationships of daytime Llareggub, which propriety and social hypocrisy thwart, displace and double, and the openly sexual night-time trysts conducted in Milk Wood by the men of the town with Polly Garter. Milk Wood, on a hill above Llareggub, is the id to its ego, and Thomas, reversing society's preference, makes the id dominant: Llareggub's values are ultimately subordinate to, *under*, those of Milk Wood. Polly is one of the play's more dubious stereotypes, of course, but she is saved from sentimentality – the earth-mother tart with a heart of gold – by her genuine pathos. Any old 'Tom Dick and Harry' mean nothing to her because the only man she has ever loved is the 'midget' 'little Willie Wee' (his name another reminder of the unthreatening nature of sex in *Under Milk Wood*).[33] Polly's lament, like Captain Cat's colloquy with the dead Rosie Probert, links sex with death in true Thomasian fashion (it appears in comic form in lines like Mae Rose Cottage's 'You just wait. I'll sin till I blow up!').[34] Together with Captain Cat, Polly is the central character in *Under Milk Wood*, while the Reverend Eli Jenkins, Thomas's surrogate in the play, bookends the action with his morning and evening hymns.

The subject of Dylan Thomas's presence in the text raises the question of the extent to which the piece derives from his own situation. Oddly, given the over-biographical readings of much of his work, *Under Milk Wood* has never been read as a *roman-à-clef*, even though there is evidence that he was seriously considering making it a far darker work very late in the composition process.

Work notes refer to 'The sadness of No-good Boyo' and 'The terrible jealousy of Mrs Cherry', and 'The poverty of the town, the idiocy, the incest'. One, headed 'What have I missed out?', lists 'Incest/ Greed/ Hate/ Envy/ Spite/ Malice'.[35] It is possible that Thomas weighed up the use of such disturbing elements because of the similarities between Llareggub and his own predicament, and that he explored his conflicted love–hate feelings about Caitlin, 'my golden loathing wife', and hers about him, via the play's relationships, from Mrs Ogmore-Pritchard's bullying of her ghostly partners to Mrs Cherry Owens's 'two husbands . . . one drunk and one sober', both of whom she loves.[36] His own puritanism, in this reading, is mocked in Jack Black, the cobbler, who chases 'the naughty couples down the grassgreen double bed of the wood'.[37] The visits to the United States became the catalyst to finish *Under Milk Wood* and also of the break-up of Dylan and Caitlin's marriage; while Dylan had his two most serious affairs with women he met out there, Caitlin, Polly Garter-like, conducted affairs in Laugharne with local men, and picked men up for casual sex during the U.S. tour in 1952.[38]

'A voice on wheels': Dylan Thomas on tour

Thomas had been asking his U.S. correspondents about work on the other side of the Atlantic, and angling for invitations to visit as early as 1945. For writers in austerity-strapped Britain, the United States at the time appeared as a land of milk and honey, with its lucrative lecture circuits, film industry and lavishly endowed university posts. Friends of Thomas, such as Ruthven Todd and the film-maker Len Lye, had moved there by the time of his first visit. Dylan already had a high profile in the States, as we have seen, and numerous admirers and contacts. The admiration was mutual, since he possessed an extensive knowledge and love of U.S. poetry and film. It was natural, then, that when he was contacted in May 1949 by John Malcolm Brinnin with the offer of a reading in the United States, he should be interested, both for literary and intellectual reasons, and as a way of solving his financial troubles.

Brinnin, in his early thirties, was an academic, poet and admirer of Thomas's work who had recently been appointed director of the Poetry Center at the Young Men's and Young Women's Hebrew Association (YM-YWHA) in New York. His offer was $500 for a reading at the YM-YWHA, plus airfare and expenses, and the opportunity to book readings elsewhere. It was a generous one. Dylan asked Brinnin to look for more dates, and once word was out, they came thick and fast.[39] By the time he flew to the United States on 21 February 1950, he was contracted to give 35 readings in roughly three months, beginning on the East Coast and travelling on to the Midwest, California and the northwest, before returning east via Florida.[40] The readings he gave were to consist of favourite poems and some of his own, but his engagements would also involve interviews, Q&A sessions and related social events: meals, receptions and parties. Brinnin made arrangements for accommodation and travel, and organized time off work so that he could accompany and socialize with his charge, but Thomas would have to travel alone to engagements away from the East Coast. Neither man had any experience of tour organization or the demands of touring, and because Brinnin was pressed to accept as many invitations as he could the programme they agreed 'would have prostrated an athlete, let alone a middle-aged poet in poor health'.[41]

Even so, Thomas's knack of being the right person in the right place at the right time was again evident in the United States of 1950. The McCarthyite witch-hunts had just begun and Cold War paranoia gripped the country. The figure of Dylan Thomas – rumpled, Dionysiac, instinctively anti-authoritarian, a bardic summoner of elemental powers with a grand reading style – acted as a cultural counterblast to repression and conservatism. His readings electrified those who heard them, shook up the staid poetry scene, and helped U.S. poetry reconnect with its own bardic tradition in ways that would bear fruit a few years later with the Beats. Thomas might dismiss himself as 'the poor man's Charles Laughton', but members of a cowed liberal intelligentsia saw him as a beacon of integrity and lyric purity in dark times, and treated him as a kind of saviour.[42] His appeal was also personal; he was a charismatic Celt, without

English *froideur* or superiority, and this endeared him to a society that liked to think of itself as classless.[43] As he toured, his warmth and self-deprecating humour won him legions of friends and admirers – and, as many have noted, he was lionized and feted to a degree approaching that of rock stars a generation later.

Yet Thomas's letters to Caitlin reveal that Manhattan struck him much as the 'insane city' of London in his letters to Vernon Watkins years before, and induced a similar anxiety and defensiveness. It was a 'dream and nightmare city' of '*noise*, all day & night', and 'huge phallic towers' driven upwards by 'the insane desire for power', where 'the imminence of death is reflected in every last powerstroke and grab of the great money bosses', the 'mad middle of the last mad Empire on earth', where 'without some drug [he] couldn't sleep at all'.[44] Although Manhattan was not the United States, he seems rarely to have relaxed anywhere in America and, as in 1930s London, strove assiduously to charm its inhabitants in order to make his way, using drink as a stimulant, a disguise and an escape. Moreover, the anxiety he had to deal with was on a correspondingly larger and hence less controllable scale. Above all, without a regular work routine, his instinctive eagerness to please his hosts meant that he was vulnerable to being overwhelmed by America's pace, its generosity and his own compulsion to satisfy its demands. He took adulation with a pinch of salt, referring ironically to his fans as 'ardents', but could not help being swayed to some degree by the flattery, and more than flattery, offered in such abundance. It was, of course, this aspect of the tours that most worried Caitlin and his friends.

The first tour set the pattern for the rest. Thomas initially sought out old acquaintances living in New York. He identified congenial local bars, such as the San Remo and the White Horse Tavern in Greenwich Village, where he could socialize and hold court. A circle of acquaintances, fellow writers and hangers-on coalesced around him. His readings were given with flair and professionalism; the first, at the YM-YWHA Poetry Center, was a triumph, attracting an audience of more than 1,000. Innumerable accounts testify to the impact the readings had on even the most jaded listeners and fellow poets. Yet, as on many subsequent occasions, this first one was preceded by a panic attack.[45] When they struck, Thomas would be reduced to prolonged coughing fits, retching and even vomiting. Often he drank to calm his nerves in advance, sometimes to a point at which it seemed impossible that he could read. But invariably he did, pulling himself together and delivering in a way that belied his condition of just minutes before.

Dylan Thomas at a BBC studio, 1948, photograph by John Gay.

Performance, it seemed, was a reflex that overrode all else, and the miraculous reversals became part of the legend.

More lurid incidents form part of the larger myth, although many were brought about by cultural differences. Just as not all Thomas's provincial young-dog antics had translated well to London, so his blend of self-deprecation, wind-up, slapstick and irony could be misunderstood in the United States. He was aware of this, and played on it in comic attempts to shock; asked by Harvey Breit, editor of the *New York Review of Books*, why he was in the United States, he quipped, 'To continue my life-long search for naked women in wet mackintoshes'.[46] This could easily backfire in places less blasé and more puritanical than New York (although it is revealing that for most of the alleged outrageous incidents there is usually also a more anodyne version).[47] Thomas's ingrained dislike of formal occasions and being paraded came to the fore in the United States, where his hosts often wished to use him in exactly this way. He sometimes missed social engagements, or, if he did attend events, challenged their protocols in ways that were not appreciated or even understood. His problems were exacerbated by a keen sense of Caitlin's disapproval of the visit, and by home-sickness. The thirst for emotional succour and the opportunities for slaking it were predictable enough, and led to two significant relationships, with Pearl Kazin on the first tour in 1950 and Liz Reitell on the tours in 1953.[48] Whether or not these reflected a genuine desire to escape his marriage, they certainly accelerated its disintegration.

On its own terms, the first U.S. tour was a huge success. Thomas became famous and established a continent-wide fund of goodwill and some notoriety, as well as an astonishing slew of artistic contacts, acquaintances and friends. (This expanded during future tours, and included not only poets as various as e. e. cummings, Elizabeth Bishop, Robinson Jeffers, Kenneth Rexroth and Theodore Roethke, but also novelists, such as William Faulkner, Anita Loos and Gore Vidal, the composer John Cage, Merce Cunningham the choreographer, Maya Deren the film-maker, the sculptor David Slivka, and Andy Warhol. To the inhabitants of Laugharne, however, by far his most notable encounter, on his first tour, was with Charlie Chaplin.[49]) Enjoyable though much of it was, however, it did not yield the hoped-for financial rewards. Brinnin was meticulous in his accounting, but Thomas was extravagant in his expenditure. His enquiries about posts at universities also drew a blank. Back in Britain, at the end of 1950 he was forced to apply for support from the Royal Literary Fund again – he was given £300 – and had to agree to visit Iran to research a documentary film for the Anglo-Iranian Oil Company.[50]

Thomas was also well aware that touring was not writing, and feared that he was becoming merely 'a voice on wheels', a performer rather than a creator. Between February 1950 and his death in November 1953 he would spend the equivalent of almost an entire year in the United States. While there he was unable to write, apart from passages he added to *Under Milk Wood* in May and October 1953. The tours therefore exacerbated his general sense of being at a crossroads, if not in crisis. The other radio pieces of the 1950s and two new stories, 'The Followers' and 'The Outing', are accomplished, but slight, and retread old ground. It was this growing impasse that Thomas had in mind when Breit asked him about his success. He answered that it was bad for him, and that he 'should be what [he] was', explaining: 'Then [in 1934] I was arrogant and lost. Now I am humble and found. I prefer that other.'[51]

Whatever the interruptions to his writing, u.s. tours guaranteed at least some money, and, despite the difficulty of holding on to the profits, their lure was irresistible. In the summer of 1951 Thomas agreed a second tour with Brinnin, to run from January to May 1952. Caitlin, aggrieved at having been left alone for so long when Dylan was on his first tour, and suspicious of his motives – she had found out about his affair with Pearl Kazin – went with him.[52] From the outset, however, she was angry, depressed and jealous of the attention he was accorded. Arguments and fights, some public, occasionally savage, punctuated the tour. The melodrama of the Thomases' dysfunctional partnership became something of a coast-to-coast soap opera. But the audiences were no less enthusiastic and, ever the professional, Thomas had augmented his repertoire.

Financial Statement on Lecture Engagements of Dylan Thomas

Fees Collected		Agent's Fees
Haverford College	225.00	33.75
Bennington College	150.00	22.50
Syracuse Univ.	200.00	30.00
Williams College	150.00	22.50
Poets' Theatre	200.00	30.00
Randolph-Macon	150.00	22.50
Mass. Inst. Tech.	150.00	22.50
Phil. Arts Council	175.00	26.25
Duke University	225.00	33.75
Amherst College	200.00	30.00
Poetry Center	200.00	30.00
	2025.00	303.75

Poetry Center 200.00
Poetry Center 800.00

Fees Forthcoming

2 925.00

Inst. Cont. Arts.	150.00	22.50
Boston University	300.00	45.00
Univ. of Conn.	80.00	--
Poetry Center	200.00	30.00
Poets' Theatre	100.00	15.00
	830.00	112.50

Total 2855.00   416.25

Travel Expenses

		Hotels, Meals, etc as living expenses for
New York - Haverford	15.00	41 days--April 21 to
Haverford - Boston	35.00	June 3,1953 @ 15.00
Boston-Bennington	7.50	per day..............
Bennington-Syracuse	6.50	$ 645.00
Syracuse-Williamstown	9.00	
Williamstown-Boston	6.00	
Boston- Washington	37.50	
Washington-Lynchburg	7.50	*Trans-Oceanic Travel Expenses–* 265.00 (ship)
Lynchburg-New York	33.00	275.00 (plane) return
New York-Philadelphia	5.00	
Philadelphia-Boston	22.00	Total earnings 2855.00
Boston-Raleigh	52.00	Agents' fees 416.25
Raleigh-Boston	52.00	2438.75
Boston-Storrs	5.00	*U.S.* Travel Expenses 320.50
Storrs-New York	7.50	2118.25
New York-Amherst	10.00	Living expenses 615.00
Amherst-New York	10.00	1503.25
	320.50	

Medical Expenses

Dr. L. Blaidin, 41 Park Ave.   *Orthopedist – 75.00*   75.00
– Medications – 23.50   23.50
Gastritis – " " – 4.20   4.20
Dr. Friedman ave. 27 Park   *X-Ray – 8.00*   8.00
Dr. Milton R. Haustein, 44 Gramercy Park   *M.D. – 66.00*   66.00
177.70

Calculations of the takings and expenses of the third U.S. tour, 1953.

Predictably, however, the money woes remained unsolved. Fewer readings meant fewer fees, two people meant more expense, and the tour had deepened the divide between husband and wife.[53]

Back in Laugharne, Thomas spent three months working on the 'Prologue', and came to an agreement with Cleverdon to finish *Under Milk Wood* for the BBC. That autumn he also agreed a third U.S. tour for spring 1953, which, since he promised to finish it in time, was to showcase a first performance of *Under Milk Wood* at the

YM-YWHA. Personal and financial problems mounted in the months leading up to his departure. Caitlin found out that she was pregnant (but was unsure whether the child was Dylan's) and had an abortion in January 1953. In the same month Margaret Taylor began charging rent on the Boat House. But the crisis provoked a solution that augured well; his agent, David Higham, took over responsibility for paying Thomas's bills, stabilizing his chaotic finances, and in the wake of D.J.'s death Nancy's husband, Gordon Summersby, promised to support Florrie. By now Caitlin's dislike of Dylan was intense, and he was living with their friends the actor Harry Locke and his partner Cordelia Sewell in their flat in Hammersmith while Caitlin remained in Laugharne. Although Dylan protested he was still in love with her, and both made further attempts to repair their marriage in summer 1953, a separation of some kind seemed unavoidable.

When he arrived in New York on 21 April 1953, Thomas was given into the keeping of Brinnin's new assistant at the YM-YWHA Poetry Center, Liz Reitell, who had been charged with getting him to finish *Under Milk Wood* in time for a first performance there on 14 May. Without Reitell it is unlikely that the play would have reached the almost-complete state in which it exists (its evening section is still under-length vis-à-vis the morning section; according to Daniel Jones, other characters would have joined Mr Waldo in singing songs in the Sailors' Arms at the close). Dylan was adding material until just minutes before the performance. But in the event it was a huge triumph. If they were expecting a daunting experimental opus, the audience's appreciation might have been amplified by relief at their realization about a quarter of an hour into the performance that they were listening to a work that was comic-subversive and life-affirming. There were fourteen curtain calls, and it was clear to everyone that a modern classic had been born, although Thomas himself was surprised by the response. A short but intense reading tour of the East Coast followed, rounding off the most successful of his tours to date (just eighteen readings, albeit in a mere 42 days); for the first time the financial returns were commensurate with the effort. In a development that boded ill for his marriage, soon after the reading of *Under Milk Wood* Thomas had also begun an affair with Reitell.

The fourth tour: death by neglect

Following the success of his third U.S. tour, Thomas agreed to a fourth, to begin just a few months later, in October 1953. An added inducement was that he had begun work on a libretto for a projected opera by Igor Stravinsky, who wished to follow up on *The Rake's Progress* (1951), the libretto for which had been written by W. H. Auden. Thomas had heard a broadcast of this opera and admired Auden's text. He was understandably flattered – the collaboration would mark a new high point in his career – and he met Stravinsky at Stravinsky's Boston hotel on 21 May, near the end of his third tour, for a preliminary discussion. It was agreed that once Thomas had completed the East Coast engagements for his fourth tour, he would fly out to stay with Stravinsky at his home in Los Angeles in early November. There they would flesh out a scenario that Thomas had already begun sketching. Accounts show that it is likely to have been a continuation of the *In Country Heaven* project. Following a nuclear disaster that has all but wiped out humanity, two survivors, a boy and a girl, emerge from a cave. As they discover the world, reborn Edenically around them, they start to name everything in it for the first time. In the process they create a new language – one lacking abstractions and consisting only of the names of 'people, objects, and things' – and devise new myths of origin. It is a vision of a fresh start for humankind, an overcoming of the Cold War's rending contradictions and threat of extinction.

Yet for all his projections of renewal, Thomas's health was worsening in the weeks before he left the UK for his fourth tour. It is highly likely that when he arrived in New York on 20 October, he already had bronchitis. He had looked and felt unwell before the journey, and he told Reitell, who met him off his flight, that he had felt 'as sick as death all the way over'. Friends who met him confirm that he looked ill. From then on he ate very little – his last full meal was on 22 October – and slept badly; lacking his past stamina, he was frequently tired. Untreated, his bronchitis seems to have become pneumonia. He was feverish and gasping for breath on 23 October, and on 25 October he was 'desperately ill', and collapsed at a performance of *Under Milk Wood*. On 27 October he had to leave his own birthday party after half an hour to return to his hotel to rest. A few days later, as Reitell later recounted, he had a hysterical breakdown in the Algonquin.

The course of the illness was not linear, however, and this contributed fatally to misdiagnosis. Thomas rallied, and indeed could seem relatively healthy, at various points during the two weeks he had left to live. He was able to take part in a symposium on film with Arthur Miller and Maya Deren, socialize and go through the motions at some engagements. He also added a few more passages to *Under Milk Wood*. But this meant that his symptoms were seen as solely drink related, when drink was a secondary factor. On 24 October he was given an injection of adrenocorticotropic hormone (ACTH), a fashionable steroid, by Reitell and Brinnin's physician, Dr Morton Feltenstein. The aim was to reduce Dylan's gout-related inflammation and give him an adrenaline boost. Feltenstein neglected to check for respiratory illness, despite Thomas's symptoms and medical history, but the surge of adrenaline gave both Thomas and Reitell faith in the efficacy of his 'winking needle', as Thomas called it.

Eleven days later, when Reitell called Dr Feltenstein back to deal with Dylan's renewed nausea and vomiting, he assumed the symptoms were wholly alcohol related.[54] On three occasions on that day, Wednesday, 4 November, he injected Thomas with ACTH and morphine (contraindicated in any case for delirium tremens, which Feltenstein assumed he was dealing with). Almost the last words Thomas spoke, late that evening, involved a play on 'roses', as both flower and the Rose's brand of lime cordial, punning to the last. Half an hour after the morphine injection – a hefty half a grain (30 mg) dose – he stopped breathing properly, went 'blue in the face' and fell into the coma from which he would never recover. It then took two hours to get him to St Vincent's Hospital, in the small hours of Thursday, 5 November. Once he was there, Feltenstein's authority ensured that for two days the coma continued to be treated as purely alcohol related. At that stage, however, it is likely that hypoxia and cerebral oedema had starved Thomas's brain of oxygen so badly that his death was inevitable.

Worse still, no one seems to have noticed that his hospital notes recorded X-rays taken on admission which showed he was suffering from bronchial pneumonia.[55]

Caitlin flew to New York, arriving on Sunday, 8 November, and was given a police escort from the airport to the hospital. She then went to rest from her flight with David and Rose Slivka, two of the Thomases' artist friends, before returning to the hospital later that day. By this time she was drunk, swore, attacked staff and smashed some of the hospital's religious trappings. She was straitjacketed and taken to a private psychiatric institution. As a result she was absent when Dylan died, peacefully, the next day. Liz Reitell had resumed her vigil by his bedside but, perhaps aptly – she and the duty nurse were taking a break at the time – the one person who would witness Dylan Thomas taking his very last 'station of the breath', around 12.45 p.m. on Monday, 9 November 1953, was John Berryman, a friend and fellow poet.

Conclusion:
Afterlife and Popular Culture

It is a bitter irony that, had he survived the fourth u.s. tour, Dylan Thomas would probably have solved all of his immediate and medium-term financial problems.[1] Most poignant of all, he was on the verge of developing in new directions as a writer. A follow-up radio play to *Under Milk Wood* was envisaged, and on the day of his death he had been due to fly to California to meet Stravinsky. Instead, accompanied by Caitlin, his body was shipped back from New York to Southampton. Daniel Jones and Ebie Williams, the landlord of Brown's Hotel and Laugharne's sole taxi-driver, were waiting to convey it back to Laugharne. On the morning of his funeral, at St Martin's Church in Laugharne, Thomas lay in an open coffin in Florrie's house. Florrie, who had lost her husband and daughter in the previous year, and now her son, showed remarkable composure; 'He's nice' was her verdict on the work of the American morticians who had made up his face with rouge and lipstick. Caitlin, who was consumed by grief, kept the children away from the funeral. A Pathé newsreel shows scores of mourners – Thomas's old Swansea friends, locals and acquaintances from London and the bbc, among them Louis MacNeice, who wrote the funeral into his long poem *Autumn Sequel* – following the coffin up the churchyard path.[2]

Dylan Thomas's death was a major public event, reported on in the international press as it was occurring, and lamented and raked over long afterwards. The unusual scope of his fame was reflected in the fact that obituaries appeared in both the mass-circulation *Daily Mirror* and *The Times*. For the u.s. poet and critic Karl Shapiro, it was 'the most singular demonstration of suffering in modern literary history'; Thomas had been 'the idol of writers of every description and the darling of the press', 'the first poet who was popular and obscure', one who had singlehandedly created '[the] impossible . . . a general audience for a barely understandable poet'.[3] His passing, at a time of Cold War tension and grey cultural conformity, was felt to have a significance that exceeded the merely literary. He had burned brightly in defiance of convention, and with his departure it seemed as if an important ideal – of uninhibited expression and romantic ardour – had also departed. One of the few last sparks of resistance to a soulless, administered society had been snuffed out. Lyric poetry – youth itself, it was claimed by some – had suffered a fatal blow, and the world had sustained 'a psychic wound'.

Dylan Thomas died intestate, and Daniel Jones took charge of the funeral arrangements and of putting his estate in order. With the help of Thomas's agent, David Higham, his publisher Dent, and Thomas's many friends, including leading literary figures in Britain and the United States – among them Edith Sitwell, Arthur Miller,

Dylan Thomas, *Self-Portrait*, 1953, pencil on paper.

The Reverend Leon Atkin with gravedigger at Dylan Thomas's grave, St Martin's Church, Laugharne, 1953.

W. H. Auden, Louis MacNeice and T. S. Eliot – fundraising events were organized to defray medical and funeral expenses and set up a trust fund for his family.[4] Memorial services were held in New York, on 13 November 1953, and at the Royal Festival Hall in London on 14 February 1954. *Under Milk Wood*, with Richard Burton as First Voice, was broadcast by the BBC on 25 January 1954. (The Welsh Service of the BBC deemed it unsuitable 'for family or home listening' and did not join in, one of the first signs of the puritanical disapproval of Thomas in his native land that would last for decades.) Dan Jones edited the play, and it was published later in the year.[5] Two selections of work Thomas had been planning to issue – *A Prospect of the Sea* and *Quite Early One Morning* – were also hurried out by Dent in 1954.

Disturbed by Caitlin's behaviour in Laugharne and suffering from the impact of her bereavements, Florence Thomas moved to Carmarthen, but later returned to live in the Boat House. Her health declined rapidly and she died there in 1958. At the end of 1954 Caitlin left England for Elba, returning the following year but moving to

Rome permanently in the spring of 1957. She took Colm with her, but Llewelyn and Aeronwy would spend much of their adolescence in boarding schools. Italy was a place where Caitlin was able to escape the past to some extent; she had enjoyed it during the visit in 1947, when she had had an affair, and in the late 1950s she entered into a relationship with Giuseppe Fazio, with whom she had a son, Francesco, in 1963. Fazio, a strong character, helped her to deal with her grief and her suicidal impulses, and eventually cure her alcoholism. But on her death in 1994, according to her final wishes, she was buried with Dylan in the grave in Laugharne.

The controversy over Thomas as a man and writer was prolonged by the publication of *Dylan Thomas in America* (1955), John Brinnin's account of the tours and of his relationship with Dylan, in which he mourned him and attempted to clear himself of responsibility for his death. Brinnin's graphic detailing of excess was in many cases exaggerated or based on hearsay, although his account of a confused and sometimes lost soul at a crossroads in his life rang true. The controversy was extended by Caitlin's *Leftover Life to Kill* (1957), the first of several angry memoirs. Full of insight into Thomas's character, and demonstrating her own substantial literary talent, it nevertheless had much the same defensive purpose as Brinnin's book.

The outpouring of grief and posthumous lionization inevitably shaped Thomas's reputation, and in different ways on either side of the Atlantic. In America, where he was taken most seriously as a writer – perhaps too seriously at times – he inspired numerous poets and fed the energy of the nascent Beat movement, just as his personal life, as revealed by Brinnin and by Caitlin, would provide a template for the candour of Confessional poetry. In U.S. academia, too, Thomas was treated as a modern master, his poems scrupulously analysed and interpreted, launching many dissertations and doctoral theses. In Britain the response to his death also proved to be one of the hinges on which post-war literary culture turned, but in a mixed and generally negative way. In particular, the backlash against the outpouring of emotion on Thomas's death gave added impetus to the Movement. While Philip Larkin, the group's main poetic voice, quietly admired Thomas's work, Kingsley Amis consistently mocked and traduced him throughout his career. The virulent hostility bespoke an indebtedness, of course, and Thomas continued to be the ghost that haunted the spartan feast of Movement poetry. The split transatlantic response was summed up by the reception of *Letters to Vernon Watkins* (1957), Watkins's defence of Thomas and his artistry, in which the painstaking, sober craftsman was revealed in fine-grained detail that should have been impossible to gainsay. It was, however, derided by British reviewers even as it was welcomed as a corrective in the United States. If Thomas still had powerful intellectual advocates at home – William Empson and Raymond Williams among them – they were beginning to thin out as the 1960s wore on.

The backlash in Britain can be partly understood as the price to be paid for bucking the trend for a poet's work to be undervalued immediately following their death. And yet, in a characteristic paradox, the opposite was about to happen among general readers, with whom Dylan Thomas had never fallen out of favour. With the onset of the new political, cultural and sexual freedoms of the 1960s he suddenly seemed to be a prophet of the zeitgeist, a victim of Establishment hypocrisy and meanness.[6] As an exemplary proto-rebel for the counterculture his star rose even higher, and he achieved the iconic status he retains to some extent to this day. Robert Zimmerman, AKA Bob Dylan, adopted his name in 1962, Stan Tracey composed the *Under Milk Wood* jazz suite in 1965, and the Beatles had Peter Blake put him on their *Sgt Pepper's Lonely Hearts Club Band* album cover in 1967 (Thomas was John Lennon's favourite author). Thomas became, and continues to be, a favoured genius-martyr for painters, composers, rock stars and actors from Richard Burton to Patti Smith and Johnny Depp to David Bowie, as well as a genuine creative touchstone. His work still features in popular cultural forms, including in advertisements for Volkswagen cars, and comic books, such as Garth Ennis and Steve Dillon's *The Preacher*, and it is quoted regularly in memes and social media.[7] One of the world's biggest stars, Dwayne 'The Rock' Johnson, motivated his fitness followers in 2014 to 'rage against the dying of the light' in a post that received over half a million likes. (Although his appropriateness for contemporary healthism might have made some sense for Thomas in his cross-country-running teens, the irony of his recruitment, given his later lifestyle, would surely not have been lost on him.) Another, Taylor Swift, refers to Thomas directly in the title song of her album *The Tortured Poets Department* (2024), where the narrator/singer chastises her lover for imagining them to be following in the footsteps of Thomas and Patti Smith.

Importantly, Thomas's work is used extensively in film. Two poems are particularly prominent: 'And death shall have no dominion' and 'Do not go gentle into that good night'. The first, for example, is declaimed in full by George Clooney in Steven Soderbergh's *Solaris* (2002), while the second features in Alan Metter's *Back to School* (1986), John N. Smith's *Dangerous Minds* (1995) and Roland Emmerich's *Independence Day* (1996), and it is threaded through Christopher Nolan's *Interstellar* (2014), recited by Michael Caine. Indeed, raging 'against the dying of the light' is now common sci-fi currency to signal standing resolute against any civilization-ending apocalypse. Thomas's appeal for science fiction may also underpin the largest of all popular-culture universes, that of George Lucas's *Star Wars*, whose Force, the 'energy field created by all living things . . . [that] surrounds us and penetrates us . . . [and] brings the galaxy together', has its antecedent in the one that 'through the green fuse drives the flower'.[8] Nor is Thomas just part of Western culture; among the 'Misty Poets' of the post-Gang of Four Chinese poets in the early 1980s, the same poem was prized as an exemplary lyric, richly ambiguous and politically unconscriptable.[9]

Popular interest in Thomas remained buoyant in Britain and the United States, but by the end of the 1970s U.S. critical interest had waned and in Britain critical opinion and academia had turned against him. Thomas was now marginalized in literary histories of the 1930s, defined as 'a Forties poet', with the 1940s declared a dire decade, unworthy of attention.[10] Even as he was ignored or dismissed by academics and critics, and mainstream poets acknowledged him only in order to confess that they had long since recovered from youthful crushes on his work, Thomas was blanked by the avant-garde, with whom it might be felt he had more in common; he had failed to declare his experimentalism sufficiently resoundingly, it seemed, and was guilty of supping with the devil of populism. He continued to act as a secret leavening agent on important maverick figures, such as Roy Fisher, W. S. Graham, Ted Hughes and Sylvia Plath, but in the polarized poetry scene of the last quarter of the century he was suspended in limbo. It was not until the start of the twenty-first century that a revival of his critical fortunes began, boosted first by the fiftieth anniversary of his death, in 2003, and then, far more substantially, by his centenary in 2014.

Dylan Thomas's dual reputation, popular and critical, reflect his paradoxical, chameleonic nature, his straddling of high and low, his blend of charisma and hermeticism, and means that he will always confound boundaries.[11] But his life and work have come into better focus in recent years, and should become clearer in future. A long overdue non-Anglocentric reassessment of the poetry of the 1930s and '40s is taking place and his work is central to it (this process is reflected in two recent essay collections, which reveal that young scholars are interesting themselves in Thomas more than at any time since the 1960s).[12] Thomas's writing is now being explored in new and promising ways: in the light of the history of broadcasting, technology and science, from feminist and gender-identity perspectives, as a forerunner of eco-poetry, and as a version of Modernism from the margins. The hybrid, gothic and apocalyptic aspects highlighted in this biography are being examined more fully, as are different ways of viewing the figure of Thomas himself – in his lesser-known rural Carmarthenshire contexts, for example, or through the eyes of the women in his life.

Thomas's public reputation has also improved, as old prejudices have waned. In his home town of Swansea puritanism and self-harming begrudgery long clouded the issue; one Lord Mayor declared that the council could not consider buying his birthplace, on the grounds that Dylan Thomas was better known outside Wales than inside it – a sentiment that, applied in Stratford-upon-Avon, would have seen Anne Hathaway's Cottage turned into a multistorey

Bonnie Helen Hawkins, 'No-Good Boyo', pencil drawing from *Under Milk Wood* series, 2023.

car park or a McDonalds. Fortunately, attitudes changed markedly in the 1990s. Thomas's tourist value was realized, for one thing, and he became a posthumous beneficiary of the award to Swansea of the title UK City of Literature for 1995. Ty Llên, the Welsh national literature centre, was opened in Swansea that year and given the alternative name of the Dylan Thomas Centre. It was a thriving hub of literary events for more than a decade, many of them Thomas related, although budget cuts and austerity have taken their toll since 2008. Even so, it continues to house an impressive permanent display of Thomas memorabilia and works hard to maintain the city's literary tradition via its most famous son. The property at 5 Cwmdonkin Drive has now been refurbished in 1920s style and can be booked for tours, while plans are afoot to make 'Warmley',

Daniel Jones's former home, a similar site of literary pilgrimage. Laugharne has a Dylan Thomas Trail and the Boat House is open to the public. Websites and online Dylan Thomas groups flourish. Blue plaques dot New Quay and Tenby as well as London, Swansea and Laugharne. Last but not least, for several decades now, Thomas's legacy has been more than ably represented by two generations of his descendants, his daughter Aeronwy and her daughter, Dylan's grand-daughter, Hannah.

Such developments in Wales match the wider revision of opinion in the rest of the UK and abroad, which has gradually come round to accepting Dylan Thomas as a major figure in mid-twentieth-century poetry. While his reputation will never again stand as high as it did at the time of his death, and his colourful and sometimes rackety life will always fascinate, and at times distract, it seems reasonable to hope that future interest will temper the legend with a better grasp of the writing than hitherto. It is for the extraordinary things that Thomas was able to do with the English language that he will ultimately have lasting significance, and these are becoming clearer with the passage of time. His stories are groundbreaking, his radio scripts classics of their kind, and his poems explore the modern condition in a profound and electrifying way. From the onset of his maturity – at an age when most poets are still learning the basics – he continued, to the end, to devise original and compelling lyric forms, often perfecting them, and never repeating himself. His output was necessarily small, but the strike rate was astonishingly high.[13] And while all good writers have a verbal fingerprint, there are very few – even among the best – who have permanently expanded the stylistic scope of the language. Usually they are poets, because in poetry it is most expected that linguistic liberties will be taken. Even so, such figures are the exceptions; and Thomas, in all his ambiguities and 'intricate image', is undoubtedly a member of their very select company.

References

Introduction: An Intricate Image

1 John Goodby and Chris Wigginton, eds, *Dylan Thomas: Contemporary Critical Essays* (Basingstoke, 2001).
2 Thomas's poems take as an injunction T. S. Eliot's proposal that 'genuine poetry can communicate before it is understood.' T. S. Eliot, 'Dante', in *Selected Essays* (London, 1934), p. 238.
3 Dylan Thomas, 'Poetic Manifesto' (1951), in *The Collected Poems of Dylan Thomas*, ed. John Goodby [2014] (London, 2016), p. 225.
4 Constantine Fitzgibbon, *The Life of Dylan Thomas* (Boston, MA, and Toronto, 1965), p. 47. Fitzgibbon judges the 'protean aspect' of Thomas's character a 'cerebral and defensive one': that of the small, shy, clever boy who was 'plucky' rather than 'tough', and responded to the challenges of the world and the threat of being labelled with swagger, charm and performance.
5 James A. Davies, *Dylan Thomas's Swansea, Gower and Laugharne: A Pocket Guide* (Cardiff, 2000), p. 45.
6 This is primarily in the form of the interviews conducted by Colin Edwards in the 1950s and '60s, held at the National Library of Wales, previously neglected by biographers. These were edited and published in 2003–4 by David N. Thomas, whose other research adds significant detail concerning Thomas's wartime movements, the genesis of *Under Milk Wood* and the circumstances surrounding his death. New material has also emerged about Thomas's visit to Iran in 1951, and the discovery in 2014 of a long-lost notebook (N5) has shed important light on the development of his style.
7 W. B. Yeats, 'A General Introduction for My Work', in *Selected Criticism and Prose* (London, 1980), p. 255.

1 Young and Easy: Childhood, 1914–25

1 Dylan Thomas, 'The Countryman's Return', in *The Collected Poems of Dylan Thomas*, ed. John Goodby [2014] (London, 2016), p. 119.

2 Jeffrey Gantz, trans., *The Mabinogion* (London, 1976), p. 106.

3 There is a reverse pun on Arianrhod in 'A grief ago' ('the rod the aaron') and a play on Dylan in 'Over Sir John's hill' ('Dilly dilly call the birds'). Thomas, *Collected Poems*, pp. 81, 185.

4 Dylan was entered in the 1921 Census, presumably by D.J., as Welsh-speaking, in another anti-authoritarian gesture.

5 Elocution lessons were given at a small establishment in nearby Brynymor Crescent run by Miss Gwen James, who had studied at the Central School of Speech and Drama in London. According to her sister Esther, she thought Dylan had 'a naturally good voice', 'a big [one] for a small boy'. David N. Thomas, ed., *Dylan Remembered*, vol. I: *1914–1930, Interviews by Colin Edwards* (Bridgend, 2003), p. 41.

6 James A. Davies, *Dylan Thomas's Swansea, Gower and Laugharne: A Pocket Guide* (Cardiff, 2000), p. 60.

7 Constantine Fitzgibbon, *The Life of Dylan Thomas* (Boston, MA, and Toronto, 1965), p. 33.

8 Dylan Thomas, *Reminiscences of Childhood*, in *The Broadcasts*, ed. Ralph Maud (London, 1991), pp. 3, 5.

9 Thomas, *Collected Poems*, p. 107. The 'uglier side of a hill' refers to the built-up side of the hill up which Cwmdonkin Drive ran; the other side was farmland until the 1930s, when the Townhill estate was built on it.

10 Dylan Thomas, *Return Journey*, in *Broadcasts*, p. 188.

11 Dylan Thomas, *Reminiscences of Childhood*, in *Broadcasts*, p. 3.

12 Dylan Thomas, *Collected Stories*, ed. Walford Davies (London, 1983), pp. 137–8.

13 Dylan Thomas, *Reminiscences of Childhood*, in *Broadcasts*, p. 19.

14 Fitzgibbon, *Dylan Thomas*, p. 40. These are a slightly different version of the statement made in 'Poetic Manifesto', in Dylan Thomas, *Early Prose Writings*, ed. Walford Davies (London, 1971), p. 156.

15 Dylan Thomas, *Collected Stories*, p. 139.

16 Andrew Lycett, *Dylan Thomas: A New Life* (London, 2003), pp. 19–20.

17 Fitzgibbon, *Dylan Thomas*, p. 13.

18 Thomas, 'Poetic Manifesto', pp. 157–8.

19 Thomas, *Collected Poems*, p. 161.

20 David N. Thomas, *Dylan Remembered*, p. 166.

21 Thomas, *Collected Poems*, p. 61.

22 Ibid., p. 39. See also Chris Wigginton, *Modernism from the Margins: The 1930s Poetry of Louis MacNeice and Dylan Thomas* (Cardiff, 2007), pp. 36–7.

23 Dylan Thomas, *The Collected Letters*, ed. Paul Ferris, 2nd edn (London, 2000), p. 40.

24 Thomas, *Collected Poems*, p. 57.

25 Ibid., p. 56.

26 Ibid., p. 52.

27 Ibid., p. 65.

28 Ibid., p. 61.

29 Thomas, *Broadcasts*, p. 3.

30 Thomas, *Collected Poems*, p. 83.

31 Ibid., pp. 98–9.

32 Ibid., p. 90.

33 Ibid., p. 53.

34 Ibid., pp. 44–5.

35 Ibid.

36 Thomas, 'Poetic Manifesto', pp. 154–5.

37 Mutlu Konuk Blasing, *Lyric Poetry: The Pain and the Pleasure of Words* (Princeton, NJ, 2007), p. 13.

38 Ibid.

2 Eggs Laid by Tigers: The Apprentice Poet, 1925–32

1 Dylan Thomas, *Return Journey*, in *The Broadcasts*, ed. Ralph Maud (London, 1991), p. 185.

2 Andrew Lycett, *Dylan Thomas: A New Life* (London, 2003), p. 50.

3 Constantine Fitzgibbon, *The Life of Dylan Thomas* (Boston, MA, and Toronto, 1965), pp. 47–9. Fitzgibbon gives the full text of the essays 'Modern Poetry' and 'The Films' (these may also be found in Dylan Thomas, *Early Prose Writings*, ed. Walford Davies (London, 1971)) and of three very early poems; for others, see Dylan Thomas, *The Poems*, ed. Daniel Jones (London, 1971).

4 *Swansea Grammar School Magazine* (April 1930), p. 24.

5 Heather Holt, *Dylan Thomas: The Actor* (Llandybie, 2003), p. 18.

6 David N. Thomas, ed., *Dylan Remembered*, vol. I: *1914–1930, Interviews by Colin Edwards* (Bridgend, 2003), pp. 260–67; Holt, *The Actor*, pp. 26–71.

7 Dylan Thomas, *Collected Poems*, ed. John Goodby (London, 2014), p. 12.

8 Ibid., p. 13.

9 Dylan Thomas, *The Collected Letters*, ed. Paul Ferris, 2nd edn (London, 2000), pp. 113–20. See also Ethel Ross, *Ugly, Lovely: Dylan Thomas's Swansea and Carmarthenshire of the 1950s in Pictures*, ed. Hilly Janes (Cardigan, 2016), pp. 80–83.

10 Dylan Thomas, *Collected Stories*, ed. Walford Davies (London, 1983), p. 159.

11 Ibid., pp. 163, 169. After leaving school, Jones gained a First Class Honours BA in English from Swansea University, followed by a Masters degree, and studied music in Vienna before returning to Britain to become a composer; he went on to devise his own 'Complex Metres' rhythmic system and compose thirteen symphonies, the fourth of which was dedicated to Thomas's memory. During the Second World War he was a good enough linguist to work as a cryptanalyst at Bletchley Park.

12 Daniel Jones's first letter to Thomas, dated 30 December 1927, contains 'Persephone', a ballad in fourteeners, and ends, 'acknowledging your superiority in this Art'. Lycett, *A New Life*, p. 36.

13 David N. Thomas, *Dylan Remembered*, vol. i, p. 17.

14 Ibid., pp. 146–7; Lycett, *A New Life*, p. 37.

15 Rayner Heppenstall, for example, recalled Thomas being 'very keen', in his early days in London, in 1935, on '*Wozzeck* . . . the opera [by Alban Berg]'. David N. Thomas, *Dylan Remembered*, vol. i, p. 64.

16 Thomas, *Collected Letters*, p. 91.

17 Thomas, *Collected Stories*, p. 164.

18 Daniel Jones, quoted in Fitzgibbon, *Dylan Thomas*, pp. 60–61.

19 Ibid., p. 54.

20 Ibid., p. 38.

21 Thomas, *Collected Letters*, pp. 222–6. In August 1935, alone in Donegal and wrestling with 'Altarwise by owl-light', Thomas wrote his longest and most revealing letter to Jones, 'from one WARMDANDYLANLY man to another'. A bravura piece, comic, frankly nostalgic and insightful, it celebrates the creative zest and humour they had shared. Despite projecting a return to Swansea as successful artists in later life, however, it accepts that their friendship has already been arrested by the onset of adulthood.

22 Thomas, *Early Prose Writings*, p. 156.

23 Robert Graves, 'These Be Your Gods, O Israel!', *Essays in Criticism*, v/2 (1955), p. 148.

24 Thomas, *Collected Stories*, p. 161.

25 Jeff Towns, '"Borrowed Plumes" – Requiem for a Plagiarist', in *Dylan Thomas: A Centenary Celebration*, ed. Hannah Ellis (London, 2014), p. 47.

26 Percy Smart, quoted in *Poet in the Making: The Notebooks of Dylan Thomas*, ed. Ralph Maud (London, 1968), p. 11. For corroborative comments by Smart, see David N. Thomas, *Dylan Remembered*, vol. 1, pp. 77–8.

27 Thomas, *Broadcasts*, p. 183.

28 Ibid., p. 182.

29 Thomas, *Collected Stories*, p. 212.

30 Ibid., p. 211.

31 Dylan Thomas, 'The Poets of Swansea', in *Early Prose Writings*, p. 118.

32 Thomas, *Collected Letters*, p. 28.

33 Ibid., p. 24.

34 Thomas, *Broadcasts*, p. 184.

35 Ibid., pp. 183–4.

36 David N. Thomas, *Dylan Remembered*, vol. 1, p. 84. The first (N4) version of 'The force that through the green fuse' is dedicated to 'E.P.'

37 Vera fell out with the Thomases as a result of the so-called Majoda Incident (see Chapter Six).

38 Thomas, *Broadcasts*, p. 6.

39 See note to 'I have longed to move away', in Thomas, *Collected Poems*, pp. 239–40.

40 See David N. Thomas, *Dylan Remembered*, vol. 1, pp. 118–33.

3 The Rimbaud of Cwmdonkin Drive: The Poetics of Process, 1933–4

1 Dylan Thomas, *The Collected Letters*, ed. Paul Ferris, 2nd edn (London, 2000), p. 101.

2 Ibid., p. 102.

3 Andrew Lycett, *Dylan Thomas: A New Life* (London, 2003), p. 65.

4 Dismissing literary 'pseudo-revolutionaries', Thomas observed in a letter to Bert Trick of February 1935 that they 'have no idea at all of what they priggishly call "the class struggle"' and are 'bogus from navel to skull'. Thomas, *Collected Letters*, p. 212.

5 Thomas's review of Stephen Spender's *Vienna* in *New Verse*, December 1934, sets out his differences with New Country poets more generally: poetry requires an acute sensitivity to verbal context, and no amount

of 'historically emotional significance' will make up for a lack of it. Indeed, lack of verbal sensitivity will paradoxically rob the poetry of the propaganda impact it aspires to by jettisoning it. Dylan Thomas, *Early Prose Writings*, ed. Walford Davies (London, 1971), pp. 169–70.

6 In 'Gaspar, Melchior, and Balthasar', an unfinished story of this period, it is the same; revolution will come under attack by the forces of reaction, leading to bombing, street fighting, looting, murder and rape. Dylan Thomas, *Collected Stories*, ed. Walford Davies (London, 1983), pp. 365–7.

7 Paul Ferris, *Dylan Thomas* (London, 1978), p. 81.

8 Thomas, *Collected Letters*, p. 192.

9 Ibid., p. 103.

10 David N. Thomas, ed., *Dylan Remembered*, vol. I: *1914–1930, Interviews by Colin Edwards* (Bridgend, 2003), p. 164.

11 Thomas, *Collected Letters*, p. 185.

12 Both Paul Ferris and Andrew Lycett are patronizing towards Thomas's politics, and seem determined to prove that his socialism – which admittedly had admixtures of anarchism and secularized Christianity – must have been naive.

13 Dylan Thomas, *Return Journey*, in *The Broadcasts*, ed. Ralph Maud (London, 1991), p. 188.

14 Thomas, *Collected Letters*, p. 417.

15 Jack Lindsay, *Meetings with Poets* (London, 1968), p. 41.

16 David N. Thomas, *Dylan Remembered*, vol. I, p. 165.

17 Dylan Thomas, *The Notebook Poems, 1930–1934*, ed. Ralph Maud [1989] (London, 1990), pp. 146–7.

18 Thomas, *Collected Poems*, ed. John Goodby (London, 2014), p. 23.

19 Ibid., p. 33.

20 Thomas, *Collected Letters*, p. 49.

21 Thomas, *Collected Poems*, p. 31.

22 Pamela Hansford Johnson (1912–1981) was another young writer. She was two years older than Thomas, lived with her mother in Clapham and worked in a bank. She introduced Thomas to the literary circle around Victor Neuburg, his entrée to literary London. Starting out as a poet, she would make her name as a novelist; her first novel, *This Bed Thy Centre* (1935), took its title from Donne's 'The Sun Rising' at Thomas's suggestion.

23 The other poem was 'The Woman Speaks', published in *The Adelphi* the following March. It elicited another fan letter, from Glyn Jones, later one of Wales's leading writers. Jones was flummoxed by

'Dylan', which pleased Thomas: 'your doubt as to my sex was quite complimentary, proving (or was it merely my uncommon name?) that I do not write with too masculine a pen' – an indication of the interest in hermaphroditism and gender-switching that is a feature of his work. Thomas, *Collected Letters*, p. 120.

24 Ibid., p. 40.

25 Thomas, *Collected Poems*, p. 39.

26 'Answering Johnson's objection to "doublecrossed", he noted "I . . . have always been struggling with . . . the idea of poetry as a thing entirely removed from such accomplishments as 'word-painting' . . . There must be no compromise; there is always only the one right word: use it, despite its foul or merely ludicrous associations.'" Thomas, *Collected Letters*, p. 43.

27 Ibid., p. 43.

28 Thomas, *Collected Poems*, pp. 51–2.

29 David Aivaz, 'The Poetry of Dylan Thomas', *Hudson Review*, VIII/3 (Autumn 1950), repr. in *Dylan Thomas: The Legend and the Poet*, ed. E. W. Tedlock (London, 1963), p. 195.

30 Thomas is likely to have read a volume of essays by Huxley on Darwinism in D.J.'s library, and had read Freud's *The Interpretation of Dreams*. He also read Alfred North Whitehead, the Stephen Hawking of his day, who had set out a philosophy of 'process' in 1920, as recalled by W. Emlyn Davies, in *Dylan Remembered*, vol. I: *Interviews with Colin Edwards*, ed. David N. Thomas, p. 145. It is highly likely that he was also aware of the work of other cosmologists who popularized Einsteinian concepts at the time, such as James Jeans and Arthur Eddington.

31 William Blake, 'The Everlasting Gospel', in *The Complete Poems*, ed. W. H. Stevenson (London, 1972), p. 854.

32 Thomas, *Collected Poems*, p. 51.

33 Thomas, *Collected Letters*, p. 121.

34 Ibid., p. 122.

35 Ibid., p. 57.

36 Thomas, *Collected Poems*, p. 60.

37 Thomas, *Collected Letters*, pp. 76–7.

38 Thomas, *Collected Stories*, pp. 75, 78.

39 Ibid., p. 33.

40 Thomas, *Collected Poems*, p. 60.

41 Thomas, *Collected Letters*, pp. 72–3.

42 Thomas, *Collected Poems*, p. 7.

43 Tony Conran, *Frontiers in Anglo-Welsh Poetry* (Cardiff, 1997), p. 113.

44 Thomas, *Collected Poems*, p. 58.

45 Ibid., pp. 73–4.

46 Ibid., p. 63.

47 Sigmund Freud, *The Interpretation of Dreams*, Pelican Freud Library, vol. IV (Harmondsworth, 1983), p. 366.

48 William Empson, *Argufying: Essays on Literature and Culture*, ed. John Haffenden (London, 1988), p. 394.

49 Karl Shapiro, 'Dylan Thomas', in *Dylan Thomas: A Collection of Critical Essays*, ed. C. B. Cox [1957] (Englewood Cliffs, NJ, 1966), p. 172.

50 Process may even extend to the internal workings of a single word. 'Drives' in the first stanza of 'The force that through the green fuse', for example, loses a letter to become 'dries' in the second, enacting the waning of energy.

51 Thomas, *Collected Letters*, pp. 147–8, 208.

52 One of the best descriptions is by Vernon Watkins: 'Dylan worked upon a symmetrical abstract with tactile delicacy; out of a lump of [verbal] texture or nest of phrases he created music, testing everything by physical feeling, working from the concrete image outwards.' Dylan Thomas, *Letters to Vernon Watkins*, ed. Vernon Watkins (London, 1957), p. 13.

53 Thomas, *Collected Letters*, p. 328. Thomas typically qualifies this statement ('preciously like nonsense'), and stresses 'my critical part in the business' of 'letting' images breed – although he does not discount the permission given to unbidden linguistic agency.

54 Linden Huddlestone, 'An Approach to Dylan Thomas', *Penguin New Writing*, 35 (1948), pp. 123–60.

55 Thomas, *Collected Poems*, p. 208.

56 Thomas, *Letters to Vernon Watkins*, p. 29.

57 Ibid., p. 55.

58 See James J. Balakiev, 'The Ambiguous Reversal of Dylan Thomas's "In Country Sleep"', *Papers on Language and Literature*, XXXII/1 (1996), p. 21.

59 Thomas, *Collected Poems*, p. 64.

60 Thomas, *Collected Letters*, p. 33.

61 See R. George Thomas, 'Dylan Thomas and Some Early Readers', *Poetry Wales: Dylan Thomas Special Issue*, IX/2 (Autumn 1973), p. 12: '['The force that through the green fuse'] was accepted [by 1930s readers] as a fairly clear realization of unknown physical suffering that must lie ahead of us, most probably in gas warfare or Guernica-like devastation. None of us felt uneasy about the macabre images in

the poem . . . there was a nightmare quality in the drift towards Hitler's war which was echoed more closely in Thomas's non-political verse than in any of the [MacSpaunday] verse.'

62 Thomas, *Collected Letters*, p. 132.

63 Ibid., pp. 162, 164.

64 Answering the question 'Do you take your stand with any political or politico-economic party or creed?', Thomas answered: 'I take my stand with any revolutionary body that asserts it to be the right of all men to share equally and impartially, every production of man from man and from the sources of production at man's disposal, for only through such an essentially revolutionary body can there be the possibility of a communal art.' Thomas, *Collected Poems*, p. 224.

65 Thomas, *Collected Letters*, p. 198. It was on this occasion that Jones told Thomas about Dr William Price (1800–1893), the self-styled bard and druid who, in 1883, had fathered a son named Jesu Grist and who, when his son died at the age of five, had cremated him on the hillside above Pontypridd. Thomas immediately adapted it in his story 'The Burning Baby', adding incest and an attack on Nonconformism for good measure.

66 Glyn Jones, "Three Poets: Huw Menai, Idris Davies, Dylan Thomas', in *The Dragon Has Two Tongues: Essays in Anglo-Welsh Writers and Writing,* ed. Tony Brown (Cardiff, 2001), pp. 161–91 (p. 166).

4 The Direction of the Elementary Town: London, Surrealism and Love, 1935–7

1 For vivid details of the move and their London digs, see Hilly Janes, *The Three Lives of Dylan Thomas* (London, 2014), pp. 4–19, and Dylan Thomas, *The Broadcasts*, ed. Ralph Maud (London, 1991), p. 264.

2 Dylan Thomas, *The Collected Letters*, ed. Paul Ferris, 2nd edn (London, 2000), p. 215.

3 Miron Grindea, ed., *Adam International Review*: *Our Dylan Thomas Memorial Number*, XXI/238 (Winter 1953), p. 23.

4 Thomas, *Collected Letters*, p. 212.

5 Janes, *The Three Lives*, pp. 4, 11; Andrew Lycett, *Dylan Thomas: A New Life* (London, 2003), p. 113. Thomas told Glyn Jones in March 1935 that he had 'little real work to my credit' after four months in London, but N5 shows that he had written four or five poems. Thomas, *Collected Letters*, p. 213.

6 Dylan Thomas, *Poet in the Making: The Notebooks of Dylan Thomas*, ed. Ralph Maud (London, 1968), p. 39.

7 On 'night custard', see Thomas, *Collected Letters*, p. 144, and Lycett, *A New Life*, p. 106. One example of the collective fantastical speculations engaged in by Dylan, Fred Janes, Mervyn Levy and others who dropped in on their first digs involved an ongoing calculations of how many mice it would take to pull the Glasgow to London express train. One million? Five? How would the mice be harnessed to the engine? With what? And so on.

8 Desmond Hawkins, *When I Was: A Memoir of the Years between the Wars* (London, 1989), p. 118.

9 Thomas, *Collected Letters*, p. 380.

10 New Country poets were among those most baffled. Spender called *18 Poems* 'just poetic stuff with no beginning nor end, or intelligent or intelligible control'. MacNeice, less dismissively, described 'a series of nonsense images, the cumulative effect of which is usually vital and sometimes seems to have a message'. The inability of either to notice Thomas's intricate rhyme schemes and strict syllabic forms reveals the ideological blind spot. See Chris Wigginton, *Modernism from the Margins: The 1930s Poetry of Louis MacNeice and Dylan Thomas* (Cardiff, 2007), p. 40.

11 See John Goodby, *The Poetry of Dylan Thomas: Under the Spelling Wall* (Liverpool, 2013), p. 62.

12 Dylan Thomas, 'How To Be a Poet', in *A Prospect of the Sea* (London, 1955), p. 114.

13 Thomas, *Collected Letters*, p. 258.

14 Ibid., pp. 392–3.

15 Ibid., pp. 248–9.

16 Wigginton, *Modernism from the Margins*, p. 40.

17 David N. Thomas, ed., *Dylan Remembered*, vol. II: *1935–1953, Interviews by Colin Edwards* (Bridgend, 2004), p. 66.

18 Thomas, *Collected Letters*, p. 214.

19 Ibid., p. 217.

20 Norman Cameron, *Collected Poems and Selected Translations*, ed. Warren Hope and Jonathan Barker (London, 1990), p. 71.

21 Dylan Thomas, *Collected Poems*, ed. John Goodby (London, 2014), p. 75.

22 Don McKay, 'Crafty Dylan and the Altarwise Sonnets: "I Build a Flying Tower and I Pull It Down"', *University of Toronto Quarterly*, LV/4 (1985/6), pp. 373–94 (p. 383).

23 Thomas, *Collected Letters*, p. 160.

24 Ibid., p. 272. In reality, at least one parody of 'Altarwise' by a member of Thomas's circle had already appeared at this point; see Goodby, *The Poetry*, pp. 279, 298 n. 99.

25 Thomas, *Collected Poems*, pp. 80, 46, 95.

26 Ibid., pp. 68–9.

27 Ibid., p. 72.

28 Silvano Levy, *Sheila Legge: Phantom of Surrealism* (Rhos-on-Sea, 2014), pp. 30–51.

29 Dylan Thomas, *Early Prose Writings*, ed. Walford Davies (London, 1971), p. 160.

30 Quoted in Constantine Fitzgibbon, *The Life of Dylan Thomas* (Boston, MA, and Toronto, 1965), p. 176.

31 Reprinted in Henry Treece, *Dylan Thomas: 'Dog Among the Fairies'* (London, 1949), pp. 145–8.

32 Watkins immediately fell under Thomas's spell. As Gwen Watkins later observed, 'it was like love at first sight.' Gwen Watkins, *Dylan Thomas: Portrait of a Friend*, 2nd edn (Talybont, 2005), p. 19. Watkins's account of their first meeting has an air of the *coup de foudre*: 'He was slight, shorter than I expected, shy, rather flushed and eager in manner, deep-voiced, restless, humorous, with large, wondering, yet acutely intelligent eyes, gold curls, snub nose, and the face of a cherub . . . In thought and words he was anarchic, challenging, with the certainty of that instinct which knows its own freshly-discovered truth.' Dylan Thomas, *Letters to Vernon Watkins*, ed. Vernon Watkins (London, 1957), pp. 12–13.

33 Thomas, *Collected Letters*, pp. 325–6.

34 Watkins, *Portrait of a Friend*, p. 22.

35 Linda Evans, 'Polgigga – Cornwall: Part 1', Canolfan Dylan Thomas Centre blog, 29 June 2020, www.dylanthomas.com.

36 Augustus John (1878–1961) had, in the decade before the First World War, been considered the leading artist in Britain. After the war he worked chiefly as a portraitist, and painted both Caitlin and Dylan.

37 John's account comes from a letter to his partner, Dorelia; his correspondence is held in the National Library of Wales. Quoted in Lycett, *A New Life*, p. 133.

38 Thomas, *Collected Letters*, pp. 269, 262, 271.

39 Emily Holmes Coleman (1899–1974) was a writer and diarist who, following her conversion to mystical Catholicism in 1944, devoted herself to the religious life. Her pioneering poetic novel was based on her recovery from post-natal breakdown.

40 See Thomas, *Early Prose Writings*, p. 183.
41 Lycett, *A New Life*, p. 139.
42 Thomas, *Collected Poems*, pp. 91–2.
43 At the end of 1936 D.J. retired from Swansea Grammar School. Thomas returned to Swansea in January and again in April 1937 to help his parents move from Cwmdonkin Drive to 'Marston', a small semi-detached house in Bishopston, a Gower village near Mumbles.
44 Thomas, *Collected Letters*, pp. 284, 285.
45 Lycett, *A New Life*, p. 144.
46 Thomas, *Collected Poems*, p. 93.
47 Thomas, *Collected Letters*, p. 287, n. 1.

5 Loving Presences, Warring Absences: Marriage, Wales and War, 1938–41

1 Dylan Thomas, *The Collected Letters*, ed. Paul Ferris, 2nd edn (London, 2000), p. 340.
2 Caitlin Thomas with George Tremlett, *Caitlin: A Warring Absence* (London, 1986), p. 70.
3 David N. Thomas, ed., *Dylan Remembered*, vol. II: *1935–1953, Interviews by Colin Edwards* (Bridgend, 2004), pp. 211–12.
4 Thomas, *Collected Letters*, p. 449.
5 Dylan Thomas, *Collected Poems*, ed. John Goodby (London, 2014), p. 94.
6 Ibid., p. 95.
7 Thomas, *Collected Letters*, p. 305.
8 Ibid., p. 336.
9 Thomas, *Collected Poems*, p. 101.
10 Ibid., p. 102.
11 Thomas had signalled his awareness of the need to open his poetry out in this way as early as April 1936, to Watkins: 'Perhaps, as you once said, I should stop writing altogether . . . I'm almost afraid of all the once-necessary artifices . . . and can't, for the life or the death of me, get any real liberation, any diffusion or dilution or anything, into the churning bulk of the words.' Thomas, *Collected Letters*, p. 249.
12 Ibid., p. 368.
13 Ibid., p. 324.
14 Thomas, *Collected Poems*, p. 104.

15 Ibid., p. 109.
16 Ibid., pp. 105–7.
17 Ibid., pp. 107–8.
18 Thomas, *Collected Letters*, p. 420.
19 They included Lynette Roberts, Keidrych Rhys, Alun Lewis, Davies Aberpennar, Idris Davies and Vernon Watkins among the poets, and the novelists Lewis Jones, Jack Jones, Richard Llewellyn and Margiad Evans. Glyn Jones, like Thomas, was a poet and writer of fiction.
20 Saunders Lewis, lecture, 'Is There an Anglo-Welsh Literature?' (Cardiff, 1939), p. 6.
21 In a review in 1934 he wrote: 'The true future of English poetry, poetry . . . that comes to life out of the red heart through the brain, lies in the Celtic countries . . . Wales, Ireland, and, in particular, Scotland, are building up . . . a poetry that is as serious and as genuine as the poetry in Mr Pound's *Active Anthology*.' Dylan Thomas, *Early Prose Writings*, ed. Walford Davies (London, 1971), pp. 165–6.
22 Thomas, *Collected Letters*, p. 349.
23 Quoted in Ralph Maud with Albert Glover, *Dylan Thomas in Print: A Bibliographical History* (Pittsburgh, PA, 1970), pp. 123–4.
24 Thomas felt, or said he felt, that *A Portrait* was a capitulation to the marketplace, describing it as 'vulgar'. He also viewed *Adventures in the Skin Trade* – which began where *A Portrait* left off and was in the same style – as 'a mixture of Oliver Twist, Little Dorrit, Beachcomber, and good old 3-adjectives-a-penny belly-churning Thomas, the Rimbaud of Cwmdonkin Drive'. Thomas, *Collected Letters*, p. 493.
25 The stories 'mix "high" culture with "low" life', and gradually lead us into an 'underworld of fantastic metamorphosis (comical, farcical, plangent and Circean-sinister by turns)'. M. Wynn Thomas, *Corresponding Cultures: The Two Literatures of Wales* (Cardiff, 1999), pp. 75–6.
26 Dylan Thomas, *Collected Stories*, ed. Walford Davies (London, 1983), pp. 160, 163.
27 Ibid., p. 210.
28 Thomas, *Collected Letters*, p. 461.
29 Ibid., pp. 462, 454.
30 Ibid., p. 453.
31 C. Day-Lewis, 'Where Are the War Poets?', quoted in *Poetry of the Forties*, ed. Robin Skelton (Harmondsworth, 1968), p. 19.
32 Thomas, *Collected Letters*, p. 508.
33 Ibid., p. 490.

34 Ibid., p. 540.

35 Ibid., p. 465.

36 Ibid., p. 518.

37 Ibid., p. 513.

38 John Davenport (1908–1966) was a Cambridge-educated critic, teacher, screenwriter and BBC employee; he was renowned for his strength, pugnacious temperament and wit, and was one of Thomas's best friends during the war years.

39 Apocalypse and neo-romantic poetry, which dominated the 1940s, is still too little understood, after long misrepresentation by Movement-influenced critics. In reality it was responsible for much good, even great, poetry, from Lynette Roberts's *Gods with Stainless Ears* and W. S. Graham's *The Nightfishing* to major works – *Four Quartets*, *The Towers Fall*, *The Anathemata* – by older, re-energized Modernists. T.S. Eliot, *Four Quartets* (published separately in London, by Faber & Faber, between 1936 and 1942 ('Burnt Norton', 1936; 'East Coker', 1940; 'The Dry Salvages', 1941; 'Little Gidding', 1942); first collected and published in book form as *Four Quartets* (New York, 1943); H.D. (Hilda Doolittle), *The Walls Do Not Fall* (Oxford, 1944); Lynette Roberts, *Gods with Stainless Ears: A Heroic Poem* (London, 1951); David Jones, *The Anathemata* (London, 1952); W. S. Graham, *The Nightfishing* (London, 1955).

40 The two other Apocalypse anthologies were *The White Horseman* (1941) and *The Crown and Sickle* (1944). The influence on university poets is reflected in *Eight Oxford Poets* (1941), and in the work of English Regionalist poets, and those in Wales, Scotland and Northern Ireland. See James Keery, *Apocalypse: An Anthology* (Manchester, 2020).

41 Keery's seminal articles on Apocalypse and 1940s poetry, 'The Burning Baby and the Bathwater', appeared in *P. N. Review* issues 150, 151, 152, 154, 156, 159, 164, 170 and 171 between 2003 and 2006. See John Goodby, '"My Jack of Christ": Hybridity, the Gothic-Grotesque and Surregionalism', in *The Poetry of Dylan Thomas: Under the Spelling Wall* (Liverpool, 2013), pp. 238–301, for a discussion of their implications.

42 Thomas, *Collected Poems*, p. 117.

43 Vernon Watkins, 'Notes on Dylan Thomas', in *Vernon Watkins on Dylan Thomas and Other Poets and Poetry*, ed. Gwen Watkins and Jeff Towns (Cardigan, 2013), p. 45.

44 Thomas, *Collected Letters*, p. 524.

6 Singing in Chains: Apocalypse and Fame, 1942–7

1 The poem, in four stanzas, was published in *Poetry London* in January 1941; see John Goodby, *Discovering Dylan Thomas: A Companion to the Collected Poems and Notebook Poems* (Cardiff, 2017), p. 174. A shorter, more pungent three-stanza version appeared in *Deaths and Entrances* and *Collected Poems, 1934–1952*: see Dylan Thomas, *Collected Poems*, ed. John Goodby (London, 2014), p. 124.

2 Thomas, *Collected Poems*, p. 120.

3 Ibid., pp. 121–2.

4 Ibid., p. 137. It may or may not be a coincidence that Gwen Watkins said of Caitlin that 'being with her was like being in the same room with a tiger which has not been very strongly chained.' Gwen Watkins, *Dylan Thomas: Portrait of a Friend*, 2nd edn (Talybont, 2005), p. 118.

5 Thomas, *Collected Poems*, pp. 132, 136, 137.

6 Vernon Watkins, *Vernon Watkins on Dylan Thomas and Other Poets and Poetry*, ed. Gwen Watkins and Jeff Towns (Cardigan, 2013), p. 49.

7 Dylan Thomas, *The Complete Screenplays*, ed. John Ackerman (New York, 1995), p. viii.

8 Ibid., p. viii.

9 Thomas, *Collected Poems*, p. 127.

10 Thomas, *Complete Screenplays*, pp. 39–40.

11 Ibid., p. 31.

12 Ibid., p. 71.

13 Ibid., p. 72.

14 Ibid., p. 123.

15 Quoted in Thomas, *Complete Screenplays*, p. xv.

16 Dylan Thomas, *The Collected Letters*, ed. Paul Ferris, 2nd edn (London, 2000), pp. 559–61, 563–4, 569–70.

17 For a contrary view, see Andrew Sinclair, *Dylan Thomas: No Man More Magical* (New York, 1975), p. 118.

18 Thomas, *Collected Poems*, p. 161.

19 Ibid., p. 178.

20 Ibid., p. 140.

21 Ibid., p. 165.

22 Dylan Thomas, *Selected Poems*, intro. Derek Mahon (London, 2004), p. xiv.

23 Thomas, *Collected Poems*, p. 171.

24 Ibid., p. 143.

25 Ibid., pp. 133, 134.

26 Ibid., p. 85.

27 Ibid., pp. 144–5.

28 Ibid., p. 173.

29 Jankel Adler (1895–1949) was a left-wing painter, influenced by Paul
    Klee, Fernand Léger and Pablo Picasso, who left Cologne when the
    Nazis took power in 1933, thereafter living in exile in France and
    Britain. His work had been included in the notorious Nazi 'Entartete
    Kunst' ('Degenerate Art') exhibition of 1937.

30 For the first draft of 'A Refusal to Mourn', see Goodby, *Discovering
    Dylan Thomas*, p. 204.

31 Laurence Stapleton, *Some Poets and Their Resources: The Future Agenda*
    (Lanham, MD, 1995), p. 46.

32 Dylan Thomas, *The Broadcasts*, ed. Ralph Maud (London, 1991), p. xiv.

33 Ibid., p. 92.

34 Jack Lindsay, *Meetings with Poets* (London, 1968), p. 22.

35 Quoted in David N. Thomas, ed., *Dylan Remembered*, vol. II: *1935–1953,
    Interviews by Colin Edwards* (Bridgend, 2004), p. 92.

36 Dylan Thomas, *Collected Stories*, ed. Walford Davies (London, 1983),
    p. 338.

37 Ibid., p. 304.

38 Ibid., p. 307.

39 The name Majoda was an amalgam of the first two letters of the
    landlord's children's names: Thomas suggested that he would rename it
    'Catllewdylaer'.

40 David Daiches, 'The Poetry of Dylan Thomas', in *Dylan Thomas:
    A Collection of Critical Essays*, ed. C. B. Cox (Englewood Cliffs, NJ, 1966),
    p. 17.

41 Watkins, *Portrait of a Friend*, pp. 115–17.

42 David N. Thomas, *Dylan Remembered*, vol. II, p. 257. As David Thomas
    proves, the 'alcoholic gastritis' diagnosis previously alleged by the
    poet's biographers is not supported by the hospital records.

43 Thomas, *Collected Poems*, pp. 259–63.

44 Kenneth Rexroth, ed., *The New British Poets: An Anthology* (New York,
    1949), pp. xvii–xxi. A U.S. audience craving exuberance and dissidence
    was primed by such comments as 'He [Thomas] hits you across the face
    with a reeking, bloody heart, a heart full of needles and black blood and
    thorns, a werewolf heart.'

7 Against the Dying of the Light: Pastoral and America, 1948–53

1 Dylan Thomas, *Collected Poems*, ed. John Goodby (London, 2014), p. 192.

2 Margaret Taylor bought the Boat House for £2,500, allowing the Thomases to live in it at a low rent. She was tolerant of periods of non-payment until January 1953, when she began charging £2 per week.

3 There were similarly laudatory reviews by Cyril Connolly, Stephen Spender and other notables; the Foyles Prize was worth £250.

4 At the time of Thomas's death two more critical studies were in preparation (both appeared in 1954), as was a bibliography (published in 1956).

5 Caedmon Records was set up in 1952 by two young university graduates, Barbara Holdridge and Marianne Roney. The very first recording for the label was of Thomas, and it was largely by virtue of its success that Caedmon became leaders in the U.S. LP recorded voice and audio-book market.

6 The trip to Prague – no more than a long weekend – came as the result of an invitation by a friend who worked at the Czech Embassy in London and with whom Thomas had discussed translations of the Czech poet Vítězslav Nezval. Thomas gave a brief address to a writers' conference and enjoyed an intoxicated and empathetic meeting of minds with the great Czech poet Vladimír Holan.

7 The National Insurance authorities discovered in 1947 that Thomas had not paid them for several years, and took to deducting a chunk of his earnings annually.

8 The classic instance is Kenneth Rexroth's angry memorial poem 'Thou Shalt Not Kill', a major departure point for Allen Ginsberg's *Howl* (1956).

9 Further evidence of Thomas's unexceptional lifestyle in Laugharne in 1938–40 and 1949–53 emerged in 2016 in the form of an account of the Thomas family by the family's GP, David Hughes, written for Charles Barber, the son of a friend, in 1961. See Adrian Osbourne, 'The Poet, the GP, the Publican and a Pig Named Wallis', *New Welsh Reader*, 114 (Summer 2017), pp. 26–44.

10 Nancy later took D.J. back to Brixham until Florrie was discharged. The dates are uncertain, but it is likely that after spending most of the war in India, where she had met her new husband, Nancy spent 1946–50 in England, before they returned to India. After a further brief visit to England for an operation for cancer in 1952, she died in Bombay (Mumbai) in April 1953, just months before her brother. See Katie

Bowman, 'Nancy Thomas: Part 5', Canolfan Dylan Thomas Centre
blog, 16 December 2020, www.dylanthomas.com.

11 Dylan Thomas, *The Collected Letters*, ed. Paul Ferris, 2nd edn (London,
2000), pp. 938, 639, 1005. Julius and Ethel Rosenberg were convicted of
spying for the Soviet Union and sent to the electric chair on 19 June 1953
despite a widespread campaign for a pardon; Thomas described it as a
'murder . . . which should make all men sick and mad'.

12 Ibid., pp. 221–2.

13 Ibid., p. 201. 'Prologue' was Thomas's final poem, and one of the most
demanding he ever wrote. Sending the poem to Ernest Bozman, his
editor at Dent, on 10 September 1952, he noted: 'I set myself . . . a most
difficult technical task: The Prologue is in two verses . . . of 51 lines each.
And the second verse rhymes *backward* with the first. The first & last
lines of the poem rhyme; the second and last but one; & so on & so on.
Why I acrosticked myself like this, don't ask me.' Whatever the reason,
it serves its function as an introduction perfectly, and is patently not
the work of a poet whose powers are on the wane, as some have argued.
Thomas, *Collected Letters*, p. 935.

14 Ibid., pp. 184–5. The poem has five twelve-line stanzas, with syllable
counts per line of 5–6–14–14–5–1–14–5–14–5–14–14 and a complex
AABCCBDEAEDD end-rhyme scheme.

15 Thomas, *Collected Letters*, p. 881.

16 Thomas, *Collected Poems*, pp. 192–3.

17 Thomas, *Collected Letters*, p. 892.

18 Comment by Thomas introducing the poem at the University of Utah
on 18 April 1952, cited in *Dylan Thomas: The Legend and the Poet*,
ed. E. W. Tedlock (London, 1963), p. 66.

19 Thomas, *Collected Poems*, p. 195.

20 Ibid., p. 197.

21 Ibid., p. 198.

22 Ibid., p. 199.

23 Ibid., p. 200.

24 For various accounts of the genesis of *Under Milk Wood*, see David N.
Thomas, ed., *Dylan Remembered*, vol. I: *1914–1930, Interviews by Colin
Edwards* (Bridgend, 2003), p. 165, and David N. Thomas, ed., *Dylan
Remembered*, vol. II: *1935–1953, Interviews by Colin Edwards* (Bridgend,
2004), pp. 74–5.

25 Ibid., vol. II, p. 292.

26 Constantine Fitzgibbon, *The Life of Dylan Thomas* (Boston, MA, and
Toronto, 1965), p. 237.

27 The most recent research, by David N. Thomas, suggests strongly that most of the play was written in New Quay, Oxfordshire and the United States, rather than in Laugharne itself; nor was Laugharne the only model for Llareggub, which is a composite of all the Welsh seaside towns Thomas knew but is, above all, an imaginary creation.

28 Thomas, *Collected Letters*, p. 905.

29 *Under Milk Wood* is suffused with a more genial form of the Surrealism of Thomas's earlier work, and occasionally echoes it directly: 'The bagpipe dugs of the mother sow' are a recognizable descendent of the more forbidding 'bagpipe-breasted ladies in the deadweed' of 'Altarwise', for example. Dylan Thomas, *Under Milk Wood*, ed. Walford Davies and Ralph Maud (London, 1995), p. 50.

30 Ibid., p. 61.

31 Ibid., p. 46.

32 Thomas, *Collected Letters*, p. 905.

33 Thomas, *Under Milk Wood*, p. 41.

34 Ibid., p. 57.

35 Ibid., p. xxxviii.

36 Ibid., p. 58.

37 Ibid., p. 8.

38 According to Rose Slivka, Caitlin would sometimes go to the waterfront and pick up a sailor or longshoreman. See Andrew Lycett, *Dylan Thomas: A New Life* (London, 2003), p. 328.

39 Thomas's readings were almost all given at universities and colleges. The average fee for a reading was about $150 (£57 14s) in 1950, or just over £2,300 in 2023 prices. Brinnin took a 15 per cent commission, a good deal less than a commercial agent would have charged.

40 This made 19,300 km (12,000 mi.) of travel in all, by road, rail and air, plus a 9,655-kilometre (6,000 mi.) transatlantic round trip. On his first tour Thomas flew to the United States, but the flight took seventeen hours. Unable to face a repeat, he returned on the liner *Queen Elizabeth*.

41 Martin E. Gingerich, 'Dylan Thomas and America', in *Dylan Thomas Remembered* (Cowbridge and Bridgend, 1977), p. 26.

42 John Malcolm Brinnin, *Dylan Thomas in America: An Intimate Journal* (Boston, MA, 1955), p. 15. Brinnin describes the phenomenon clearly, but equally clearly succumbed to it himself: 'Some of his listeners were moved by the almost sacred sense of his approach to language; some by the bravado of a modern poet whose themes dealt directly and

unapologetically with birth and death and the presence of God; some
were entertained merely by the plangent virtuosity of an actor with a
great voice.' Ibid., p. 24.

43 Rexroth, like many U.S. commentators, hit on an essential truth about
Thomas while at the same time being amusingly wide of the mark: 'A
vast relief after these nasty English poets. He is Welsh and proletarian
to the core.' Kenneth Rexroth, ed., *The New British Poets: An Anthology*
(New York, 1949), p. xviii.

44 Thomas, *Collected Letters*, pp. 832–4.

45 Brinnin, *America*, pp. 23, 25.

46 Ibid., p. 15.

47 Brinnin's account is unreliable in many respects, but not malicious,
and gives some of the flavour of Thomas's pranksterish and sometimes
offensive behaviour. Although more often than not indulgent of
the demands placed upon him, Thomas found questions about the
meaning of his poetry particularly trying. Asked at a party hosted by
the critic Marshall Stearns what 'Ballad of the long-legged bait' was
about, he allegedly bellowed 'A gigantic fuck!'

48 Pearl Kazin was a friend of Brinnin, and junior literary editor at
Harper's Bazaar. She was 27 when she met Thomas (he was 35),
a politically Left Jewish-American Brooklynite. She was a close
friend of Truman Capote and Elizabeth Bishop, and herself a gifted
but occasional writer. Liz Reitell was 32 when Thomas met her in
April 1953; she had been married twice, and had worked as an actor,
costume designer and painter. Thomas's relationship with Kazin
seems to have continued into his third tour, although by that point
it was probably no longer sexual; that with Reitell began during the
third tour.

49 Thomas visited Chaplin at his California home. Realizing his friends
in Laugharne might not believe him on his return, he had Chaplin
send them a confirmatory telegram.

50 He was in Iran from 17 January to 14 February 1951, hot, thirsty and
depressed by a letter from Caitlin declaring their marriage to be over.
In response he wrote virtuosic descriptive replies declaring his love
and begging forgiveness (as he did simultaneously to Kazin). Some
of the purple passages became a radio feature in 1952. At Abadan
refinery, Thomas chanced to meet Ebrahim Golestan, a short-story
writer who became one of Iran's leading film directors in the 1960s
(in 2008 Golestan wrote a long blog detailing their encounter). The
harsh inequalities of Iranian society and the company employees' racist

attitudes triggered Thomas's radicalism, entering his letters and radio script. Aware of his disapproval, Anglo-Iranian paid the agreed fee, but did not pursue the film project. In 2023 Thomas's Iran visit was the subject of a documentary by Nariman Massoumi, *Pouring Water on Troubled Oil*; see www.etudoverdade.com.br.

51   Quoted in Lycett, *A New Life*, p. 283.

52   In September 1950 Thomas travelled to London to meet Brinnin and Kazin, who were en route to Italy. Caitlin had confronted him that summer with letters from Kazin. Thomas, who escorted Kazin around his London haunts and to Brighton, was careless; Margaret Taylor found out about the affair and, jealous, travelled to Laugharne to tell Caitlin. The result was their greatest marital crisis yet. It lasted for several months and sometimes erupted in fights that could leave Dylan temporarily unconscious and Caitlin with a black eye. To crown their misery, in September 1950 Dylan contracted pleurisy and Caitlin had an abortion.

53   By the summer of 1952 the marriage seemed broken beyond repair, with Caitlin unable to trust Dylan and permanently resentful. Nevertheless, attempts by both to patch it up continued into 1953.

54   Thomas's jokey boast to Reitell of the evening before, the 3–4 November – 'I've just drunk eighteen straight whiskies. I believe that's the record' – may have sealed his fate. Later investigation would show that he had drunk far fewer; the bartender at the White Horse remembered six measures, or six units in today's reckoning, spread over two hours. But the bravado was believed and it shaped his subsequent treatment.

55   Hilly Janes, *The Three Lives of Dylan Thomas* (London, 2014), pp. 212–13. As Janes notes, the full story of Thomas's medical treatment was only pieced together decades later by the painstaking researches of David N. Thomas.

Conclusion: Afterlife and Popular Culture

1   '[I]n four years after his death Dylan's works earned two million dollars,' Martin E. Gingerich has noted; 10,000 copies of the *Collected Poems* had already been sold at the time of his death, and 53,000 copies of *Under Milk Wood* were sold in the year after it was published. Thomas's first Caedmon LP, issued by RCA in April 1952, was followed by several more; by 1963, total LP sales had reached 400,000. The Caedmon contract, a generous one, gave Thomas a $500 advance

against the first 1,000 LPS sold and 10 per cent on all sales thereafter. Martin E. Gingerich, 'Dylan Thomas and America', in *Dylan Thomas Remembered* (Cowbridge and Bridgend, 1977), p. 34.

2　See Pathé, 'Funeral of Dylan Thomas (1953)', www.youtube.com.

3　Karl Shapiro, 'Dylan Thomas', in *Dylan Thomas: A Collection of Critical Essays*, ed. C. B. Cox (Englewood Cliffs, NJ, 1966), pp. 178, 176.

4　The fund raised $20,000 (£7,000) in two months – about £250,000 in 2023 values. Because of Caitlin's fragile mental state and propensity for drink and wild behaviour, Jones, Higham and Stuart Thomas (an old school friend) set up a trust to administer the fund and future royalties. Caitlin signed a deed entitling her to 50 per cent of the funds during her lifetime, the other 50 per cent to be held in trust and divided equally between the children when they were of age. But, as Hilly Janes notes, while 'the trustees had the best of motives . . . Dylan's financial legacy was to cause bitter disputes for years to come.' See Hilly Janes, *The Three Lives of Dylan Thomas* (London, 2014), p. 225.

5　Thomas was a valuable property for his agent and publisher; records show that in 1976, for example, sales of his books were worth £50,000 per annum to Dent (£460,000 in 2023 prices). Royalties were larger than expected, reaching £16,731 by 1956–7 (£516,000 in 2023 prices); by the 1990s they were running at about £120,000 per annum.

6　One of the more surprising converts to Dylan Thomas's writings at this time was Jimmy Carter, later 39th President of the United States. It was Carter who, on an official visit to the UK in 1977, asked why Thomas was not represented in Poets' Corner at Westminster Abbey. The UK Prime Minister James Callaghan promised to make amends, and a stone inscribed with the last two lines of 'Fern Hill' was unveiled there on 1 March 1982. In 1995 Carter honoured Thomas by opening the Dylan Thomas Centre in Swansea.

7　The VW Golf advert of 2007, 'Night Driving', a masterpiece of its kind, can be found on YouTube.

8　The connection goes beyond a single word to a deeper entanglement; Lucas acknowledges a debt to Roman Kroitor and Arthur Lipsett's use of 'the force' in *21-87* (1964), and Lipsett's *Free Fall* (also 1964) is a filmic response to Thomas's 'The force that through the green fuse'. And, equally suggestive, Kroitor would develop IMAX technology with Graeme Ferguson, with whom he worked on the film *The Days of Dylan Thomas* (1965).

9　From a conversation between John Goodby and the Chinese poet Yang Lian in 2017.

10 See James Keery, 'Introduction', *Apocalypse: An Anthology* (Manchester, 2020).

11 Empson's claim that Thomas's death had robbed the public of work that would have been 'very profound and very box-office' makes a point that applies beyond marketability; equally revealingly, he remarked that, when he and the faculty and students of Beijing University were 'refugeeing' in western China during the Japanese invasion in 1937–9, he took just two books with him: 'school Problem Papers [and] the poems of Dylan Thomas as well because they were equally inexhaustible'. William Empson, '*Collected Poems* and *Under Milk Wood*', in Cox, ed., *Dylan Thomas*, p. 86.

12 These are the essay collections edited by Rhian Barfoot and Kieron Smith, and by Edward Allen (see Select Bibliography).

13 American critics of the 1950s and '60s often made a point of listing the Thomas poems they felt 'stood with the best poems of their time' – often, in their estimation, up to a third of those he published.

Select Bibliography

Books, publications and broadcasts by Dylan Thomas

For many years after his death, Dylan Thomas's work – the *Collected Poems* of 1952 apart – appeared incompletely and haphazardly, in miscellany form. Ralph Maud's edition of four of the notebooks (N1–N4) in 1967 was the exception that proved the rule to this benign neglect. However, following Paul Ferris's biography (1977) and edition of the *Collected Letters* (1985) there was a revival of editorial effort that resulted in editions of the collected stories (1983), broadcasts (1991) and screenplays (1995), and a complete version of *Under Milk Wood* (1995). A further wave of editorial work in the 2000s and 2010s produced a fully annotated edition of the *Collected Poems* (2014) and an annotated facsimile edition of the newly discovered fifth notebook (2020).

Much of Thomas's work is still in print, and the most recent miscellany includes poems, stories, *Return Journey* and *A Child's Christmas in Wales*, as well as *Under Milk Wood*. Recent additions to the corpus include *A Pearl Beyond Price*, six letters from Thomas to Pearl Kazin. A *Selected Poems*, edited by Leo Mellor, is in preparation with Faber, as is a new Dent edition of *Under Milk Wood* edited by Nerys Williams. The Caedmon recordings and many of those Thomas made for the BBC are available on CD. Much of this material can also be found on Spotify, YouTube and other online platforms. The Discovering Dylan website, set up by Thomas's granddaughter Hannah Ellis, contains much invaluable information.

Timeline of selected publications, broadcasts and recordings by Dylan Thomas

1933 'And death shall have no dominion' (in *New English Review*); 'The force that through the green fuse drives the flower' (in the *Sunday Referee*)

1934 *18 Poems*

1936 *Twenty-Five Poems*

1937 First radio broadcast: *Life and the Modern Poet*

1939 *The Map of Love*; *The World I Breathe* (USA only)

1940 *A Portrait of the Artist as a Young Dog*

1943 Broadcast of *Reminiscences of Childhood* (published in *The Listener*); *New Poems* (USA only)

1944 Broadcast of *Quite Early One Morning*

1945 Broadcast of *Memories of Christmas*

1946 *Deaths and Entrances* (London); *Selected Writings* (USA only); broadcasts of *Holiday Memory*, *The Londoner*, *Margate: Past and Present* and *The Crumbs of One Man's Year* (published in *The Listener*)

1947 Broadcast of *Return Journey*

1950 Broadcast of *Three Poems*; *A Child's Christmas in Wales* in *Harper's Bazaar* (combines 'Memories of Christmas' and 'Conversation about Christmas'); *Twenty-Six Poems* (selected poems in a limited U.S. edition)

1952 *In Country Sleep* (USA only); first Caedmon recording 22 February, LP issued 1 April; *Collected Poems 1934–1952*

1953 *The Doctor and the Devils* (filmscript); second Caedmon recording, 2 June; reads 'The Outing' on television, 10 August

1954 *Quite Early One Morning* (prose miscellany); *Under Milk Wood* (broadcast version)

1955 *Adventures in the Skin Trade*; *A Prospect of the Sea* (prose miscellany)

1957 *Letters to Vernon Watkins*, ed. Vernon Watkins

1963 *The Beach at Falesá*

1964 *Twenty Years A-Growing*; *The Selected Letters of Dylan Thomas*, ed. Constantine Fitzgibbon

1967 *The Notebooks of Dylan Thomas*, ed. Ralph Maud (U.S. edition); a UK edition, titled *Poet in the Making: The Notebooks of Dylan Thomas*, was published 1968

1971 *Early Prose Writings*, ed. Walford Davies; *The Poems*, ed. Daniel Jones

1976 *The Death of the King's Canary*, with John Davenport

1983 *Collected Stories*, ed. Walford Davies

1985   *The Collected Letters*, ed. Paul Ferris (2nd edn 2000: repr. in
        2 vols 2017)
1989   *The Notebook Poems, 1930–1934*, ed. Ralph Maud; *Collected Poems
        1934–1953*, ed. Walford Davies and Ralph Maud
1991   *The Broadcasts*, ed. Ralph Maud
1995   *The Complete Screenplays*, ed. John Ackerman; *Under Milk Wood*,
        ed. Walford Davies and Ralph Maud
2004   Eleven-CD set *The Caedmon Collection*, of Caedmon LP
        recordings in the 1950s and '60s, plus BBC, CBC and other
        archive material
2006   *Dylan Thomas: A War Films Anthology*, DVD (eight films)
        introduction by John Goodby (Imperial War Museum:
        The Official Collection)
2014   *Collected Poems*, annotated centenary edition, ed. John Goodby
        (2nd edn 2016; U.S. edn 2017)
2020   *The Fifth Notebook of Dylan Thomas*, ed. John Goodby and
        Adrian Osbourne

Sources

Biography

Ackerman, John, *Welsh Dylan: Dylan Thomas' Life, Writing, and
    His Wales* (Cardiff, 1979)
Brinnin, John Malcolm, *Dylan Thomas in America: An Intimate Journal*
    (Boston, MA, 1955)
Davies, Walford, *Dylan Thomas* (Cardiff, 2014)
Ferris, Paul, *Dylan Thomas* [1977] (London, 1985)
Fitzgibbon, Constantine, *The Life of Dylan Thomas* (Boston, MA,
    and Toronto, 1965)
Hardwick, Elizabeth, 'America and Dylan Thomas', in *Dylan Thomas
    in America*, ed. John Malcolm Brinnin (Boston, MA, 1961)
Hawkins, Desmond, *When I Was: A Memoir of the Years between
    the Wars* (London, 1989)
Heppenstall, Rayner, *Four Absentees* (London, 1960)
Holt, Heather, *Dylan Thomas: The Actor* (Llandybie, 2003)
Janes, Hilly, *The Three Lives of Dylan Thomas* (London, 2014)
Jones, Daniel, *My Friend Dylan Thomas* (London, 1977)
Lindsay, Jack, *Meetings with Poets* (London, 1968)

Lycett, Andrew, *Dylan Thomas: A New Life* (London, 2003)

Ross, Ethel, *Ugly, Lovely: Dylan Thomas's Swansea and Carmarthenshire of the 1950s in Pictures*, ed. Hilly Janes (Cardigan, 2016)

Sinclair, Andrew, *Dylan Thomas: No Man More Magical* (New York, 1975)

——, *Dylan the Bard: A Life of Dylan Thomas* (London, 1999)

Thomas, Caitlin, *Leftover Life to Kill* (New York, 1957)

——, with George Tremlett, *Caitlin: A Warring Absence* (London, 1986)

Thomas, David N., *Dylan Thomas: A Farm, Two Mansions and a Bungalow* (Bridgend, 2000)

——, ed., *Dylan Remembered*, vol. I: *1914–1930, Interviews by Colin Edwards*, transcribed by Joan Miller (Bridgend, 2003)

——, ed., *Dylan Remembered*, vol. II: *1935–1953, Interviews by Colin Edwards*, transcribed by Joan Miller (Bridgend, 2004)

Watkins, Gwen, *Dylan Thomas: Portrait of a Friend* [1983], 2nd edn (Talybont, 2005)

Book-length critical studies

Barfoot, Rhian, *Liberating Dylan Thomas* (Cardiff, 2014)

Davies, Walford, *Dylan Thomas* (Milton Keynes, 1986)

Goodby, John, *The Poetry of Dylan Thomas: Under the Spelling Wall* (Liverpool, 2013)

Hardy, Barbara, *Dylan Thomas: An Original Language* (Athens, GA, and London, 2000)

Korg, Jacob, *Dylan Thomas* (New York, 1972)

Maud, Ralph, *Entrances to Dylan Thomas' Poetry* (Pittsburgh, PA, 1963)

Moynihan, William T., *The Craft and Art of Dylan Thomas* (Oxford, 1966)

Olson, Elder, *The Poetry of Dylan Thomas* (Chicago, IL, 1954)

Pratt, Annis, *Dylan Thomas' Early Prose: A Study in Creative Mythology* (Pittsburgh, PA, 1970)

Wigginton, Chris, *Modernism from the Margins: The 1930s Poetry of Louis MacNeice and Dylan Thomas* (Cardiff, 2007)

Collections of critical essays

Allen, Edward, ed., *Reading Dylan Thomas* (Edinburgh, 2018)

Bold, Alan, ed., *Dylan Thomas: Craft or Sullen Art* (London and New York, 1990)

Brinnin, John Malcolm, ed., *A Casebook on Dylan Thomas* (New York, 1960)

Cox, C. B., ed., *Dylan Thomas: A Collection of Critical Essays* [1957] (Englewood Cliffs, NJ, 1966)

Davies, Walford, ed., *Dylan Thomas: New Critical Essays* (London, 1972)

Ellis, Hannah, ed., *Dylan Thomas: A Centenary Celebration* (London, 2014)

Goodby, John, and Chris Wigginton, eds, *Dylan Thomas: Contemporary Critical Essays* (Basingstoke, 2001)

Smith, Kieron, and Rhian Barfoot, eds, *New Theoretical Perspectives on Dylan Thomas: 'A Writer of Words, and Nothing Else'?* (Cardiff, 2020)

Tedlock, E. W., ed., *Dylan Thomas: The Legend and the Poet* (London, 1963)

Companions and reference works

Ackerman, John, *A Dylan Thomas Companion: Life, Poetry and Prose* (London, 1991)

Davies, James A., *Dylan Thomas's Swansea, Gower and Laugharne: A Pocket Guide* (Cardiff, 2000)

Emery, Clark, *The World of Dylan Thomas* (Miami, FL, 1962)

Goodby, John, *Discovering Dylan Thomas: A Companion to the Collected Poems and Notebook Poems* (Cardiff, 2017)

Kershner, R. B. Jr, *Dylan Thomas: The Poet and His Critics* (Chicago, IL, 1976)

Maud, Ralph, *Where Have the Old Words Got Me?* (Cardiff, 2003)

—, with Albert Glover, *Dylan Thomas in Print: A Bibliographical History* (Pittsburgh, PA, 1970)

Tindall, William York, *A Reader's Guide to Dylan Thomas* [1962] (New York, 1996)

Critical essays and journal articles

Aivaz, David, 'The Poetry of Dylan Thomas', *Hudson Review*, VIII/3 (Autumn 1950); repr. in E. W. Tedlock, ed., *Dylan Thomas: The Legend and the Poet* (London, 1963), pp. 382–404

Balakiev, James J., 'The Ambiguous Reversal of Dylan Thomas's "In Country Sleep"', *Papers on Language and Literature*, XXXII/1 (1996), pp. 21–44

Empson, William, 'Review of the *Collected Poems* of Dylan Thomas', *New Statesman and Nation*, 15 May 1954, pp. 643–6

Horan, Robert, 'In Defense of Dylan Thomas', *Kenyon Review*, VII/3
    (Spring 1945), pp. 304–10
Huddlestone, Linden, 'An Approach to Dylan Thomas', *Penguin New
    Writing*, XXXV (1948), pp. 123–60
Keery, James, 'The Burning Baby and the Bathwater', *P. N. Review*, 150
    (March–April 2003), pp. 33–8; *P. N. Review*, 151 (May–June 2003),
    pp. 49–54; *P. N. Review*, 152 (July–August 2003), pp. 57–62; *P. N.
    Review*, 154 (November–December 2003), pp. 26–32; *P. N Review*,
    156 (March–April 2004), pp. 40–42; *P. N. Review*, 159 (September–
    October 2004), pp. 45–9; *P. N Review*, 164 (July–August 2005),
    pp. 57–61; *P. N. Review*, 170 (July–August 2006), pp. 59–65; *P. N. Review*,
    171 (September–October 2006), pp. 56–62
McKay, Don, 'Crafty Dylan and the Altarwise Sonnets: "I Build
    a Flying Tower and I Pull It Down"', *University of Toronto Quarterly*,
    LV (1985/6), pp. 357–94
——, 'What Shall We Do with a Drunken Poet?: Dylan Thomas' Poetic
    Language', *Queen's Quarterly*, XCIII/4 (1986), pp. 794–807
Mills, Ralph J., 'Dylan Thomas: The Endless Monologue', *Accent*, XX
    (Spring 1960), pp. 114–36
Morgan, George, 'Dylan Thomas and the Ghost of Shakespeare',
    Cycnos, 5 (1989), pp. 113–21
——, 'Dylan Thomas's "In the Direction of the Beginning": Towards or
    Beyond Meaning?', *Cycnos*, XX/2 (2003), pp. 1–17, available at https://
    epi-revel.univ-cotedazur.fr
Neill, Michael, 'Dylan Thomas's "Tailor Age"', *Notes and Queries*, XVII/2
    (February 1970), pp. 59–63
Riley, Peter, 'Thomas and Apocalypse', *Poetry Wales*, XLIV/3 (Winter
    2008–9), pp. 12–16
Thomas, R. George, 'Dylan Thomas and Some Early Readers',
    Poetry Wales: Dylan Thomas Special Issue, IX/2 (Autumn 1973),
    pp. 3–19

Book chapters

Bayley, John, 'Dylan Thomas', in *The Romantic Survival* (London, 1957),
    pp. 186–227
Conran, Tony, '"After the Funeral": The Praise-Poetry of Dylan Thomas',
    in *The Cost of Strangeness: Essays on the English Poets of Wales* (Llandysul,
    1982), pp. 180–87

—, '"I Saw Time Murder Me": Dylan Thomas and the Tragic Soliloquy', in *Frontiers in Anglo-Welsh Poetry* (Cardiff, 1997), pp. 120–33

Crehan, Stewart, 'The Lips of Time', in *Dylan Thomas: Craft or Sullen Art*, ed. Alan Bold (New York and London, 1990; repr. in John Goodby and Chris Wigginton, *Dylan Thomas: Contemporary Critical Essays* (Basingstoke, 2001), pp. 46–64)

Goodby, John, '"The Rimbaud of Cwmdonkin Drive": Dylan Thomas as Surrealist', in *Dada and Beyond*, vol. II: *Dada and Its Legacies*, ed. Elza Adamowicz and Eric Robertson (Amsterdam and New York, 2012), pp. 199–223

—, and Chris Wigginton, '"Shut, too, in a tower of words": Dylan Thomas' Modernism', in *Locations of Literary Modernism: Region and Nation in British and American Modernist Poetry*, ed. Alex Davis and Lee Jenkins (Cambridge, 2000), pp. 89–12

—, and Chris Wigginton, 'Welsh Modernist Poetry: Dylan Thomas, David Jones, and Lynette Roberts', in *Regional Modernisms*, ed. Neal Alexander and James Moran (Edinburgh, 2013), pp. 160–83

Heaney, Seamus, 'Dylan the Durable? On Dylan Thomas', in *The Redress of Poetry* (London, 1995), pp. 124–5

Jones, Glyn, 'Three Poets: Huw Menai, Idris Davies, Dylan Thomas', in *The Dragon Has Two Tongues: Essays in Anglo-Welsh Writers and Writing*, ed. Tony Brown (Cardiff, 2001), pp. 161–91

Lewis, Peter, 'The Radio Road to Llareggub', in *British Radio Drama*, ed. John Drakakis (Cambridge, 1981), pp. 72–110

Miller, J. Hillis, 'Dylan Thomas', in *Poets of Reality: Six Twentieth Century Writers* (Cambridge, MA, 1966), pp. 190–216

Nowottny, Winifred, *The Language Poets Use* [1962] (London, 1975), pp. 187–219

Thomas, M. Wynn, 'Portraits of the Artist as a Young Welshman', in *Corresponding Cultures: The Two Literatures of Wales* (Cardiff, 1999), pp. 75–94

—, '"Marlais": Dylan Thomas and the "Tin Bethels"', in *In the Shadow of the Pulpit: Literature and Nonconformist Wales* (Cardiff, 2010), pp. 226–55

Selected online material

BBC Dylan Thomas page: www.bbc.co.uk

The Boathouse, Laugharne: www.dylanthomasboathouse.com

'Thomas, Dylan Marlais', *Dictionary of Welsh Biography*: www.biography. wales

Dally, Andrew, *Dylan Thomas News* blog: www.dylanthomasnews.com; @dylanthomasnews

Dylan Thomas Centre, Swansea: www.dylanthomas.com

Dylan Thomas Collection, Margaret Lockwood Memorial Library Poetry Collection, State University of New York, Buffalo: https://digital.lib. buffalo.edu

Dylan Thomas collection, Harry Ransom Center, Digital Collections, University of Texas at Austin: https://hrc.contentdm.oclc.org/digital/ collection/p15878coll98

Ellis, Hannah, Discovering Dylan website (includes blog articles by David N. Thomas): www.discoverdylanthomas.com

Goodby, John, Oxford Bibliographies Online: www.oxfordbibliographies. com

National Library of Wales: https://dylan.llgc.org.uk. See also the papers of Dylan Thomas and Veronica Sibthorp, National Library of Wales: https://archives.library.wales

Audio material

The recording of *Under Milk Wood* in the Caedmon CD set is of the (rather ragged) first performance in New York in May 1953, chiefly of interest because it is the only version featuring Thomas himself. What was long agreed to be the definitive version is the classic BBC production of 1954 with Richard Burton as First Voice and a Welsh cast, available in Naxos and BBC versions.

Dylan Thomas at the BBC, two CDs, intro. Paul Ferris (London, 2003)

Dylan Thomas: The Caedmon Collection, eleven CDs, intro. Billy Collins (New York, 2002)

Acknowledgements

This book draws on many years of reading, teaching, writing and thinking about Dylan Thomas, and we record here our debts to the scholars, critics and other biographers of Dylan Thomas mentioned in the References and in the Select Bibliography. Although Dylan Thomas's work is now mostly out of copyright, we would also like to thank David Higham and the Dylan Thomas Estate for their co-operation with us in our labours over many years, and New Directions Press, Dylan Thomas's u.s. publishers. Grateful mention must also be made to the staff of the libraries with manuscript holdings of Thomas's writings: the Richard Burton Archive at Swansea University, the National Library of Wales, Aberystwyth, the British Library, the Harry Ransom Center at the University of Texas at Austin, and the Poetry Special Collection in the Margaret Lockwood Memorial Library at the State University of New York, Buffalo. As always, to work on Dylan Thomas is to become aware of and incur debts to fellow-Dylanites; there are too many to mention all except a few of them here, but we would particularly like to thank Hilly Janes, David N. Thomas, Adrian Osbourne, Hannah Ellis, Bonnie Hawkins, and Katie Bowman of the Dylan Thomas Centre, Swansea, for their contributions, direct and indirect, to the writing of this book. Last, but never least, thanks are due to our families for their unfailing tolerance and support while it was being written.

Permissions

Photo Acknowledgements

The author and publishers wish to express their thanks to the sources listed below for illustrative material and/or permission to reproduce it. Some locations of works are also given below, in the interest of brevity:

Erich Auerbach/Popperfoto via Getty Images: p. 8; courtesy Susan Deacon: p. 17; Dylan Thomas Society, Swansea: p. 113; © Estate of Alfred Janes, all rights reserved 2024/Bridgeman Images: pp. 84 (National Museums Wales), 132 (private collection); Harry Ransom Center, The University of Texas at Austin: pp. 19, 82, 120, 150, 157, 162, 176, 182, 183; © Bonnie Helen Hawkins: p. 188; courtesy Hilly Janes: pp. 20, 34, 110, 137, 154; David Matthew Lyons/ AdobeStock: p. 164; National Library of Wales, Aberystwyth: pp. 71, 166; © National Portrait Gallery, London: p. 173; Richard Burton Archives, Swansea University: pp. 80, 94; West Glamorgan Archive Service, Swansea: p. 38; courtesy William Scott Foundation 2024: p. 90.